Jim Twelves has captured the essence of many of the social ills besetting Australia and the Western world at the current time. He has drawn on well recognised experts who have shared their observations and motivations for involvement in their fields. No-one could claim to be unaffected by most of the topics in this far-ranging book. It seeks to wake us up to the deceptions we have unwittingly swallowed before it is too late. Maybe in the past we have been comfortable that topics such as climate change, abortion, euthanasia or moral question around sexuality, were outside our purview. We could just get on with our lives and let others deal with these unseemly questions.

Well, the chickens have come home to roost. No-one can claim to be unaffected because our ability to worship, to pray, even to discuss in our own homes is being challenged. Several instances are documented of faithful, hard-working, highly respected practitioners who have already been dragged through the courts. Unwittingly you may be next.

It behoves us all to remember: It is 'by the blood of the Lamb and by the word of their testimony' (Revelation 12:11) that the devil is defeated. Will you accept the challenge? Will you prepare your testimony? You need to gather the facts to prepare your case. This relevant and highly informative book will give you a starting place and incentive to wake up.

Teri Kempe,
Christian author.

Jim Twelves is right. Large segments of the church have indeed been asleep as Western nations have sought to eradicate God from every part of public life. The result is a disaster. The church is God's solution still. Jim has offered a voice of clarity for many years at *The Daily Declaration*. Now he offers the church a resounding wake-up call. Hear the sober warning in his words, but most of all, be encouraged by the testimonies of those making a difference for God's kingdom, and Jim's reminder that our nations need not perish but can return to the Lord and be restored.

Kurt Mahlburg,
Senior Editor, The Daily Declaration.

In a world where multitudes are being called to wake up to the serious dangers of a woke and occultic culture, Jim Twelves has gifted lovers and seekers of truth, a timely publication that tackles the major social ills facing his own nation Australia and yet is universal in nature. From the first chapter to the thirteenth chapter on Spiritual Warfare, before discussing the two important components of the Middle East Conflict in the last two chapters, Jim has captivated us to think through, ponder deeply, and take action towards addressing the pertinent issues raised and the need for humanity to seek the only Saviour and Master who is able to save them (Acts 4:12).

With an apt title, *While We Were Sleeping*, the book addresses in modern times an ancient parable recorded in Scripture and addressed by The King of The Kingdom in Matthew 13:24-30, concerning the seeds sowed by the enemy while the servants of the Kingdom slept. The reality is *now,* and we as Kingdom Ambassadors are called to arise and shine, as light, in the darkness that has come in a woke culture that tries to envelope the areas we live in. We either take heed, act, and overcome, or we are instead overcome by the enemy. The choice is yours and mine to make now, as we move towards the restoration of all things, the great harvest, and the return of the King. As He had already commanded through Joshua 24:15, 'choose for yourselves this day whom you will serve.' Your choice determines your destiny. Jim Twelves has written with brilliant living testimonies, and the Word, to help us make the right choice in the midst of the great deception. 'Awake, you who sleep…' (Ephesians 5:14).

Mikaele Mudreilagi,
Chair Melanesian One New Man,
Co-Chair – Scripture Union Fiji, Former National Director ICEJ Fiji,
Former School Principal.

This book is a deep dive. Each topic's interviewee has lived and breathed the issue, and just when it starts to feel overwhelming; faith arises with the hope of the gospel. It encourages each of us to have a significant role in upholding truth to the lost, and the truth in the person, Jesus Christ, the way the truth and the life.

Jodie Pickard,
Founding Director of Love Australia, a leading pro-life organisation.

While We Were Sleeping: A Wake-up Call for All Christians

Jim Twelves, PhD

Dedicated to my wife Gillian, our four children, Sarah, Clare, Peter and Timothy and our six grandchildren, Laura, Benjamin, William, Joshua, Levi and Charlotte.

CONTENTS

PREFACE

Do not be conformed to this world, but be transformed by the renewing of your mind, that you may prove what is that good and acceptable and perfect will of God. (Romans 12:2)

W e have been hypnotised, distracted, and deceived. Our foundational life principles have been undermined with the result that we can no longer discern right from wrong, and good from evil. It would seem many of us are sleepwalking and ignoring the war around us.

While We Were Sleeping: A Wake-up Call for All Christians is my alarm clock to announce that we have slept long enough. It's time to wake up, get up, and take a stand. To return to biblical principles and proclaim, *Enough! We are taking back what the enemy has stolen from us.*

Back in the 1970s when I became a Christian, society still adhered to Christan values and principles. Today, however, our society has profoundly changed and no longer knows what it believes or accepts absolute values. *While We Were Sleeping* is a book about right and wrong, good and evil and considers many topics on which the church has been largely silent.

It has been my own despair, disappointment, and growing frustration at the silence on these key issues impacting all Christians and society at large that has driven me to write this book. I believe the church has been intimidated out of fear of causing hurt or offence at the same time as Western culture, founded on Judeo-Christian principles, has been dismantled from within by the twin assaults of neo-Marxism and the global Islamic Jihadist agenda.

My desire in writing this book is to give us tools to engage in lively debate about these issues, for discussions within our families, our Bible study groups and with the wider community. My dream is that preachers and teachers might be empowered to raise these issues to equip their people and their students to do likewise.

While planning for this book, I discovered Megan Basham's 2024 book *Shepherds for Sale: How Evangelical Leaders Traded The Truth for a Leftist Agenda*. She reveals how well-funded forces from outside the Christian church have silenced, distracted, or redirected Christians away from their core values and beliefs. Rosaria Butterfield, former lesbian's endorsement of Megan's book:

Shepherds for Sale offers an urgent wake-up call for all faithful Christians. With brave reporting and translucent writing, Megan Basham reveals that some of the most trusted ministry leaders have proven to be liars and charlatans, bought by the world's filthy lucre and flattery. It's not too late to repent and believe in the Gospel of our Lord Jesus Christ and drive out the wolves.

While We Were Sleeping acknowledges and feels for the pain, of individuals and families struggling with the impact of gender ideology, just one of the crises addressed from education, marriage, family, the right to life, politics, health, spiritual warfare, Islam, Israel, and more.

In Chapter 7, Transgenderism, I quote from Kirralie Smith's 2024 book, *Devastated: How gender ideology is tearing Australian families apart*:

Parents' stories have been silenced by a system that prohibits any dissent or questioning of a child expressing a desire to 'transition their gender.' Their stories shed light on the sinister tactics of the gender industry and the activists working to separate children from their families. (Kirralie Smith)

So many churches are afraid of biblical prophecy and the book of Revelation in particular, for fear of being labelled divisive, unbalanced, or radical. With the result, many Christians are unable to condemn the barbarism of the Hamas terrorists' onslaught on Israel on 7th October 2023; instead, they sympathise with those who accuse Israel of genocide toward the Palestinians in Gaza.

While We Were Sleeping has been designed for Christians, church leaders and congregations alike, looking for Christian answers to a range of challenging issues. While directed to a Christian audience, it is also accessible to anyone anxious about the state of the world and concerned for the future of their children and grandchildren. While each chapter quotes the Holy Bible, it does so to establish common ground, it does not claim to be a theological study.

Each topic begins with a personal testimony from a Christian who has experience in the relevant field. They tell their story of *waking up* and of their passion for the issue. Their accounts are inspirational, for example:

Christians hold the key. They have a secure hope, and they can point to reality. They can demonstrate the need to love and to sacrifice and to put others first, and to invest in their children. Or they can sit on the fence and hope it all goes away, but one day we will all be called to account. (John Anderson, Chapter 10, Politics)

I have been an educator for half a century. In the early part of my career, I taught mostly Physical Geography, specialising in Ice Ages, Climatology, Meteorology, and Biology. Later I became a Christian school principal and then a teacher of teachers. My doctoral work examined a successful Christian school in Australia, which gave me training and experience in professional research, but this book is not written for academics - it is designed to be accessible by all.

In the last four years I have been a regular contributor to *The Daily Declaration*, Australia's largest online Christian news platform; this book taps extensively into their resources.

Western Christians have had it so easy. There has been little overt opposition to their Christian faith, and many churches have seen remarkable growth. Western Christians have been captivated by the grace of God, and the Lord was adding 'daily those who were being saved' (Acts 2:47). However, at the same time, *While We Were Sleeping* the 'devil has come to steal, kill, and destroy' (John 10:10).

Critical thinking is a foundation of this book, a practice missing from much of current discourse that has been saturated and stultified with simplistic binaries, of agreement or rejection. Typically, today issues are introduced in soundbites, of invariably less than eight seconds, sidelining and silencing alternative perspectives and debate.

I invite you to step aside from conventional thinking and any tendency for compromised faith. Jesus reminded His followers to expect hostility from mainstream thinking:

If you were of the world, the world would love its own. Yet because you are not of the world, but I chose you out of the world, therefore the world hates you. (John 15:19)

However, Jesus also said:

...in Me you may have peace. In the world you will have tribulation, but be of good cheer, I have overcome the world. (John 16:33)

The battle has been won; we just need to accept it without compromise. This is a call to boldness, courage, and active engagement in these issues.

Dr Jim Twelves,
Sydney, Australia,
16 October 2025

CHAPTER 1 - MARRIAGE

Lyle Shelton's Story

Lyle is the National Director of the recently re-birthed Family First political party. His previous work included serving the Australian Christian Lobby for 10 years, five as managing director. For more than 20 years he has been a keen participant in Australia's culture wars, first as an elected member of the Toowoomba City Council through to his present involvement in minor party politics. During the 2017 same-sex marriage plebiscite he was a director and spokesperson for the Coalition for Marriage. Lyle has written for The Australian, The Courier Mail, The ABC online, The Spectator and has been a regular media commentator, appearing on Sky News, the ABC's Q&A, Channel 7's Sunrise, ABC News Breakfast and Channel 10's The Project. Lyle's book, *I Kid You Not – Notes from 20 Years in the Trenches of the Culture Wars* (2020) is still selling very well.[1] Lyle has a Bachelor of Arts in journalism and was a former Group Commodities Editor for Rural Press Limited. He lives in Sydney with his wife Wendy. They have four adult children and one grandchild.

Lyle picks up the story:

I first got involved in flighting for the preservation of traditional marriage when I was a teenager. People in my church introduced me to Francis Schaeffer, who was encouraging Christians to engage in politics. We watched his films, 'How then should we live?'[2] Schaeffer was raising the issue of abortion and the impact of the sexual revolution on marriage and the family. In those days, I became aware and developed a passion, as we saw divorce rates skyrocketing. I became concerned with the impact of social policies on society's breakdown, including the liberalisation of pornography, for example.

While I was still at school, I would take every opportunity to practice public speaking, raising social issues. That was probably the start of my political journey. I followed politicians, for example, Alasdair Webster, a Liberal member in Federal Parliament, who was outspoken in favour of traditional family values.[3] Such politicians were few and far between. On the back of this, I went into rural journalism, campaigning for social issues. My parents were very encouraging of my passion. My dad was also into these things. We would often discuss such matters around the meal table. My dad has been in ministry for fifty years and pastored a church for most of that time. He was unique in that he could see that Christians and politics needed to engage. He would read theologians with this disposition. This got me reading and thinking in a similar direction.

I ran for the local council in Toowoomba, Queensland. I took on many of the social issues affecting local government. For example, the legalisation of brothels and its impact on marriage and family. I took a stand for anything that would damage the traditional family unit. This was back in the year 2000. There was an issue about wanting to legalise strip clubs. I have written about these issues in my book (Chapter 4 Entertaining Men).[1] I fought against public policy that had a negative impact on the dignity of women.

In 2003/4 I became aware there were moves being made overseas to allow same sex marriage. The Howard government recognised this was about to become a problem. The Australian Christian Lobby (ACL) was still very new in those days, but a big meeting was called in Parliament House in 2004. I was still living in Toowoomba at the time, but I flew down. About a thousand people gathered in the Great Hall, and lobbied the Howard government, to confirm, in the Marriage Act, that marriage is between one man and one woman. Homosexual couples had gone overseas to be 'married' and come back wanting their same sex marriages recognised here.[4]

Because of that meeting in Parliament House, John Howard and the opposition leader, Kim Beasley, made a bi-partisan agreement, to amend the Marriage Act, by writing into it, what everyone knew marriage to be, namely, a union between one man and one woman. This amendment sailed through with bi-partisan support. The gay lobby went berserk but they were only tiny then. Everyone felt that protecting traditional marriage was more important than the demands of a small activist group.

However, this whole scenario in 2004, woke me and many others, to the fact that there was a real threat to marriage on the horizon. I believe it goes back to 1974 and the introduction of no-fault divorce. This is when marriage was really undermined. Then in the 1990s the changes to the Family Law Act recognised in law that if you co-habited with someone for twelve months, you were deemed to be married. But the gay lobby was always after so called equality, despite already having equality under the law. That wasn't enough for them.

I went to work for ACL in 2007. By 2009 when the Rudd Government was in Canberra, they were against same sex marriage, however, they agreed to amend 84 laws to take away any doubt over equality. These changes allowed same sex couples to share their Centrelink benefits and have all the benefits of a de-facto couple. ACL supported all these changes, not because we think homosexuality is good, but our position was that we were not interested in what people did in their bedroom, but if they want to cohabit and this helped their domestic circumstances, we had no objection to them having a fully functional life. Those 84 law reforms ensured that there was no inequality for them.

The only part of the law we objected to was that children could be a product of a same-sex couple relationship. That was nonsense. Children can only be the product of a male and female relationship.

But confirming that there was no inequality was not enough for the gay lobby. They came back for more, they kept coming! They kept using the political system to get what they wanted. They got equality under the law in 2009. Then in 2010 Adam Bandt (Greens) was elected to parliament. The first thing he did was to propose a motion that everyone survey their electorates on what they thought about gay marriage. That got the ball rolling. The Greens entry into the lower house of parliament was very much a seminal moment as it gave them great leverage. They had a toxic influence, first of all on Labor and then on some Liberals.

The gay lobby was never about equality; it was about deconstructing society. We have to see this through the prism of Cultural Marxism and Identity Politics. Some in parliament knew what was going on but others were useful idiots, and the rest were too scared to stand up for what they knew to be true in their hearts. There are some who are true believers in the deconstructionist cause, such as the Greens, some in Labor and a handful of Liberals. The rest were just too timid, who thought it was just progress and didn't have a well-informed worldview to know what the consequences of their actions would be.

The gay lobby just lied. They said there would be no consequences for letting two gay people get legally married because they love each other. In the ACL, we tried very hard to point these things out. Marriage is a compound right to found and form a family. So how then do same sex couples get access to children? They can't have children naturally, but they can get overseas surrogacy. The first thing the gay lobby went for after legalising gay marriage was legalising altruistic surrogacy and now, they are pushing for commercial surrogacy. Why? Altruistic surrogacy is wrong in and of itself because you are creating a child that has a biological or emotional stake in who that child is, but no way of resolving that. It completely confuses the child's identity in terms of its mother and father. If you inject money payment into the mix, that's another level of ethical and diabolical confusion. If this is legalised two men can pay a woman, inevitably from a lower socio-economic background, to carry their baby. They will do cute things like mix the sperm, but in the end, it will be one person's genetic material. They might get their eggs from yet another woman and implant them into the surrogate womb. It reduces mothers to gestational carriers. The only thing a baby knows when it's born is its mother, but two blokes come along and take them from the breast of the actual mother, so that they can be the 'parents' of the child.

I would say it's a deeply unethical, evil agenda. These are the consequences of same sex marriage to which the politicians turned a blind eye. When marriage is de-gendered, you pave the way for the whole transgender onslaught. It was building before the same sex marriage victory but that gave their agenda a turbo charge. The consequences have been enormous, and our politicians have been useful idiots in this project, and some are only just waking up to the deconstruction of our society.

Pretty much all the time I was at ACL, we were trying to get ahead of the gay agenda. We could tell that the same sex marriage agenda was going to be the main cultural issue for us. The gay lobby were very active in the parliament the whole time I was there as a lobbyist. It was a constant struggle. They had cultural momentum on their side, they had the media, they had academia, and they were working with global resources. They leveraged every piece of global news they could, they were very well co-ordinated. We were in a pitched battled from 2007 right up to 2017 when the plebiscite happened. We spent a lot of time working with the church trying to wake them up, we were warning that this would be a big threat to their religious freedom. The Sydney Anglicans were very good, also the Sydney Roman Catholic Archdiocese, some of the Eastern Orthodox churches and the Coptics. Pentecostals and Baptists were involved but not very vocal.

The biggest challenge we had was getting our supporters to make the case in public, there were very few voices out there. It was very hard to get secular people involved in the fight as they didn't see the importance, they couldn't see it as a core issue as they couldn't see the consequences. They knew that we had already had 40 or 50 years of the sexual revolution, why make an issue of a few gay people who wanted to get married. No one was thinking about the children and their right to the love of their mother and father. We live in a very selfish society, marked by very high divorce rates, and many living for sexual and hedonistic pleasures. Children for decades have had to suffer the consequences of this. Society had already trashed heterosexual marriage so there was no appetite to preserve its definition.

I think that, despite the loss of this debate in 2017, Christians should never give up. We should redouble our efforts to strengthen our own marriages; it starts with us and our church communities. Then we have to find a way to speak to our culture, to the wider society, to people who aren't Christians, about the public good of marriage, why it's good for all people as individuals, their children and society at large.

The sociological research is incontrovertible. Where you have marriage breakdown you have higher prison populations, lower educational outcomes, mental health problems, teenage pregnancy, and drug abuse. Everything stems from the breakdown of the family, that's why I have been passionate about it from being a teenager. I could see it breaking down, before the gays came along. The 1960s have a lot to answer for.

Strong families make strong communities that make strong nations. We have become so individualistic as a society, and this has contributed to the breakdown of marriage and the family. We have grown to rely on government to manage our lives. We have to come back to the principle of subsidiarity, namely, the government should only do what we can't do for ourselves.[5] Churches, charities, and localism must be championed.

Why don't we talk about this, why don't we recognise there are issues that can be addressed? Let's aim for what is optimal. Let's put in place public policy that helps rather than hinders the family. At the moment, the tax and childcare systems discriminate against the family. This is crazy. We have accepted radical individualism. Let's structure the tax system so it helps the family unit. Family income tax splitting: if there are going to be childcare subsidies, they should go to the family, not to a day care centre, so that people have the economic choice to care for the kids the way they want. Also, there are social policy things we can do. Let's stigmatise pornography, let's stigmatise prostitution, let's stigmatise things that cause unfaithfulness in marriage.

As a society, we have torn down the fences of protection around family, in the name of sexual expressionism, it's been a toxic, terrible thing for society.

In 2013, the Gillard government took out the meaning of male and female in the Sex Discrimination Act and put in the words 'gender identity' instead. Neither major party, the Greens or the Teals have any appetite to repeal this. The Liberal party supported Gillard at the time and could not see the ramifications down the track. The Liberal party make it clear they won't fix this. Family First will, if we are elected, and certainly lobby for it. The major parties don't have the courage.[6]

President Trump's policies in America are very encouraging, but time will tell if they really gain traction over there. I am sure there will be a flow-on in Australia in time. If you ask the average Australian what a man is and what a woman is, they know. They are generally sick of this nonsense, and they would expect their politicians to have that reflected properly in law.

J D Vance's speech at the Munich Security Conference, early in 2024, was very significant. He asked: Why would America defend Europe when they don't even defend Western values of freedom of speech? Australia is exactly the same. We have the same laws that stop people praying outside abortion clinics, even silently. I know people who have gone to the High Court because of this. I have been dragged through a five-year legal battle. We don't even support the values the ANZACs fought and died for, and no one, on either side of politics, will fight for them. America is looking at everyone and saying: Why would we go and save everyone when they won't save themselves.

The biggest problem with our politicians at the moment is their lack of courage. Most politicians know what is right, but they are timid and lack conviction. We could sort out the gender issue; we could have policies that support marriage and family. It's the libertarian right and the radical left that are the enemies of marriage and family. For example, the new Libertarian party has a view of freedom as licence. It's not freedom from something; it's freedom for a principle. It's freedom to live in community and fulfil our obligations towards others.

We need people to get married! I would encourage young people to not worry about whether they can afford a house, or whether they have the right furniture, just get married and enjoy being poor together. Have fun! You will be more prosperous in the long term, don't let economics stop you getting married. Marry young and stay faithful to the one person. Marriage is not try-before-you-buy, it's not till we fall out of love, it's in sickness and in health.

❀   ❀   ❀

Feminism's Assault on Marriage

During the Enlightenment (17th and 18th centuries) gender became an unavoidable topic as anatomical studies of our bodies developed, and an understanding of the fundamental differences between men and women gained wider recognition.

> *The male is male only at certain moments; the female is female her whole life… everything constantly recalls her sex to her, and to fulfil its functions, an appropriate physical constitution is necessary to her… she needs a soft sedentary life to suckle her babies. How much care and tenderness does she need to hold her family together!… The rigid strictness of the duties owed by the sexes is not and cannot be the same.* (Jean-Jacques Rousseau, Emile, 1762)[7]

The first wave of feminism was triggered by Christian women, arguably articulating the egalitarianism demonstrated by Jesus in his earthly ministry. The equality between women with men is God's truth, not a secular idea that infiltrated the Church. Many historians highlight Mary Wollstonecraft's *A Vindication of the Rights of Woman* (1792)[8] as pivotal in starting the movement.[9]

Today we are in the fourth wave of feminism, epitomised by the #MeToo movement. There is a strong emphasis on inclusivity in all aspects of life, intersectionality (*the complex, cumulative way in which the effects of multiple forms of discrimination such as racism, sexism, and classism, overlap, or intersect, especially in the experiences of marginalised individuals or groups*),[10] and the recognition of and advocacy for the rights of transgender women.[11]

The late Doctor Voddie Baucham, Dean of Theology, African Christian University, Lusaka, Zambia, in conversation with Ben Shapiro, argued that today's toxic feminism has much to answer for in the destruction of marriage in our society.[12]

Our society now disparages the value of fathers and mothers. We are asked to accept any family formation as equal; you don't need a mother or a father, two mothers will do, or two fathers are just as good. But data proves that the best outcome for young men is to have a father in the home.[13] Society now has the idea that people who appeal to absolute truth are part of this hegemonic oppressive power which fourth wave feminism is determined to overthrow.

On top of this we have the powerful narrative that men are viewed with suspicion and by default must be unsafe, and consequently patriarchy is inherently oppressive. The passionate feminist sees patriarchy as the root of all evil.

Baucham believed this denigration of men has led to the idea of toxic masculinity, resulting in men behaving badly, creating a negative feedback loop confirming the feminist's worst fears. The more muscular, arrogant, and lacking in self-control men behave the more they fit the feminist stereotype, while some consciously or subconsciously act as if they were female, the metrosexual, fuelling the transgender movement (Chapter 7).

Men have lost their way, and some good men have been feminised. What men were supposed to do has been taken from them. The result, many become as promiscuous as they want, they do not have kids unless they can help it, they don't settle down and don't take responsibility. Men are in crisis, they are not going to university as much as they used to, and they are not in the workforce as much as women. (In all 38 countries in the OECD, 25–34-year-old women are more likely to have a tertiary degree than men (New York Times 23 November 2021)).

God created us male and female, we can't understand maleness apart from femaleness, we are not the same. We must understand what it means to be a man and what it means to be their 'counterpart' a woman. God designed men to be priests, prophets, providers, and protectors for women. Men have all these God-given attributes that allow them to take advantage of women including to get them pregnant. If these male characteristics are left unchecked, they produce the toxic masculinity that feminists like to fear.

Society now directs us to be self-centred, in contrast, being God focused draws us outside of ourselves. For example, being a man or a woman is not just about who we think we are or who we want to be. It's better for us to reflect on the one Who made us, for what purpose, and for the relationships He intends for us to have with the opposite sex.

Baucham went further to say that, because of the toxic culture created by modern feminism many men don't want to be married. The God idea is that men should be in a relationship, the head of a household as their priest, prophet, provider, and protector; all these roles give men purpose. But our world now leaves women unprotected and men unchecked in their toxic masculinity.

Couples don't have to have everything figured out before tying the knot. That's one of its joys, the adventure of trusting God and not being reliant on self. Men are not called to do this by themselves, 'iron sharpens iron' (Proverbs 27:17). Men need other men in their lives, as mentors and as disciplers, especially young men need to be accountable to someone.

The plethora of dating apps and the try-before-you-buy culture has cemented the idea of *birds of a feather flock together* meaning marriage will only work if personality, interests, and skills are compatible. I would argue that the idea of *opposites attract* sits better with God's design.

During my own wedding service in 1976 our pastor stood before us with his two hands outstretched, palms facing toward him. He then brought his hands together, interlocking his fingers. Each hand represented each of us, the fingers our strengths, the gaps between, our weaknesses. He then demonstrated how strong we were together, when each of our strengths made up for the other's weakness, confirming *opposites attract*.

Finally, our pastor quoted:

Though one may be overpowered by another, two can withstand him. And a threefold cord is not quickly broken. (Ecclesiastes 4:12)

Marriage is not just two very different people supporting each other, but there is a third invisible element, the presence of the Lord, the designer of marriage.

Church Leadership Largely Silent

Commenting on the same sex marriage debate Lyle said: 'We spent a lot of time working with the church trying to wake them up, we were warning that this would be a big threat to their religious freedom. The Sydney Anglicans were very good, also the Sydney Roman Catholic Archdiocese, some of the Eastern Orthodox churches and the Coptics. Pentecostals and Baptists were involved but not very vocal.'

Baucham believed a lot of pastors become enamoured with their own success. They like to be liked, we all like to be liked. They start carving off the sharp edges of biblical truth until eventually they are doing things for clicks and likes.[12]

The other thing is academia and our education system, that has been taken over by the Neo-Marxists (Chapter 3 Education). Most pastors have been educated by the government all the way through to university and then they go to seminary, but the worldview they have imbibed is a Neo-Marxist worldview. It infects the way they view the Scriptures, and it infects the way they view their calling.

Religious leaders became worried about members of their flock wandering away, so they went after them and then broadened the fence to make sure they still felt included. But if we abandon our boundaries, we are left with nothing to stand on other than shifting sand. The church growth movement in the 80s and 90s, was all about doing whatever was necessary to get people into the doors. As the saying goes, whatever you do to get them in, is what you're going to have to do to keep them in!

Baucham was optimistic, he knew a lot of pastors who hadn't *bowed the knee* and there are now many people following them online.

Another reason for pastor's silence has been the accusation of being a Christian Nationalist. Yes, this pejorative was born in the USA but can equally be applied in other nations:

> ...*a cultural framework that idealises and advocates a fusion of Christianity with American civic life. It contends that America has been and should always be distinctively Christian from top to bottom—in its self-identity, interpretations of its own history, sacred symbols, cherished values, and public policies—and it aims to keep it that way. But the Christian in Christian Nationalism is more about identity than religion. It carries with it assumptions about nativism, white supremacy, authoritarianism, patriarchy, and militarism.* (Andrew Whitehead)[14]

It is easy to see why pastors would shy away from such an accusation despite it being obviously penned from a Neo-Marxist, fourth wave feminist standpoint. Sadly, rejecting Christian Nationalism also rejects our own history, sacred symbols, and cherished values, including marriage and the nuclear family.

How Can We Respond

Lyle's exhortation is for us to 'get married! To encourage young people, to not worry about whether they can afford a house, or whether they have the right furniture, just get married and enjoy being poor together. Have fun!'

We don't have to settle for *what-will-be-will-be*. Take Turley's research which highlights Poland's recent experience where Christianity is beginning to infuse every aspect of political life.[15] Their parliament proposed legislation to ban abortion. The bill didn't pass but pro-life advocates are not giving up.

There was extreme pressure to accept so-called 'same -sex marriage,' but Poland has said 'no.' Its constitution is one of seven in the EU that bans same-sex marriage and is one of six that refuse to recognise civil same-sex unions. Turley goes on to correlate *open borders* with *open values*. Poland has successfully restricted mass immigration as its conservative government wants to preserve their national personal and moral order.

All of us can stand up against the tide. We can plant our feet firmly onto the unshakable facts surrounding our creation in God's image and seek to live out His purposes for our lives and those around us. For young Christians, I see two impediments to marriage that we should start to demolish if ever we see them. Firstly, *peer pressure*, the subconscious call to conform to the rest of society stemming from the fear of being an outcast. Secondly *beguiling consumerism* that convinces us to have all the trimmings before we can get married and start a family.

What Does God Say?

I am indebted to Gary Hamrick, Pastor Cornerstone Chapel, Leesburg, Virginia, USA for his review of 1 Corinthians 7:1-9.[16]

In this passage Paul is addressing two errant philosophies that had crept into the church, *Gnosticism* (only the spirt matters, you can do anything you like with your body, it doesn't matter) and *Asceticism* (the belief that all pleasures are wrong, you should deny yourself physical pleasures, that includes sex within marriage).

> *Now concerning the things of which you wrote to me: It is good for a man not to touch a woman.* (v 1)

Here Paul is not saying it is best to be single, but he is saying it's fine to be single if that's you're calling. But if you are single here are the guard rails. Literally Paul is saying, it is good for the man not to 'kindle a fire in a woman.' In other words, this is the answer to the question, 'how far can you go?' The answer is not beyond the point of arousal. Therefore, if you can't exercise self-control, it's better that you marry. This is a great Scriptural antidote to *try-before-you-buy*.

> *Nevertheless, because of sexual immorality, let each man have his own wife, and let each woman have her own husband. Let the husband render to his wife the affection due her, and likewise also the wife to her husband.* (v 2-3)

Paul is here firmly advocating for marriage. Afterall, God ordained marriage from the very beginning with Adam and Eve. Back in Genesis, the pattern was established, 'be fruitful and multiply' (Genesis 1:28).

Therefore, a man shall leave his father and mother and be joined to his wife, and they shall become one flesh. (Genesis 2:24)

God celebrates sex in a marriage, each giving authority of their body to the other. When we get married, we give up exclusive right to ourselves and our bodies. So, we never should demand what we want. It means we must understand what the other needs.

The wife does not have authority over her own body but yields it to her husband. In the same way, the husband does not have authority over his own body but yields it to his wife. Do not deprive each other except perhaps by mutual consent and for a time, so that you may devote yourselves to prayer. Then come together again so that Satan will not tempt you because of your lack of self-control. (v 4-5)

Finally, Paul seems to contradict himself with his wish that everyone should be single like him:

I wish that all of you were as I am. But each of you has your own gift from God; one has this gift, another has that. (v 7)

Yes, it could be taken at face value that Paul was wishing everyone single but the context of this chapter and the whole narrative of Scripture makes clear that can't be true. Hamrick's take is that Paul knows about the demands of family life so it's easier for the spread of the Gospel if people are single and unencumbered. But if that is the case, then it's a specific gift from God for that purpose; while others are gifted to be husbands, wives, fathers, and mothers.

Footnotes

[1] Shelton, Lyle (2020). *'I Kid You Not': Notes from 20 years in the trenches of the culture wars.* Connor Court Publishing Pty Ltd. https://www.amazon.com.au/Kid-You-Not-Trenches-Culture/dp/1925826953?ie=UTF8&useRedirectOnSuccess=1&ref_=dex_glow_signin&path=%2FKid-You-Not-Trenches-Culture%2Fdp%2F1925826953

[2] Schaeffer, Francis & Schaeffer, Edith (2020, November 10). *How Should We Then Live?* Vision Video. [Video]. YouTube. https://www.youtube.com/watch?v=5QeOrzGbLkU&t=82s

[3] Parliamentary Handbook. (n.d.). *Webster, Alasdair OAM.* Retrieved October 17, 2025, from https://handbook.aph.gov.au/Parliamentarian/WJ4

[4] Iles, Martyn (2010, August 14). What's happening in Canada over a decade after same-sex marriage was legalised? *Australian Christian Lobby (ACL).* https://www.acl.org.au/blog/what-s-happening-canada-over-a-decade-after-same-sex-marriage-was-legalised/

[5] Caritas Australia. (n.d.). *The Principle of Subsidiarity.* Retrieved October 17, 2025, from https://www.caritas.org.au/media/0xopvo0g/cst-subsidiarity.pdf?Download=True

[6] Family First Party. (n.d.). Retrieved October 17, 2025, from https://www.familyfirstparty.org.au/

[7] Rousseau, Jean-Jacques (n.d.). *Emile, or On Education.* Carleton College Female Identity and Gender Equality during the Enlightenment, HIST 139 - Early Modern Europe. Retrieved October 17, 2025, from https://earlymoderneurope.hist.sites.carleton.edu/exhibits/show/women-and-gender-in-early-mode/thoughts-about-female-identity

[8] Wollstonecraft, Mary (n.d.). *A Vindication of the Rights of Woman by Mary Wollstonecraft.* Project Gutenberg. Retrieved October 17, 2025, from https://www.gutenberg.org/ebooks/3420

[9] Wallace Nunneley, Kate (2015, March 6). Origins & First Wave Feminism. *The Junia Project.* https://juniaproject.com/feminist-friday-the-first-wave/

[10] Miriam-Webster. (n.d.). *Intersectionality.* Retrieved October 17, 2025, from https://www.merriam-webster.com/dictionary/intersectionality

[11] Varrial, Angi (2023, November 16). What Is Feminism and Why Is It Important? *Global Citizen.* https://www.globalcitizen.org/en/content/what-is-feminism-and-why-is-it-important/

[12] Baucham, Voddie (2023, July 31). *What Does It Mean to Be a Man?* Ben Shapiro. [Video]. YouTube. https://www.youtube.com/watch?v=CMiXQ-iODyk

[13] Hart, Dan (2023, June 27). Fathers Are Crucial to Healthy Outcomes for Kids, Studies Confirm. *Dads4Kids.* https://dads4kids.org.au/fathers-are-crucial-to-healthy-outcomes-for-kids-studies-confirm/

[14] Baker, Lisa Loraine (2022, August 1). What Is the Meaning of Christian Nationalism? *Christianity.com.* https://www.christianity.com/wiki/christian-terms/what-is-the-meaning-of-christian-nationalism.html

[15] Turley, Stephen R. (2019). *The Return of Christendom: Demography, Politics, and the Coming Christian Majority.* Turley Talks. https://www.amazon.com.au/Return-Christendom-Demography-Politics-Christian/dp/1796658707

[16] Hamrick, Gary (2024, November 12). *God's View of Singleness & Marriage: 1 Corinthians 7 Part 1.* Cornerstone Chapel – Leesburg VA. [Video]. YouTube. https://www.youtube.com/watch?v=24GE0ehe028&t=18s

CHAPTER 2 - FAMILY

Warwick Marsh's Story

Warwick married Alison in 1975. Together, they have five children and ten grandchildren, and they live in Wollongong, New South Wales, Australia. Warwick is a family and faith advocate, social reformer, musician, TV producer, writer, and public speaker. In 1998, he received a Father of the Year Award in the New South Wales Parliament, and in 2001, he was awarded a Centenary Medal by Prime Minister John Howard for his mission work and his contributions to Aboriginal communities and youth.

In 2002, Warwick and Alison founded the *Dads4Kids Fatherhood Foundation*[1] to encourage fathers and promote excellence in fathering. The foundation delivers its mission through web, TV, radio, research, policy development, education programs, and training initiatives. In 2010, Warwick worked with various faith leaders to draft the *Canberra Declaration*,[2] a statement supporting family, faith, life, and freedom. This movement later launched *The Daily Declaration*,[3] now Australia's largest Christian news site.

Although that's a summary of Warwick's public accomplishments, he prefers a simpler introduction: 'God's donkey from Wollongong.'

Warwick picks up the story:

There's a saying in Christian circles: 'Your mess becomes your ministry.' Henri Nouwen, the great Catholic thinker, labelled this phenomenon *The Wounded Healer*.[4]

I had a wonderful father and mother, but they couldn't get along. My mum was from Scotland and my dad from Australia, with strong English roots. No one had taught them that marriage is the process of two people dying to themselves. Many people don't realise this. Marriage is the death of two so that one may live. As Scripture says, the two shall become one. This aligns with the Christian principle that out of death comes life. Paul wrote in his letters, 'Death is working in us, but life in you' (2 Corinthians 4:12), and Jesus said, 'Unless a grain of wheat falls into the ground and dies, it remains alone; but if it dies, it produces much grain' (John 12:24). Family is multiplication, but it comes through death. Love is a continual rhythm of death and life. Jesus also said, 'Greater love has no one than this, than to lay down one's life for his friends' (John 15:13).

We speak our marriage vows thinking it will be *happily ever after*, but in Australia today, one in three marriages ends in divorce. And that's only counting marriages. Many couples don't even marry anymore, and these attempted long-term relationships are three times more likely to end and breakup. Our children pay the price. We're facing a massive breakdown of family life in our society. This was never God's intention. God is a family God. He created marriage to be *till death do us part*.

God made the family before He made the Church. I remember sitting in a sidewalk café in the hot tropical air of Kuala Lumpur, Malaysia, talking with an American preacher. We were discussing how best to explain the Bible to people who didn't have much background in it. He paused, then said something that struck me deeply: 'The Bible can be summed up in one sentence, the Father is looking for a Bride for His Son.'

That simple phrase hit me like a thunderbolt. I couldn't shake it. For the next two weeks, I thought about it constantly. The Bible begins with a marriage, Adam and Eve in the Garden of Eden, and ends with one, the wedding of the Lamb, Christ united with His Church in the book of Revelation. From Genesis to Revelation, the story of Scripture is wrapped around the idea of covenant, love, and divine union. It's profound when you realise the whole narrative of God and humanity is framed in terms of family and marriage.

But even as I pondered that insight, I sensed there was more. I kept praying, reflecting, and searching the Scriptures. And then it came to me, an addition that completely summarises the Bible, in two sentences:

The Father is looking for a Bride for His Son.
The Father wants a big family filled with many children.

Usually, in a family, the bride is secured first, and then the family comes along. But God did things differently. He sent Jesus to this earth to give His life as a ransom for many, and through that sacrifice, we have the opportunity to be born again, born into the family of God as adopted children.

So, God has a big, big family. That's His final plan: a great family, united in love, living together in harmony, caring for one another, getting along, and showing kindness. This family, this body, is called the *ecclesia*, the Church of the Living God, the Body of Christ. Families come from heaven and strong families are foundational to our society.

A family begins when a man and a woman say, 'I do.' The man puts a ring on the woman's finger, the woman puts a ring on the man's finger, and they say to each other, 'Baby, I'm with you for the rest of my life. Here we go, good or bad, better or worse, richer or poorer, we're going to do this thing together.' They have children, and that creates a family. That family becomes a microcosm of the community, the church, and the nation. So, if you have strong families, you'll have a strong community, a strong church, and a strong nation.

Back to my story, my mess became my ministry. I grew up amidst tension between my parents, shuffled between Scotland and Australia. At one point, a welfare officer wanted to take us kids away and put us in a home in Bowral. I was about nine. I cried so much. In the end, they didn't go through with it, but I didn't realise until my mid-thirties how deeply broken my heart was.

At that time, I was playing in a Christian band. I had a wife and four kids, and we were preparing to perform at a school the next day, sharing Jesus' love. That night, I had a dream. I saw a man and a woman walking down a road, silhouetted against the setting sun. I didn't know who they were. In one of their arms, either the father's or the mother's, I couldn't tell, was a little boy, about three years old. As the couple walked, they started to drift further and further apart. The boy began calling out, maybe for Mummy, maybe for Daddy, I wasn't sure. The dream tore my heart in two. I wasn't just crying, I was bawling. Tears were streaming down my face. When I woke up, my pillow was soaked. I was shaking. I said to myself,

'What's going on? You're a grown man, a carpenter. You've got four kids. You love your wife. What's wrong with you?'

Then I heard a voice from heaven: 'You're the little boy.' That dream exposed my wound. The trauma from my parents' conflict, the police, the instability, and brokenness, it all came flooding back. I knew then that family was so very important. From that moment on, my mission was to love my wife and children well. Everything else, even my ministry, became secondary.

Men often tie their identity to what they do. But God never intended that. He is a family God. All through Scripture, He speaks of tribes, clans, lineages. In Ephesians 3:14–15, Paul writes, 'I bow my knees to the Father of our Lord Jesus Christ, from whom the whole family in heaven and earth is named.' That means family didn't start on earth, it started in heaven.

The Trinity itself is a heavenly family. In Genesis, God said, 'Let Us make man in Our image, according to Our likeness' (Genesis 1:26). And in Jesus' prayer (perhaps the most unanswered prayer in history) He pleads, 'That they all may be one, as You, Father, are in Me, and I in You; that they also may be one in Us, that the world may believe that You sent Me' (John 17:21). God is a family God.

That vision I had in my mid-thirties changed the trajectory of my life. Back in my late teens, I didn't even want to meet a girl or get married. I said to myself, 'Why would I go through what my mum and dad went through?' That's not something most 17-year-old boys are thinking about. At that age, your hormones are raging, and your attention is usually fixed on the opposite sex. But those kinds of thoughts, hesitations, fears, are becoming more common for young men today because of the massive breakdown and heart break in modern family life.

I was on a journey to try and find what *family* really meant. I left home in Blackheath at 17 and eventually found myself in Wollongong with *Youth With a Mission*.[5] I ended up living with a pastor's family for two and a half years. Then I met my beautiful wife, who came from a beautiful family. There was this amazing family vibe in her home. I'd go over there, and they'd speak kindly to one another around the table. They'd listen to each other. It was so refreshing!

Now, Alison and I are marriage junkies. We've been to dozens of seminars. We never stop learning. One day, while waiting for an appointment with a Catholic priest, I met an elderly French priest, Father

Jacques. I asked him, 'How's the renewal going?' He looked at me with a wide-eyed loving smile and said, 'Brother, unless we are renewed every day, there is no renewal!' That applies to marriage, too. As the French writer André Maurois said, 'A successful marriage is an edifice that must be rebuilt every day.'

I've been on a journey to better understand what family really is, and to become a better husband and dad. And it was understanding my own father-wound, that became a turning point in my life, that helped set me on this path.

I remember one time; I was in a school in Albury with my Christian band sharing the gospel. Everything was going great; the young people were enjoying the music. Afterward, a boy, about 14 years old, was helping us pack up our gear. I turned to him and said, 'Father God really loves you.' I was just trying to be kind, to thank him for lending a hand.

But he spun around and said, 'Don't talk to me about your [expletive] Father God. My [expletive] father shot my mum and now he's in [expletive] jail. I don't want to hear about your [expletive] God.'

And I just stood there, stunned. I thought, what have I done? Or to paraphrase the lyrics of the song by Skillet, 'What Have we Become.'[6] But that's the reality we're living in now. So many broken homes. So much fractured pain.

As Tolstoy wrote in Anna Karenina, 'Happy families are all alike; every unhappy family is unhappy in its own way.'

The family law court is horrific. I just got an email from a man who reduced his work hours to fulfil shared parenting orders. The child support agency penalised him, saying he was just trying to avoid payments, and charged him as if he worked full-time. He's been financially crushed and is asking for help to mount a legal case.

Family law has been taken over by the cultural Marxists for the last 50 or 60 years. It's horrific. It reflects Karl Marx hatred for fathers quite beautifully, but it breaks God's heart. Marriage is meant to be something very precious. It's meant to have tension, intentional tension, between male and female. Their very difference creates the challenge. And that challenge can only ever be resolved daily, through acts of love. It's the story of dying to self. As Jesus said, 'Greater love has no one than this, than to lay down one's life for his friends' (John 15:13).

The challenge is for the man to lay down his life for the woman, but the woman's challenge is to listen to her man and respect him. That can be really hard if her man is not worthy of respect. But if they can work this out most of the time, they will have children who won't grow up in broken homes, smashed around like I did. They can multiply that love into their own children and then into the nation.

'A family without a father is like a house without a roof,' says an old Chinese proverb. Fathers make families. Mothers do too, without a mother, you can't have a family. But Pastor Allan Myer is convinced the success of marriage and family depends more on the father than the mother.[7] The statistics back this up. Maybe it's because the father has an outsized influence, or because God made the father to carry a very important role on behalf of the Father of Lights. I don't fully know why, but I know it is a reality.

I've noticed that the father-wound is often deeper than the mother-wound. Perhaps this is because it impacts the child more profoundly in the long run. When I first started Dads4Kids, I thought it was all about fathers and sons. But I've come to realise that women also get much of their identity from their father. The mother provides nurture, but the father provides identity. Involved fathers help their children develop higher IQs, perform better in school, and find better jobs and a whole host of other positive benefits besides.

By the way, statistics show that children do better overall when their parents are married, highlighting that marriage and active fatherhood go hand in hand. We started Dads4Kids in 2002 because we saw the need to encourage dads, and here we are over two decades later and still going strong!

I love music. The predominant theme by far in music is love. We all want it, but we don't know how to get it because it costs too much, and the journey of love is too arduous. That song from Foreigner, 'I want to know what love is,' is a prime example.[8]

You see love is usually staring across the other side of the kitchen table at you. True love within a marriage is too close for comfort because true love is a process of death. The man (father) has to die to self, to show love to the woman, so she can blossom, and then you (man) can blossom as well. Then you can have children that grow up in love, in the nurture of a mother and father deeply in love, and that love can change the world. Love will change the world because God is love, but love always comes at a cost, hence the high cost of the blood of Jesus.

❀   ❀   ❀

Building a Family

Warwick said, 'if you have strong families, you have a strong community, a strong church, and a strong nation.' But as a society, *While We Were Sleeping*, we have lost sight of our primary responsibilities, namely for women to have care and tenderness to hold their family together (Jean-Jacques Rousseau),[9] while men are to be priests, prophets, providers, and protectors for women (Voddie Baucham).[10]

Today a couple's transformation into a family is extremely challenging. What inhibits a couple from starting a family? The ease of contraception, the demands on personal freedom, the responsibility for another life, the rising cost of living and being unable to afford another mouth to feed, and perhaps the feeling of responsibility not to bring a new life into the world with so much pain and suffering.

As we discussed in the first chapter on marriage, men seem to have been stunted in their emotional development, often retaining childhood attitudes, and not having developed personal responsibility to the extent that they can take on the responsibility for children.

Women, advantaged by the education system, have a much better sense of personal responsibility.[11] In addition, women have retained their most powerful instinct to build family. Though some will say, 'I'm not ready to be a mum,' I think this is a stalling tactic, a nod to feminism, but deep down even they flourish in motherhood given the opportunity.[12]

Mary Eberstadt, is an American researcher and writer who draws on anthropology, intellectual history, philosophy, popular culture, sociology, and theology.[13] One of her many books, echoing some of the themes of my book is, *How the West Really Lost God: A New Theory of Secularisation.*[14] In conversation with John Anderson, Mary said:

Politicians should look at every possible experiment to make it easier to get married, easier to have families, and easier to have families of size. We are talking about incentives. Another approach is to go after some of the things we know are bad for family formation. One of the most frustrating things in the United States, for which we have very good laws, is obscenity, and yet there are no prosecutions for the creators of pornography. We need to go after this, it's a proven contributor to romantic trouble, to marital breakup, and it is often cited in divorce cases.

Outside of policy, there are grassroots experiments. In the US we have the experiment of classical[15] non-denominational private schools, and charter schools,[16] where Greek and Latin are taught, and where non-anti-American history is taught. These grassroots experiments in education, will over the long run, be all to the good of the family.

American parents seem to be waking up to the problem of what is being taught in American public schools, this is all to the good.

The privileging of motherhood would be a great thing to bring back. Hungary is experimenting with some very interesting ideas.[17,18] For example, women with four or more children do not have to pay income tax for the rest of their lives.

John supported Mary's ideas by raising the housing affordability crisis here in Australia as a major impediment for young people settling down and building families on the one hand, and on the other, the looming crisis of there being too small a population to support society into the future, as most are having smaller families or no children at all.

Stephen Turley,[19] who we referenced in the previous chapter on marriage, adds a positive perspective on family in his study of demography (the study of changes in the number of births, marriages, deaths, etc. in a particular area during a period of time). He quotes from Eric Kaufmann's 2002 study of American demographic trends, claiming that we are in the early stages of a demographic revolution, 'religious fundamentalists are on course to take over the world'; self-identified non-religious women only had 1.5 children per couple, compared with conservative evangelical women who had 2.5 children. (Replacement fertility is defined as 2.1 children).

Therefore, the socialist left; supporters of homosexuality (Chapter 6), gender transition (Chapter 7), abortion (Chapter 8), euthanasia (Chapter 9) and the fear of climate change (Chapter 12) are having fewer babies than replacement and will breed out while conservative evangelicals who trust in God are going forth and multiplying.

Turley cites encouragement and provocation from the Russian Federation. When President Putin assumed office in 1999, Russia was losing almost a million people a year, while having one of the highest abortion rates in the world. In response Putin enacted a number of policies aimed at reversing this trend, such as his ban on abortion advertising, banning abortion after 12 weeks, and promoting education programs on the dangers of abortion. Moreover, Russians are treated to an annual ceremony in the Kremlin where Vladimir Putin himself publicly honours families with eight or more children.

Notice that the initiatives discussed here are all national, not global. They are so encouraging to see, but I would argue that family is built one family at a time. Each single should look beyond themselves; each couple, as Lyle Shelton said in Chapter 1, should 'just get married and enjoy being poor together and have fun!' Let's pray that each family can celebrate the legacy they are leaving future generations.

The Rights of Children

Katy Faust is founder and president of the children's rights organisation *Them Before Us,*[20,21] a global non-profit. Together with Stacey Manning, they published *Them Before Us: Why We Need a Global Children's Rights Movement.*[22]

Their focus is on the forgotten children hit hardest by non-marital childbearing families, who are the casualties of no-fault divorce and the redefinition of marriage, or who are intentionally subjected to motherlessness or fatherlessness through reproductive technologies.

Katy observes that mothers tend to care *for* kids and dads tend to play *with* kids. Kids need both. Mum ensures they brush their teeth and go to bed on time, and dad who can say, 'let's just leave for the day and do this crazy hike in the bush.' These two caricatures complement one another, and this same division of labour exists in every society. This is what men and women do naturally because of the biological differences in their brain chemistry and this optimises their children's development.

The same-sex marriage agenda got these ladies involved as they were angry that the so-called-rights of adults were being recognised, while immense harm was being inflicted on the children, who became pawns to be traded in the marketplace of feelings. They were propelled into action when they realised that kids were being asked to do more than *tolerate* their 'parents' desires for lifestyle, they were being *required* to *sacrifice* their needs and wishes.

Kids can't organise, advocate, or defend their own interests, but we can. The book *Them Before Us,* advocates for children by focusing on the child's perspective through their own stories. It has tripped the switch on adult-focused attitudes toward marriage, parenthood, and reproductive technologies, by framing these issues around the child's right to be raised by both their biological mother and father.

Katy and Stacey recognised that the *modern family* has been all about the dreams and desires of the adults that have forced children's rights out of the picture. They argue that this is highly detrimental to their growth and development, and someone needs to stand up for the voiceless and say enough is enough.

Talking about America they said, but I am sure it's similar in Australia, 70-80 per cent of male prisoners are *fatherless*. They went on to say men who have had effective fathers don't go to prison. Prisons are 'holding tanks for fatherless men.' We are now raising a generation with extremely unstable roots. Our young men, in particular, are extremely vulnerable.

It is ironic that one of the hallmarks of the progressives has been their stand for the rights of minorities, yet they have set back children's rights decades. It's as if they have never cared about children, or they haven't wanted them at all. This demonstrates that they are simply living for the pleasures of the moment, never learning from history, nor caring about the future.

Dying to Self

Warwick began his testimony with the importance of 'dying to self.' A vital foundation for any marriage and for building family. *While We Were Sleeping,* we have become a self-centred, self-gratifying people, creating the root of many of the issues covered in this book. Everything is about *me, my* needs, and *my* wants. As our society has outlawed God, who has always been about *others*, we are left *alone*.

Pastor Brian Guerin ran a great teaching session on dying to self.[23] He used an analogy based on Romans 12:2:

> *And do not be conformed to this world, but be transformed by the renewing of your mind, that you may prove what is that good and acceptable and perfect will of God.*

If our life were a train, a locomotive; *intimacy* with God would be the fuel to make the engine run and the locomotive would run on two tracks, the one called *dying to self* and the other of the *renewed mind*. If you take out intimacy, the train doesn't run. If you pull out one of the two tracks, by being conformed to the world, or you stop denying yourself: in either case there's a train wreck.

Often, as followers of Jesus, we don't 'present your bodies a living sacrifice' (Romans 12:1) as Jesus clearly did when He died for our sins. Only when we die, can Jesus shine through us. Paul acknowledged, in the last days, 'men will be lovers of themselves' (2 Timothy 3:2), so true.

Warwick describing his parents said, no one had taught them that marriage was the process of two people dying. A lot of people don't understand that. Marriage is the ultimate death of two that one might live; the Scripture says that 'the two shall become one flesh' (Mark 10:8).

Bringing up my own family, I treasured this anonymous depiction of dying to self:

> *1. When you are forgotten, or neglected, or purposely set at naught, and you don't sting and hurt with the insult or the oversight, but your heart is happy, being counted worthy to suffer for Christ… That is dying to self.*
> *2. When your good is evil spoken of, when your wishes are crossed, your advice disregarded, your opinions ridiculed, and you refuse to let anger rise in your heart or even defend yourself, but take it all in patient loving silence… That is dying to self.*
> *3. When you lovingly and patiently bear any disorder, any irregularity, any unpunctuality, or any annoyance; when you can stand face to face with waste, folly, extravagance, spiritual*

insensibility...and endure it as Jesus endured it...That is dying to self.

4. When you are content with any food, any offering, any raiment, any climate, any society, any solitude, and interruption by the will of God...That is dying to self.

5. When you never care to refer to yourself in conversation, or to record your own good works, or itch after commendation, when you can truly love to be unknown...That is dying to self.

6. When you can see your brother prosper and have his needs met and can honestly rejoice with him in spirit and feel no envy nor question God, while your own needs are far greater and in desperate circumstances...That is dying to self.

7. When you can receive correction and reproof from one of less stature than yourself, and can humbly submit inwardly as well as outwardly, finding no rebellion or resentment rising up within your heart...That is dying to self. (Seven Laws of Dying to Self - Anon)

Some of these nails really hurt don't they! Decades have passed, and I am still learning to die to self. However, if husband and wife both die to self *simultaneously* that's wonderful, but usually they don't! My prayer is that our demonstration of dying to self will have been etched into our children's hearts, where it will take root and bear much fruit in their children's lives. Dying to self can be the salvation of so many marriages and the hedge of protection too.

What Does God Say?

Scripture has many references to family; consider these two. Paul writing to the Ephesian church:

Wives, submit to your own husbands, as to the Lord. For the husband is head of the wife, as also Christ is head of the church; and He is the Savior of the body. Therefore, just as the church is subject to Christ, so let the wives be to their own husbands in everything. (Ephesians 5:22-24)

Frequently misunderstood, especially when taken out of context, submission isn't *submission* if it's not from the heart, it's *subjugation*. If the wife recognises that two are better together and working out their cord with three stands, then submission is life and liberty.

Husbands, love your wives, just as Christ also loved the church and gave Himself for her. (Ephesians 5:25)

This is the other side of the coin, but look what this means, *dying to self,* just as the wife's submission means *dying to self.*

Children, obey your parents in the Lord, for this is right. 'Honour your father and mother,' which is <u>the first commandment with promise</u>: 'that it may be well with you, and you may live long on the earth.' And you, fathers, do not provoke your children to wrath, but bring them up in the training and admonition of the Lord. (Ephesians 6:1-4) (my emphasis)

I love this, the children being called to obedience. Unless the children are trained to be obedient to their earthly parents, how will they learn to be obedient to their Heavenly Father? We can feel the peace in the family home when this is operational. Stability and peace, the seedbed for growing personal responsibility and maturity.

Finally, consider Moses speaking to the children of Israel:

And these words which I command you today shall be <u>in your heart</u>. You shall <u>teach them diligently </u>to your children and shall <u>talk of them</u> when you sit in your house, when you walk by the way, when you lie down, and when you rise up. You shall <u>bind them</u> as a sign on your hand, and they shall be as frontlets between your eyes. You shall <u>write them</u> on the doorposts of <u>your house</u> and on <u>your gates.</u> (Deuteronomy 6:6-9) (my emphasis)

Frequently, we think of the Old Testament as *law* and the New Testament as *grace.* But this is far from the truth. The law was first in *their hearts* and then Moses describes how it was *to be worked out* in their day-to-day. They were to take every opportunity to bring the Lord into their lives, in particular, into their *homes* and into every life decision they make, in *the gate,* that is in the public square of witness and accountability.

As Warwick reminded us from Ephesians 3:14, all families in heaven and on earth take their name from our Heavenly Father. Let's honour Him while we seek to build families.

Footnotes

[1] Dads4Kids Fatherhood Foundation. (n.d.). Retrieved October 18, 2025, from https://dads4kids.org.au/

[2] Canberra Declaration. (n.d.). Retrieved October 18, 2025, from https://canberradeclaration.org.au/

[3] The Daily Declaration. (n.d.). Retrieved October 18, 2025, from https://dailydeclaration.org.au/

[4] Nouwen, Henri (2014). *Wounded Healer: Ministry in Contemporary Society - In our own woundedness, we can become a source of life for others.* Darton, Longman & Todd Ltd. https://www.amazon.com.au/Wounded-Healer-Ministry-Contemporary-woundedness/dp/0232530777

[5] Youth with a Mission. (n.d.). Retrieved October 18, 2025, from https://ywam.org/

[6] AragornPk10 (2011, April 16). *Skillet - Monster (Lyrics).* [Video]. YouTube. https://www.youtube.com/watch?v=u9NStVkSCuk

[7] Careforce Lifekeys International. (n.d.). *The Origin and Purpose of Lifekeys.* Meyer, Allan & Helen. Retrieved October 18, 2025, from https://www.careforcelifekeys.org/pages.asp?id=49

[8] RHINO. (2020, January 26). *Foreigner - I Want To Know What Love Is (Official Music Video).* [Video]. YouTube. https://www.youtube.com/watch?v=r3Pr1_v7hsw&t=45s

[9] Rousseau, Jean-Jacques (n.d.). *Emile, or On Education.* Carleton College Female Identity and Gender Equality during the Enlightenment, HIST 139 - Early Modern Europe. Retrieved October 17, 2025, from https://earlymoderneurope.hist.sites.carleton.edu/exhibits/show/women-and-gender-in-early-mode/thoughts-about-female-identity

[10] Baucham, Voddie (2023, July 31). *What Does It Mean to Be a Man?* Ben Shapiro. [Video]. YouTube. https://www.youtube.com/watch?v=CMiXQ-iODyk

[11] DiPrete, Thomas A. & Buchmann, Claudia (2013). *The Rise of Women: The growing gender gap in education and what it means for American Schools.* Russell Sage Foundation. https://www.russellsage.org/publications/rise-women

[12] Twelves, Jim (2024, February 7). What's Wrong with Feminism? *Daily Declaration.* https://dailydeclaration.org.au/2024/02/07/whats-wrong-with-feminism/

[13] Twelves, Jim (2023, February 14). Help Families, Fix Society. *Daily Declaration.* https://dailydeclaration.org.au/2023/02/14/help-families-fix-society/

[14] Eberstadt, Mary (2013). *How the West Really Lost God: A New Theory of Secularization.* Templeton Press. https://www.amazon.com/How-West-Really-Lost-Secularization/dp/1599473798/

[15] Association of Classical Christian Schools (ACCS) (n.d.). *Promote Standards of Excellence.* Retrieved October 18, 2025, from https://classicalchristian.org/

[16] Charter Schools USA (CSUSA) (n.d.). *Our Story.* Retrieved October 18, 2025, from https://www.charterschoolsusa.com/apps/pages/index.jsp?uREC_ID=415797&type=d

[17] Abbott, Tony (2024, September 26). Hungary's Place in the Global Order. *The Honourable Tony Abbott.* https://tonyabbott.com.au/2024/09/hungarys-place-in-the-global-order/

[18] Truu, Maani (2019, September 6). 'Go forth and multiply': Abbott calls for more babies, less migration at Hungarian summit. *SBS News.* https://www.sbs.com.au/news/article/go-forth-and-multiply-abbott-calls-for-more-babies-less-migration-at-hungarian-summit/tbvcqf6vg

[19] Turley, Stephen R. (2019). *The Return of Christendom: Demography, Politics, and the Coming Christian Majority.* Turley Talks. https://www.amazon.com.au/Return-Christendom-Demography-Politics-Christian/dp/1796658707

[20] Twelves, Jim (2023, April 10). A Global Children's Rights Movement: Katy Faust & Stacy Manning. *Daily Declaration.* https://dailydeclaration.org.au/2023/04/10/a-global-childrens-rights-movement-katy-faust-stacy-manning/

[21] Muehlenberg, Bill (2025, January 28). Katy Faust: Putting Children First. *Daily Declaration*. https://dailydeclaration.org.au/2025/01/28/katy-faust-children-first/

[22] Faust, Katy & Manning, Stacy (2021). *Them Before Us: Why We Need a Global Children's Rights Movement.* Post Hill Press. https://www.amazon.com.au/Them-Before-Us-Childrens-Movement/dp/1642935964

[23] Guerin, Brian (2024, October 25). *School of Dying to Self - Session Four*. Brian Guerin. [Video]. YouTube. https://www.youtube.com/watch?v=bTJ5Ey8-DDU&t=517s

CHAPTER 3 - EDUCATION

Dylan Oakley's Story

Dylan, born in Sydney, Australia, is married to Fiona and they live in Southeast Queensland. They have five children who have been, and some are still, being home schooled.

Though raised in a Christian home, by the time Dylan attended university in 1993 he was well and truly on a *runaway* from the Lord. However, in June of 1995, at 19 years of age, Dylan had a *prodigal son* epiphany and, while surrounded by sin and weakened by the effects of wild living, he reached out to the Lord with a very simple, heartfelt prayer. That day in his bedroom in Rockhampton, Dylan experienced the mercy of Jesus Christ, and it completely changed the course of his life. Within hours he led his then girlfriend, Fiona, to the Lord and just six months later they were married and were running hard after the Lord.

As a child, Dylan attended Barry Smith evangelistic crusades that opened his eyes to a globalist, antichrist agenda, and that inconvenient truth has remained with him his entire life. What Dylan witnessed while running with the world only confirmed the dark agenda against humanity that permeated the music industry, media, governments, and institutions. He knew too much to really enjoy prodigal living. Returning to the Lord as an on-fire, no-compromise Christian, Dylan discovered the strength to confront evil and call it out. Dylan recalls in 1995 submitting to the university a well-referenced paper that addressed the role of the United Nations and international efforts to bring about *a new world order.*

Then one day, when he had started his History and English teaching career in Rockhampton, Queensland, he found himself calling in sick, it was 11th September 2001. This was another pivotal moment in Dylan's life. When he called in sick, the school administrator said to him, 'Turn the TV on.' Dylan spent the rest of the day glued to the live television coverage from New York of the Twin Towers attack.

He was particularly struck by the number of reports that day that have never surfaced since. One story in particular, was about the volume of *short selling* of airline stock in the days before the attack. What did that mean? He thought, some people, apparently large numbers of people, must have been tipped off to what was about to happen. How could that be? Then, adding to Dylan's dilemma, why has this story apparently never been followed up? This was Dylan's second wake-up call.

Fast forward ten years. Now juggling a business career, lay ministry, married life and parenthood. His children's viewing habits included Disney movies that to many Christians, seemed harmless enough. But Dylan felt a check in his spirit. Why was there so often a common theme of children (or young animals) being traumatically separated from their parents? How could the fear that was generated by these storylines, and the archetypal villain, be good for his children? What was the history of Disney? Dylan noted that one of Disney's early offerings was, The Sorcerer's Apprentice (1940). Aren't Christians called to separate themselves from witchcraft and sorcery? So, what looked like, in those days, *wholesome family entertainment,* Dylan and his wife decided had a dark underbelly. The Oakley's cut their input from Disney.

Fiona, also a trained teacher, Primary and Special Education, cut short her career and began a 14-year journey of homeschooling their children. Partnering with their children so directly in education meant she could get to know them very well, and their interaction with adults brought about a maturity beyond their years compared with children in traditional schooling. Fiona is now on the board of one of the largest home-schooling providers in the country, Faith Christian School of Distance Education.[1]

The Oakley's were at pains to teach their children that it's *OK to be different*, as they have always known they were in *spiritual warfare*. Their children have grown up to be well-rounded, high achievers in sport, education, and society while maintaining their Christian distinctiveness in an increasingly perverse world.

But the rubber hit the road on 9th December 2021 when Dylan walked out of his teaching career as the *no jab, no job* mandate hit Queensland teachers, he could no longer work in the system.

At the end of that same year, their eldest, Anna, was graduating to become a teacher but she could not take up either of the jobs she was offered as she too was *not jabbed.* What madness for a profession suffering massive shortages, that healthy experienced teachers and enthusiastic new graduates were being barred from service!

Dylan, quoting from the lives of three Hebrews in exile in Babylon, approximately 600 BC, when they were called upon to bow down to Nebuchadnezzar's golden image (Daniel 3:16-18):

Shadrach, Meshach, and Abed-Nego answered and said to the king, 'O Nebuchadnezzar, we have no need to answer you in this matter. If that is the case, our God whom we serve is able to deliver us from the burning fiery furnace, and He will deliver us from your hand, O king. But if not, let it be known to you, O king, that we do not serve your gods, nor will we worship the gold image which you have set up.'

Like the three friends in the Bible, Dylan was not going to *bow the knee to bad laws.* In fact, at this time, he gained inspiration and confidence from his daughter's stand. Anna introduced Dylan to social media with the launch of his *Freedom Has A Voice* platform that now has thousands of supporters.[2]

Dylan has taken up his lay preaching in a new and vigorous way. He is also an advocate for freedom of speech and freedom of religion at rallies up and down the country. He and his wife now devote their lives to waking people up, Christians and non-Christians alike.

The foundation for their ministry is the words of Jesus:

I must work the works of Him who sent Me while it is day; the night is coming when no one can work. (John 9:4)

❀ ❀ ❀

The Long March Through The Institutions

What is education? From the moment we are born, arguable before we are born, we are all learning until the day we die. Education impacts every aspect of our lives, admiring the wonders of creation on a bush walk, holding down a stressful job, navigating school or university. I will never forget my Chemistry teacher's definition of education, (largely attributed to Albert Einstein) 'It's what you have left after you have forgotten everything you ever learned.' Good education is essential for us all to flourish and to fulfil our dreams.

Founding pastor, of Harpeth Christian Church, Nashville, Tennessee, Bobby Harrington, said:

> *On an almost daily basis, I talk to friends who lead churches around the USA who are trying to understand what is happening in our culture and how to help the people in their churches to be faithful to Jesus in light of what is happening.*[3]

My sentiment exactly. I see Christians and non-Christians alike unable to understand or articulate what is happening to our way of life. Dylan's family were awake to these issues and developed a rationale to navigate their future. *While We Were Sleeping* is my attempt to offer some tools for guiding our lives into the future.

Harrington describes the 'Long March Through the Institutions,' a phrase attributed to the Italian communist Antonio Gramsci (1891-1937) and then coined as a succinct *mission statement* by German Marxist student activist Rudi Dutschke in the 1960s. The phrase is used to describe the intellectual takeover of a society without the need to resort to military conflict. Instead, the strategy focused on slowly winning over the chief institutions that shape the culture creating an invisible revolution from within. The focus was first on the universities, then the other institutions were targeted, unions, the arts, K-12 schools, media, major corporations, and finally society as a whole.

A little booklet from 1974 that survives on the internet, *Prairie Fire: The Politics of Revolutionary Anti-Imperialism,* is most revealing about this strategy. Let's paint a picture with direct quotes from this booklet:

Our intention is to forge an underground ... a clandestine political organisation, with our final goal is the destruction of imperialism, the seizure of power, and the creation of socialism. We will develop insurgent cultures, for the overthrowing of the rotten values of male supremacy, consumerism, passivity, respectability and the rat race. For women working, forced into the marriage marketplace, trapped in oppressive relationships, raising children alone, the women's movement brought a new sense of self-worth and dignity; it explained the conditions of women's oppression.[4]

It's interesting that fifty years ago, the *manifesto* of the Long March Through The Institutions was being laid out and today we are living in its fulfilment; no longer clandestine and underground but in the hands of the powerful, and in nearly every government in the so-called democratic West. The Long March Through The Institutions has been a revolution, with its imposition of socialist ideas from the top down.[5]

This revolution would have been painfully slow and would have been ineffective had the student numbers remained at the immediate post WWII levels (the percentage of school leavers proceeding to higher education in UK in 1950 was only 3.4 per cent).[6] But the succeeding half century saw a dramatic shift in the tertiary educational landscape around the world. By 2000 the percentage in higher education in the UK had risen to 33 per cent and in Australia to 42 per cent by 2024.[7]

I believe two agendas combined to trigger this explosion of university enrolment. Firstly, governments intentionally raised the school leaving age, ostensibly to improve their population's literacy and numeracy, but the true reason, in my view, was to hide the rise in youth unemployment being created as Western governments were systematically dismantling manufacturing industries and outsourcing production to Asia and explicitly China.

The second agenda was a cover for the failure of the first. The raised school leaving age did not improve academic performance at all, in fact, the opposite;[8] hence the introduction of *the great university con, and the devaluation of academic standards.*[9] As a result, it is now easier for students to enter higher education than ever before. What is more, it's now easier to graduate with flying colours than would have been the case in previous generations. Never has Britain, had so many qualified graduates, and never before have their qualifications amounted to so little, according to Harry Lambert:

> *At a glance, British universities are a national success story. They have increased the number of undergraduate degrees they award fivefold since 1990, while the proportion of Firsts they hand out has quadrupled – from 7 per cent in 1994 to 29 per cent in 2019. For every student who got a First in the early 1990s, nearly 20 do so now. Masters' degrees, meanwhile, are nearly ten times as common as they were.*[9]

I contend that in the 1950s universities were designed to produce graduates who were great thinkers, with lifelong goals to push boundaries and, if possible, to break the mould of traditional ways of thinking and acting. Their education taught them the *love* of *learning*, *how* to gain understanding and *how* to think.

Fast forward to our day. Most degrees are designed to provide graduates with a curriculum *they need to know* to fulfil a particular career, coupled with a prescribed list of *approved skills* that employers have insisted for their workplace.

Now anyone can get a degree, and it is a rare thing for a university to create a genuine academic. Students used to be expected to *question* everything, now they are trained to be *uncritically compliant* and *submissive* to the doctrines of Marx and Lenin. This has all been by design, it is the triumph of the Long March through Education.

Baroness Caroline Cox, a member of the UK House of Lords since 1983, and an academic before that, tells a story from the mid-1970s when The Long March was just beginning. She was Head of Sociology at the then North London Polytechnic (now part of the London Metropolitan University), with a faculty of 20, 16 of whom were in the Communist Party, or even further left, with devastating consequences for one of her good friends, married to her Economics lecturer. Cox said:

> *Earlier in my life, I experienced the extensive sabotage of our political, cultural and spiritual heritage, by Marxism and Leninism in our higher education system way back in the 1970s… that included a devaluing of what was important, and that*

included the Christian faith and a political correctness that prevented you from challenging that in public.[8]

One day Cox's friend, distraught, asked to see her. The friend's husband, the Economics lecturer, had just joined the Communist Party, and he had been advised, by his party leadership, that he was obliged to ensure his wife join the party too, or he would have to divorce her! She did not become a communist. The Long March claimed her marriage.

Another way of demonstrating the Long March's success, is that in 2022 more than 80 per cent of surveyed Harvard University Faculty identify as Liberal or Very Liberal with only 1.46 per cent claiming to be Conservative,[9] a long way from Harvard's foundation principles established by the Christian Puritans in 1636, when their mission statement of 1642, read: 'Everyone shall consider as the main end of his life and studies, to know God and Jesus Christ, which is eternal life.'[10]

It is clear to me that higher education has been taken over from within. This pillar of society, once lauded and trusted, is now seen as a factory for the production of protagonists for the dismantling of Western Society and Judeo-Christian values in particular.

Teacher training, my own area of expertise, has been weaponised to infiltrate and dismantle primary and secondary school education. So much so that, *While We Were Sleeping*, our children have been indoctrinated with left leaning ideology, the death of God and the self-loathing of traditional family values.

Safe Schools Coalition Australia

The Safe Schools Coalition Australia serves as an illustration of an initiative that has taken root *While We Were Sleeping.*

I was a school principal in three Australian states between 1997 and 2008. If ever a case of bullying was brought to my attention, I immediately felt concerned that the staff and I had failed the victim, and I was at pains to root out the problem and prevent any repetition.

If one of my schools had been presented with the Safe Schools Coalition Australia, an initiative originating from Victoria, purporting to address the *growing issue of bullying in schools*, I would have been immediately sceptical. Why should individual schools need a government sponsored, one-size-fits-all initiative? Surely if we, as professional educators, cannot manage the social dynamics in our schools we are failing in our duty of care to our students and their families.

Speaking on the goal of Safe Schools at the Safe Schools Coalition National Symposium in Melbourne, 2014; co-founder Roz Ward, a self-identifying Marxist and member of the LGBTIQA+ community, and a prominent campaigner on gay, lesbian, transgender, and marriage equality, said:

> ... *Safe Schools Coalition is about supporting gender and sexual diversity. Not about celebrating diversity. Not about stopping bullying. About gender and sexual diversity. About same-sex attraction. About being transgender. About being lesbian, gay, bisexual – say the words – transgender, intersex. Not just 'Be nice to everyone. Everyone's great.'*[11]

The next year, the rhetoric was even more strident:

> *LGBTI oppression and heteronormativity are woven into the fabric of capitalism...programs like Safe Schools Coalition are making some difference, but we are still an extremely long way from liberation...only Marxism provides both the theory and the practice of genuine human liberation.*

Ward went further to connect the Safe School initiative to the same-sex marriage debate, stating: 'it's a total contradiction to say we want the Safe School Coalition, but you can't get married to the person you love.'[12] Consider some of the Safe School resources.

> *Gender fluid resources recommended for four-year-olds, only you know whether you are a boy or a girl, no one can tell you. Gender isn't quite as simple as whether you're 'male' or 'female.' Everyone has their own gender identity in relation to masculinity and femininity. Some identify with both, and some don't identify with either; it's up to the individual to describe what gender identity fits them best. The Safe Schools program promotes a biologically*

female 17-year-old, now identifying as a straight male, telling 11-14-year-olds in a class video that surgery should not be delayed for adolescents who want to transition from one gender to another.[13]

I think that's enough. So much for an *anti-bullying* initiative that should never have come from government sponsorship! So many were taken in by this false narrative; it was nearly ten years before it became widely known that there was a much more dangerous agenda.

Paul Kelly wrote in The Weekend Australian in 2017 that in the past, Australian society agreed on core values arising from the Christian tradition but recent debates on social issues such as gay marriage, abortion, euthanasia, and gender reveal a lack of direction and uncertainty when it comes to these issues. He noted that *the new progressive morality* was undermining the Christian tradition in Australia, and that at one time the laws of the state and the laws of the church co-existed, but this was no longer the case, we are witnessing:

the promotion of gay marriage, the push to legalise killing in the cause of humanitarianism, the restriction of free speech on the basis of causing offence, the promotion of gender fluidity and rejection of the boy/girl gender paradigm, and the manipulation of schools for ideological, sex, gender and climate programs.[14]

All this is evidence that schools have now become the cradle for the *new morality* and *secular fundamentalism*. The impressionable, un-churched, and un-thinking youth heading into puberty were and are the prime target.

Christian schools have not been immune to this tidal wave. Stephen Brinton[15] recently completed a significant study of the stated and actual mission of some Christian schools in Australia between 2017 and 2023. He found significant mission drift, from their founding principles, so much so that some are now asking the question, are we still a Christian school? The parallel with Harvard University is plain to see. I contend that the Safe School Coalition Australia's attack has been successful, having a significant impact on the school's capacity to be Christian.

We need not look to legislation to gauge the mores of our society. We merely need to listen to the self-censorship of the up-and-coming generations with their *new morality* and *secular fundamentalism.*

Perhaps *we were not sleeping;* but wanted to think the best of people and could not conceive that this *little initiative* out of Victoria, *designed to combat bullying,* could be a vehicle designed to demolish the Christian pillars of our society while ushering in modern day Marxism and Leninism.

What does God say?

Returning to my earlier question, what is education? I love, political commentator, Stephen Turley's description. He points out that education is not merely *informative,* the passing on of a body of knowledge, rather it is *formative*, that is, education shapes and moulds the student's character to fit into a particular culture. For Greeks, Romans, Christians and Jews education has always been *enculturation*.[16]

This was expressed in Harvard's foundation, in the 1600s, by their belief that everyone should consider their 'main end of life and studies, was to know God and Jesus Christ, which is eternal life.'[10] Christian parents have always been charged with training up their child 'in the way he should go, and when he is old he will not depart from it' (Proverbs 22:6).

All this to say, let's not be shy about our faith. Let's ensure our young are brought up in the ways of the Lord (Ephesians 6:4). But I hear you say, 'Aren't the teacher's responsible for my children's education, they are the experts, right?' No, it's the parents' primary responsibility to bring up their children in the training and instruction of the Lord, though most parents cede *some* responsibility to professional teachers under the principle of *in loco parentis.*

In loco parentis is a legal principle that embodies the responsibility of an individual or entity to take on *some* of the functions and responsibilities of a parent. Originating from Roman law, this term translates literally to 'in the place of a parent.' It is a concept that allows an individual or institution to act in the best interests of a child or young person as a parent would, assuming duties such as protection, education, and care.[17]

So, if our Christian values are being ignored, or outright contradicted, by the teachers or school in the education of our children, then *in loco parentis* is being broken and we can, and should, push back and speak up. If we don't, by our silence we are condoning the attack on our children's eternity.

In America, parents are regularly in the battlelines for their children's schooling.[18] They gather in their thousands at school board meetings. We don't have this culture in Australia, but I urge all parents to get involved in their children's education, by whatever means they can. The first step is to become informed of the various agendas competing for the hearts and minds of our children.

Few issues are as powerful to divide churches, as where to send our children to school. Should Christian parents send their children to public school? Is homeschooling the only right choice for Christian families? What about private Christian schools? These questions are never silent; everyone has an opinion, and most people feel their position is the only correct one.[19] For example, homeschooling might be right for you, as it was for Dylan and Fiona Oakley, but everyone's situation is unique. Each child is fearfully and wonderfully made, so one size can never fit all. But the responsibility of parents is clear, to ensure their young are 'brought up in the ways of the Lord.'

Let's conclude this review of education with some hope. Turley writes about the resurgence of Christian education in Hungary in recent years under prime minister Vitor Orban since 2010. It appears that their Christian schools are far better than the secular public schools and they get three times the funding per student than the standard public schools. Further, as they are run by churches and not by the state, they can choose their own textbooks and curriculum and have far more control over which students they will accept, thus they can institute very strict discipline standards as well as academic standards.[16]

Let's not close our eyes and pretend there is nothing we can do here. If the tide has turned in Hungary, it can turn for our children too! The challenge is to stay awake. We may have lost some battles in the past, but it seems to me the tide is turning. Let's identify the authors and the design of those who advance anarchy and chaos in society and seek to understand their motivation 'because He who is in us is greater than he who is in the world' (1 John 4:4).

Footnotes

[1] Faith Christian School of Distance Education. (n.d.). *Why Distance Ed?* Retrieved October 16, 2025, from https://www.faith.qld.edu.au/

[2] Freedom Has A Voice. (n.d.). *What Christian Leaders are Saying about Dylan's Ministry.* Retrieved October 16, 2025, from https://freedomhasavoice.com.au/

[3] Harrington, Bobby (2021, February 8). The Long March through the Institutions of Society. *Renew.org.* https://renew.org/the-long-march-through-the-institutions-of-society/

[4] Dohrn, Bernardine; Ayers, Billy; Jones, Jeff & Sojourn, Celia (1974). *Prairie Fire: The Politics of Revolutionary Anti-Imperialism.* Weather Underground. https://www.sds-1960s.org/PrairieFire-reprint.pdf

[5] Rufo, Christopher F. (2022, August 6). *The Long March Through the Institutions, Ep. 2.* [Video]. YouTube. https://www.youtube.com/watch?v=NEt9XepeGt4

[6] Bolton, Paul (2012, November 27). Education: Historical statistics. *Standard Note SN/SG/4252, Library House of Commons.* https://researchbriefings.files.parliament.uk/documents/SN04252/SN04252.pdf

[7] Australian Bureau of Statistics. (2024, November 8). *Education and Work, Australia.* https://www.abs.gov.au/statistics/people/education/education-and-work-australia/latest-release

[8] New South Wales Auditor-General's Report. (2012, November 1). The impact of the raised school leaving age. *Audit Office NSW.* https://www.audit.nsw.gov.au/sites/default/files/pdf-downloads/2012_Nov_Report_The_Impact_of_the_Raised_School_Leaving_Age.pdf

[9] Lambert, Harry (n.d.). *The great university con: how the British degree lost its value.* The New Statesman. Retrieved October 17, 2025, from https://www.newstatesman.com/politics/2019/08/the-great-university-con-how-the-british-degree-lost-its-value

[8] John Anderson Media. (2019, October 17). *Conversations: Featuring Baroness Caroline Cox.* [Video]. YouTube. https://www.youtube.com/watch?v=Mx7mXNBG874

[9] Xu, Meimei (2022, July 13). More than 80 Percent of Surveyed Harvard Faculty Identify as Liberal. The *Harvard Crimson*. https://www.thecrimson.com/article/2022/7/13/faculty-survey-political-leaning/

[10] Schultz, Roger (2019, February 26). Christianity and the American University. *Liberty Journal*. https://www.liberty.edu/journal/article/christianity-and-the-american-university/#:~:text=Puritans%20established%20Harvard%20College%20in,Christ%2C%20which%20is%20eternal%20life.

[11] Ward, Roz (2016, March 18). *'Safe Schools' is not about bullying, organiser admits!* End Safe Schools. [Video]. YouTube. https://www.youtube.com/watch?v=j5uNocBCw3Q&feature=youtu.be

[12] The Australian. (n.d.). *Head pans 'state homophobia.'* Retrieved October 17, 2025, from http://www.theaustralian.com.au/national-affairs/education/antibullying-head-links-safe-schools-to-samesex-marriage/news-story/6a690a2e67406b2f33d96da12c4f287b

[13] Francis, Wendy (n.d.). Safe Schools and Gender Theory. *Australian Christian Lobby*. Retrieved October 17, 2025, from https://churchandstate.com.au/wp-content/uploads/170908-Safe-Schools.pdf

[14] Bates, Winton (2017, July 12). Will individualism destroy Western Civilization? *Freedom Flourishing*. https://www.freedomandflourishing.com/2017/07/will-individualism-destroy-western.html

[15] Brinton, Stephen (2023). *A tale of two missions: the stated and perceived mission of three member schools of Christian Schools Australia.* Open Research Newcastle. [Doctoral Thesis] https://hdl.handle.net/1959.13/1471640

[16] Turley, Stephen, R. (2019). *The Return of Christendom: demography, politics, and the coming Christian majority.* Turley Talks. https://www.amazon.com.au/Return-Christendom-Demography-Politics-Christian/dp/1796658707

[17] McMurdie, Cristi (2024, February 29). Redefining Families: A Deep Dive into In Loco Parentis. *McMurdie Law & Mediation*. https://mcmurdielaw.com/redefining-families-a-deep-dive-into-in-loco-parentis-with-mcmurdie-law-mediation/

[18] CBN News. (2018, January 11). *'Mommy, Mommy, I Don't Want to Be a Boy!' Little Girl's Reaction to Radical Sex Ed Program Says It A.* [Video]. YouTube. https://www.youtube.com/watch?v=xNOBlyvaPKo

[19] Hubler, Melissa (2024, April 26). Christian Parents and the Public School Classroom. *Legacy Ministries International.* https://legacyfamilyministries.com/2024/04/26/christian-parents-and-the-public-school-classroom/

CHAPTER 4 - SCREEN ADDICTION

Lindsey Fuch's Story

Lindsey Fuchs, mother of three primary aged boys lives in Sydney, Australia. She has studied and taught Theology at tertiary level. She is now a passionate advocate for children to grow up into adulthood, free from screen addiction and its associated sociopathic adverse effects.[1]

Lindsey picks up the story:

Perhaps the first time I realised there was an issue was when I was teaching adults as a lecturer. The students were disengaged with me, and I am sure it wasn't my teaching or my material. They were also disengaged with each other. Rather, they were immersed in their screens while in my classroom.

So, one day I had every one put their devices in a bag at the door as they entered the room. They would get them back at the end of class. I thought this was simply a novel thing to do, just a sensible strategy to improve class participation. But I was met with severe aggression. From one student, a mother of teenagers, it seemed as if she was being told she couldn't have her drugs. I was shocked! This incident triggered, for me, the decision to give up teaching.

Then, one day I was at a family party. One of the children there had an iPad. The mother said to her child, 'I need to take that away.' The child, not even 18 months, shifted into aggressive behaviour. I had never seen a child behave like that over a screen.

Then with my own children, my first born, I realised this was a severe issue for childhood development. My son ended up with an addiction to screen time when he was not quite two years old. He was being looked after by a friend, while I was in hospital for five days. When my son came to see me in hospital, I thought he was a completely different kid. He had had unrestricted access to television, an iPad and an iPhone. His supervisor had permitted screentime for his first time, with the associated tantrums I had never seen before.

A year or two years later, maybe when he was four years old, he would sneak down and find our TV controller in the middle of the night. We ended up having him see a doctor for behavioural issues, because I had no idea what to do. But I did pray about it, and someone from church gifted me, Kevin Lemen's book, *How to have a New Kid by Friday: How To Change Your Child's Attitude, Behavior & Character In 5 Days.*[2]

After just one day of working on Leven's book as a family, he went from three or four full blown meltdowns a day, kicking, screaming, bashing, and thrashing to one in two weeks. So, by the time we had gotten to see the specialist, the wait time had been months, he was asking us what we had changed!

The GP who had given us the referral for the specialist had said – 'If I gave you heroin for five days, and took it away, how would you be?' He said it's the same chemical involved in your brain. Dopamine is produced in the hypothalamus. Then when the screen is removed and the dopamine takes a hit, cortisol is secreted in the adrenal glands. This triggers the rage and aggression, typical of a drug addict denied their fix.

The Lemen book gave me the courage to put on my big-girl-pants and be a mom. It reminded me of the authority that my husband and I have. We made the choices that are best for our children, and the results were remarkable.

Then when my son went to Kindergarten, I had a talk with his teacher. I said – 'How come my son has watched more TV with you, in Kindergarten, in two weeks than he has with me in our own home in eight months?' I said – 'Why is it he is watching Play School when he is at school?' And my son, who at this point was six years old, said to his teacher, showing Bluey on the screen during crunch and sip – 'Excuse me Miss, could we turn it off now and learn how to talk with each other?'

I believe that children can be helped to recognise what's happening, particularly teenagers. I personally can feel guilty looking at a screen, I don't like it. But I am not putting my guilt on anyone else. Their situation is not like mine; I respect everyone's unique circumstances.

One way of looking at screen time can be to differentiate between *entertainment* and *research,* between *candy* and *vegetables*! I view research as building on the learning I have already have; I am now going to use technology *to enhance* my understanding. So, research is what I usually use my phone for, this scrolling thing with my thumb, I can be addicted just like the next person, so I try not to touch it. One point from the high-ups in Silicon Valley, is that they don't let their own children see screens at their schools, as they understand the power of addiction, having written the algorithms that stimulate the addiction!

Talking about the connection between screen addiction and porn; I know that schools are one of the first places kids see pornography, and it's usually by Year 4, either on the devices brought in from home or on the devices that the school provides, and schools fail to install effective filters, or the kids learn how to get around them. Then peer pressure forces each other to look at it.

Someone gave me this analogy; imagine you're a high school student and your textbook is online. Equate this with a teacher handing this same student their textbook, but on top of it a Playboy magazine, and then saying to them, you need to finish Lesson 12 by tomorrow!

This illustrates the connection between internet screens and pornography. This impacts boys and girls, though perhaps the percentage take-up is higher for boys and men, but I don't think that is relevant. I think that girls are just as susceptible. They both have hormones; they are both curious.

So, my concern for screen addiction is tied so closely with porn addiction. I would love to see people educated about what is going on in their bodies and psychology.

I have read many books, one called *Stolen Focus.*[3] People's ability to focus is being taken from them, whether by diet, sleep, or screen use. The algorithms of social media platforms are designed to keep you on longer, and eventually to trigger addiction.

I am always aware of who's getting the money. I sniff out the money trail! I would love to see that everyone is as appalled as I am, but that is far from the case. When I share this with people, for instance, when we are at a playground having a chat, and they are lamenting screen use, or the fact they can't connect with their husbands anymore, or their husbands are not connecting with their kids, as they are on their phone; their reaction is often; 'it is what it is!' They feel *powerless* to do anything.

I have enough knowledge now so I would love to talk with people starting with my children's teachers. Simply ask your teachers, 'How much time is my kid on a screen in your classroom?' Don't sign the waiver for permission to go online at school. This is not to hurt the teachers, as I am sure they don't want an entire class seeing pornography on their watch. Parents, we are *powerful* and we should exercise our influence strategically to bring about change!

❀   ❀   ❀

Minecraft Education[4]

For this section I am again indebted to Lindsey. In 2024, after her wake-up call over her eldest son's experience with screens during her brief stay in hospital, she began to investigate the use of Minecraft in her children's school. She raised questions and concerns with the teachers, and then with the school principal, who eventually fobbed her off, saying that she had better take up her concerns with the Department of Education as it was specifically the *Minecraft Education* edition that she said had legitimate published educational objectives, such as:

> *Experience the balance of survival*
> *Explore the wonders of space with NASA*
> *Build AI skills with Minecraft*
> *Teach coding through game design*
> *Teach learners how to be safe online*[4]

I can imagine most teachers applauding the use of Minecraft in school, as it would tap into the comfort zone of the home. In addition, for those struggling with confidence, this could be a game changer. So, what's the harm, I hear you say?

Imagine, 'Mum, can I go on Minecraft before dinner, we are learning so much at school, I can't wait to learn more!' How many mums would say no! But school is now reenforcing screentime at home.

Lindsey was motivated to understand Minecraft, so that she could engage people intelligently in discussions, exploring the physiology and psychology of gaming, screen addiction and the specifics of Minecraft.

All video games are designed to be addictive. The euphoria experienced is due to the production of dopamine in the brain.[5] It acts on other areas of the brain to give feelings of pleasure, satisfaction and motivation. It is analogous to what happens to us after drinking alcohol, using illegal drugs and having sex.

Then, when the game is removed, our bodies crave the feelings we have lost, resulting in being aggressive and having trouble controlling our impulses. This is due to the production of cortisol by the adrenal glands creating the 'fight or flight' response, which is our healthy response to perceived threats.[6] This is an instinctive response that can't easily be controlled. Hence the child's meltdowns, kicking, screaming, bashing, and thrashing response to being taken off their drug of choice.

I contend that parents don't want this behaviour stoked by school. In addition, Minecraft competes with some of the legitimate goals of education. The developing brain, saturated with dopamine inhibits the development of the frontal lobe which is chiefly responsible for our ability to develop empathy and healthy, respectful relationships, critical thinking skills and decision-making capacity. In boys, the frontal lobe continues to be refined up to 21 years of age.

Dr. Nicholas Kardaras, an addiction expert and former Clinical Professor at Stony Brook Medicine, New York State, has also taught neuropsychology at the doctoral-level, and is the author of *Glow Kids*, says:

We've all seen them: kids hypnotically staring at glowing screens in restaurants, in playgrounds and in friends' houses and the numbers are growing. Like a virtual scourge, the illuminated glowing faces - the Glow Kids - are multiplying. But at what cost? Is this just a harmless indulgence or fad like some sort of digital hula-hoop? Some say that glowing screens might even be good for kids - a form of interactive educational tool.

> *Huge Tec conglomerates, like Apple and Microsoft amplify and*
> *perversely manipulate well intended parents into believing that*
> *iPads, tablets, smart phones, and hypnotic games like Minecraft*
> *are wonderful, educational tools that will make kids smarter.*
> *It's this combination of opportunistic tech companies, oblivious*
> *school districts, and duped parents that has led to the head down*
> *and glowing faced epidemic that any moderately observant adult*
> *has witnessed over the last few years.*[7]

Any program with these tangible adverse effects at epidemic proportions needs to be pulled. But let's consider some of the *moral* and *spiritual* messaging within Minecraft. There is a practice within the game called 'griefing,' in which one player intentionally destroys the work of another in order to cause them grief![8] As a teacher, and a parent, this is inexcusable. To justify this as child's play is intentionally feeding selfishness, spite, jealousy, deception, greed, vandalism and perhaps murder.

Another example from the game is the concept of 'respawning.' The Oxford Learner's Dictionary defines this as a character in a video game, that has been killed, has the capacity to respawn or is respawned, so that their character appears again in the game.

Minecraft participants become more at home in the reality of the game than in their physical reality. If 'rebirthing' is a natural part of the game it denies our experience of *one* birth, *one* death and *one* 'rebirth' in Jesus Christ. The game's term is not 'rebirthing' or being 'born-again' with its Christian connotation, but rather 'respawning,' which is impossible in the physical world, but has echoes of the animal kingdom.

The End of Minecraft is a dimension in the game where you can go to after gathering some rare items and fighting monsters. You defeat the Ender Dragon and jump into a portal. After this *fun achievement*, you read (or ignore) a poem on the screen and continue playing the game as normal.

The poem is a conversation between two voices. It was written by Julian Gough at the request of Markus Persson, the creator of the game. It draws parallels between the game and real life by calling them both *dreams*. In real life, you eat, you walk, you work — for what? What is the point of life? Don't many people ask themselves this question today?

According to the poem, life is a journey to achieve the highest level (of understanding).[9]

Consider these phrases from the End Poem:

> *and the universe said I love you*
> *and the universe said you are stronger than you know*
> *and the universe said the light you seek is within you*
> *and the universe said you are not alone*
> *and the universe said I love you because you are love*
> *You are the player. Wake up*

If it isn't clear by now, the game is essentially telling the player, 'You are god.' 'The player is the universe. The player is love.' After all the hours of mining, all the hours of building, all the hours of someone else asking, 'Can I use the computer yet?'—the culmination of your effort is meant to be the realisation that you are the godlike universe.[9]

Parents, I know this is counter intuitive and a daunting task but take a deep dive into the design and philosophy of Minecraft. How much of a *hold* does it have on your children? Do you use it to *manage* your children? Does your school us it and why?

It appears to me that Minecraft is being used as a *control mechanism* for future generations. It is designed to dull the child's intellect, *addict* them to screen time and indoctrinate them against the Christian faith and its traditional mores.

Distraction or Addiction

Can we tell the difference between *distraction* and *addiction*? I guess we can at the extremes, but what about the boundary. There are so many competing views and emotions around the word *addiction*. Many might point the self-righteous finger at the addict and subconsciously build a wall, building an ever-growing hurdle for the addict to overcome.[10]

My aim is not to spread moral panic but rather to stimulate our asking questions and sharpening our powers of observation.[11] If we can't decide between distraction and addiction, examine some of the potential adverse effects:

Hyperarousal looks different for each person. It can include difficulties with paying attention, managing emotions, controlling impulses, following directions and tolerating frustration. Some adults or children struggle with expressing compassion and creativity, and have a decreased interest in learning. This can lead to a lack of empathy for others, which can lead to violence. Also, kids who rely on screens and social media to interact with others typically feel lonelier than kids who interact in person.[12]

Further, the imbalance in brain chemistry of young people addicted to smartphones and the internet, has been shown to correlate with significantly higher scores in depression, anxiety, insomnia severity and impulsivity.[13]

Bjorn Bull-Hansen takes a broad view of society today and claims that, 'They're adults but still children!'[14] Have we become a society hypnotised by entertainment with little capacity left for creativity and striving to achieve visions and goals:[15]

We can see the immaturity on social media; we are losing something of what it means to be a grownup. There is a reluctance in interest in gaining knowledge and wisdom. Instead, people have become very opinionated. People these days are very quick to get angry. Maybe people are no longer as good as they were at listening to others. There is so much me first, my opinions, my enjoyment.[14]

So rather than going with the flow, shrugging and saying, 'it is what it is!' Let's take a stand and push back against the tide at our doorway. There are helpful tips we can seek to implement. As adults we can model the healthy use of screens and video games to our young. We can unplug when we first get home from work, at dinner and when driving. We can intentionally explore alternative methods of relaxation and entertainment, such as bushwalking, playing games, having a dance party or reading a book. We can keep all screens out of bedrooms and require that all devices be charged outside of bedrooms overnight.[12,16]

I wonder how many households achieve calm, supportive conversations around screen time. I suspect 50 per cent have a *laisse fair landscape*, with no acknowledgement of any problem; 25 per cent represent battle fields with missiles being launched daily with many casualties on both sides; and finally, a further 25 per cent, where seeking after truth is the hallmark, and joy and peace are the objectives.

What does God say?

Screen distraction has been growing for decades (Postman's diagnosis in the 1980s)[15] as more and more of our lives have become dependent on our screens, which may have brought us to the tipping point into addiction. I am most concerned about the young; firstly, the most vulnerable, the pre-teens, then the teens, so easily manipulated by peer pressure.

The habit of sitting at home around the meal table with others is a significant theme in the Bible, often representing fellowship, sharing, and the importance of hospitality. Several verses highlight this idea, including those in Luke 14:10, 1 Corinthians 11:34, and Matthew 8:11. Sitting around the table with no screens is such a wonderful time for building positive memories, especially when putting into practice Lindsey's son's request to, 'learn how to talk with each other.'

Let's make the reclaiming of our *personal responsibility* one of our goals and let's model this to the young around us. Let's search our hearts; are there areas of our responsibility that we have abdicated to others or to the state? Let's pray that as Christians, we will not be deceived, finding our *personal responsibility* taken away without our knowledge.[17]

Beware lest anyone cheat you through philosophy and empty deceit, according to the tradition of men, according to the basic principles of the world, and not according to Christ. (Colossians 2:8)

David Murrow demonstrates how screen time weakens our faith in God.[18] For example:

Screens have become the objects of our worship. Anything that commands our attention nine hours a day can be accurately described as an idol. Christians now spend the vast majority of their free time interacting with screens. Not God. Not people. Screens are the true object of our worship.

Screen time is displacing spiritual disciplines. Take prayer for example. In the pre-iPhone era, I used to spend idle moments communing with God. Now, if I have a few minutes standing in line or waiting at the baggage carousel I tend to reach for my phone. Instead of turning my heart toward Christ or praying for people I meet, I find myself scrolling social media or playing Candy Crush. We miss opportunities to fulfill our mission in life. If our noses are buried in our screens, we pay less attention to the world around us. Time that could be spent fulfilling our God-given mission is instead devoted to watching reruns or blasting imaginary on-screen foes.

Screens tempt us. 1 John 2:16 says, 'For all that is in the world— the lust of the flesh, the lust of the eyes, and the pride of life—is not of the Father but is of the world.' No single verse better describes what screens do to us. They inflame our lusts with an endless gallery of sensual images (desires of the flesh), objects and lifestyles to covet (desires of the eyes), and people to look down upon (the pride of life).

Murrow says, 'If our noses are buried in our screens, we pay less attention to the world around us.'[18] So true and isn't that the pandemic surrounding us? No more conversations at bus stops, no more conversions at the checkout, no more conversions with our bank, and diminishing conversations with our spouse and our children.

The theme of this book is to encourage us to *wake-up* to the world that surrounds us, that so desperately needs us. From the words of Melody Green, sung by her husband Keith:[19]

> *Oh, I wanna thank You now*
> *For being patient with me*
> *Oh, it's so hard to see*
> *When my eyes are on me.*

Footnotes

[1] Juby, Bethany (2024, February 8). What It Actually Means to Be a 'Sociopath.' *Healthline.* https://www.healthline.com/health/mental-health/sociopath#What-is-a-sociopath

[2] Lemen, Kevin (2012). *How to have a New Kid by Friday: How To Change Your Child's Attitude, Behavior & Character In 5 Days.* Revell. https://www.goodreads.com/book/show/3152629-have-a-new-kid-by-friday

[3] Hari, Johann (2022). *Stolen Focus: Why You Can't Pay Attention.* Bloomsbury. https://johannhari.com/

[4] Minecraft Education. (n.d.). *Welcome to Minecraft Education.* Retrieved October 19, 2025, from https://education.minecraft.net/en-us

[5] Health Direct, Free Australian health advice you can count on. (n.d.). *Dopamine.* Retrieved October 19, 2025, from https://www.healthdirect.gov.au/dopamine

[6] Health Direct, Free Australian health advice you can count on. (n.d.). *Cortisol.* Retrieved October 19, 2025, from https://www.healthdirect.gov.au/the-role-of-cortisol-in-the-body

[7] Kardaras, Nicholas (2016). *Glow Kids: How Screen Addiction Is Hijacking Our Kids – And How To Break The Trance.* St Martin's Press. https://www.amazon.com.au/Glow-Kids-Nicholas-Kardaras/dp/1250097991

[8] Kerby, Carl, Jr. & Thorwall, Drew (2014, July 1). Minecraft: Friend or Foe? *The Berean Call.* https://www.thebereancall.org/content/july-2014-extra-minecraft

[9] Reinier (2021, September 20). A Christian Perspective on Minecraft's End Poem. *Medium.* https://medium.com/@reinier_/a-christian-perspective-on-minecrafts-end-poem-1fce2d9f2de1

[10] Twelves, Jim (2025, January 23). *Addiction Ep 51.* Jim Twelves. [Video]. YouTube. https://www.youtube.com/watch?v=C_95ToqOHlM&t=228s

[11] Bradley Ruder, Debra (2019, June 19). Screen Time and the Brain: Digital devices can interfere with everything from sleep to creativity. *Harvard Medical School.* https://hms.harvard.edu/news/screen-time-brain

[12] Luker, Edward (2022, July 1). Are video games, screens another addiction? *Mayo Clinic Health Systems.* https://www.mayoclinichealthsystem.org/hometown-health/speaking-of-health/are-video-games-and-screens-another-addiction

[13] Seo, Hyung Suk (2017, November 30). Smartphone Addiction Creates Imbalance in Brain. *Radiological Society of North America (RSNA).* https://www.rsna.org/media/press/i/1989

[14] Bull-Hansen, Bjorn, Andreas (2025, February 28). *They're Adults But Still Children: A Grumpy Gen X-ers Opinion.* Bjorn Andreas Bull-Hansen. [Video]. YouTube. https://www.youtube.com/watch?v=wabrfO1onzo

[15] Postman, Neil (1985). *Amusing Ourselves to Death: Public Discourse in the Age of Show Business.* Penguin Books. https://www.amazon.com.au/Amusing-Ourselves-Death-Discourse-Business-ebook/dp/B0023ZLLH6

[16] Alavi, Seyyed Salman (2012). Behavioral Addiction versus Substance Addiction: Correspondence of Psychiatric and Psychological Views *Int J Prev Med, April, 3*(4), 290–294. https://pmc.ncbi.nlm.nih.gov/articles/PMC3354400/

[17] Twelves, Jim (2024, February 14). The World Has Gone Mad! Part 7: Personal Responsibility. *Daily Declaration.* *https://dailydeclaration.org.au/2024/02/14/the-world-has-gone-mad-part-7-personal-responsibility/*

[18] Murrow, David (2020, December 3). How Screen Time Weakens Our Faith. *David Murrow.* https://davidmurrow.com/how-screen-time-weakens-our-faith/

[19] Green, Keith (2024, March 22). *Make My Life a Prayer to You (Lyric Video).* Mission of Grace Church. [Video]. YouTube. https://www.youtube.com/watch?v=BgCw2rRX0IE

CHAPTER 5 - ARTIFICIAL INTELLIGENCE

Akos Balogh's Story

Akos was born in Budapest, Hungary, under communist rule. Hungarians are very patriotic, and hated Russian control, which included censorship, their vicious secret police and Russian control of what the schools taught.

In 1981, this oppression drove the Balogh family to migrate to Australia when Akos was four years old. They settled in Sydney, and upon finishing high school, where he came to faith, Akos joined the Australian Army (as a Combat Engineer). After the army, he completed a degree in Aerospace Engineering at the University of New South Wales and worked in the Royal Australian Air Force as an Aerospace Engineering Officer for five years.

After the Air Force, I went from fixing broken aeroplanes to fixing broken people, through speaking the news of the Christian gospel to them: and so I undertook ministry training. I did a ministry apprenticeship with Campus Bible Study, also at the University of New South Wales, and then completed a Bachelor of Divinity at Moore Theological College, Sydney.

This part of his testimony was a dramatic U-turn! In 2010, Akos moved his family to north-eastern New South Wales, where he worked for six years with the Australian Fellowship of Evangelical Students (AFES) as a chaplain with the staff and student body of Southern Cross University, Lismore.

So far in his Christian walk Akos had experienced respect for and fulfilment in his ministry, but while pastoring there in the university, his Christian activities came under a concerted attack from a middle-aged gay guy in the university. Akos was accused of spreading homophobic attitudes in his meetings.

At first the university authorities tried to support Akos with mediation, but this didn't last. The authorities began to show their cards, bias against Christians and favour toward the aggrieved student.

This was a startling wake-up call for Akos. He now began to recognise Christians have a forceful, belligerent enemy, academia, that had initially given him an open door into the university community, were actually on the attacking side.

He left Lismore at the end of 2015, and by 2017 finished his Masters of Arts (Theology), through the Queensland Theological College. It was around this time that Akos became aware of the all-pervasive elements of Woke Culture.

What does woke mean? The old meaning of the word defines woke as simply the past tense of the verb 'to wake,' as in to wake up, or awaken. Described by Merriam-Webster as 'chiefly US slang,' the dictionary defines the word as: 'Aware of and actively attentive to important facts and issues (especially issues of racial and social justice).'

In a modern sense, the meaning of the word has changed significantly, and in 2017, the new meaning of the word 'woke' was officially added to the dictionary. Woke nowadays refers to being aware or well informed in a political or cultural sense, especially regarding issues surrounding marginalised communities; it describes someone who has 'woken up' to issues of social injustice.[1]

From this eye-opening experience, Akos developed a passion for religious freedom. He developed an acute eye for any move seeking to limit the expression and practice of the Christian faith. And to this end, he conducted a good deal of research around Article 18 of the United Nations Universal Declaration of Human Rights:

Everyone has the right to freedom of thought, conscience and religion; this right includes freedom to change his religion or belief, and freedom, either alone or in community with others and in public or private, to manifest his religion or belief in teaching, practice, worship and observance. (UN Universal Declaration of Human Rights – Article 18)[2]

Akos became the CEO of The Gospel Coalition Australia, a fellowship of evangelical churches in the Reformed tradition, deeply committed to the renewing of faith in the gospel of Jesus Christ and to reforming ministry practices to conform to those expressed in Scripture.

More recently Akos returned to Moore Theological College, where he worked as the External Engagement Manager. Today, Akos is a blogger, researcher, and ghost writer. His weekly blogs focus on the intersection of culture and Christianity with a particular focus on developments in Artificial Intelligence (AI).

Prior to 2010, he had a radical change of heart with his transition from life in the armed services to taking up his Christian ministry. But the assault on his work in Lismore was at a whole deeper level. It challenged his core beliefs about the place of God in society.

Do you not know that friendship with the world is enmity with God? Whoever therefore wants to be a friend of the world makes himself an enemy of God. (James 4:4)

Akos understood this world has always been against Jesus, and therefore against him as he preached the gospel.

Five years later, he recognised his second wake-up-call as he came face the face with the woke philosophy. This in turn drove him to research the perception of religious freedom which ultimately propelled him into his current calling to equip his brothers and sisters in Christ, in their fight for the gospel:

And do not be conformed to this world, but be transformed by the renewing of your mind, that you may prove what is that good and acceptable and perfect will of God. (Romans 12:2)

Akos sets the stage for our consideration of AI with this great scenario. He asks us to examine the impact on the user of a bicycle and a car as a means of transport. Both, efficiently transport the user from A to B. Yes, the car will normally take the user much further and faster than the bicycle, but, with regular use, the cyclist will become a healthy, fit, lean, muscle machine, while the driver will most likely become unfit, lacking muscle tone, and overweight.

Our use of AI shapes us. As Christians, we need to use 'disciplined discernment' to understand this shaping, limiting as far as we can any negative aspects while making the most of the positives. Let's look into AI with eyes wide open.

❀　　❀　　❀

What do we feel about AI?

Many of us are super excited about AI, we avidly explore as much information as we can about AI and we are quick to download the latest software to try it ourselves. However, it has been said that AI may well eclipse the industrial revolution by its pace of rollout and its impact on the human race.[3] It certainly seems set to have the potential for greater disruption than the advent of the internet or the impact of the atomic bomb.

The inevitability of dramatic change across our lives is the reason I start this book with a consideration of AI. I hope to be able to show that developments in AI are creating the stage upon which each of my topics play out.

Types of AI

It is common to refer to AI as if it is a single entity, the breathtaking new software that can write student's essays and draft the perfect sermon for the pastor. However, there is much more to AI than this.

John Lennox, Irish mathematician, bioethicist, and Christian apologist; gives us three types of AI.[4]

Narrow AI creates an outcome that can already be done by human intelligence, but much faster and more accurately than any human. For example, the interpretation of X-ray images. AI compares images with a massive database that has already been analysed by experts from around the globe. This gives doctors a much better result than any local hospital or a single specialist could ever hope to achieve. In this case the *intelligence* lies in the intellect of the people who designed the software, and the specialists who've given their data to the AI system.

Naturally, everyone, the medical fraternity, and the patient, are thrilled with this development of AI. It can be a life saver for those in rural communities with very limited medical facilities and personnel.

China's social credit system is another example of Narrow AI. This is a development from the digital tracker system in mobile phones, coupled with facial, or gait, recognition software. All movements and behaviours are monitored and fed into the individual's account, creating a positive, or negative, score that will permit, or block, the individual's future movements or behaviours.

Most of us would be appalled to live under such *big brother* control. But if you have grown up with this and have never known anything else, you might feel a sense of security, because you know that your *best interests* are being *protected*. You would not know your human rights had been removed.

Artificial General Intelligence (AGI) is the quest to build systems, which some believe will surpass human intelligence. This is the stuff of dreams and science fiction, so people love it, a type of AI that possesses the capability to understand, learn, and apply knowledge across a broad range of tasks, simultaneously. AGI aims to exhibit general cognitive abilities, allowing it to solve new problems and adapt to new environments, autonomously, without the need for additional programming by a human. In other words, it will teach itself. It aims to surpass human cognitive processes, including learning, reasoning, and problem-solving.[5]

AGI is an enormous step up from Narrow AI. We are not there yet, though some believe we are very close. Definitions vary and terms differ, so it's very hard to pin down. However, for me, the crux of AGI seems to be the concept of the 'cascade effect,' a scenario where a single action or development by an AGI triggers a chain reaction of events, rapidly impacting multiple systems and potentially leading to significant, unforeseen consequences across various aspects of society, often with escalating intensity, much like a waterfall cascading down a series of steps. Narrow AI is *controlled* by us, AGI is not![6]

Transhumanism describes the idea of taking existing human beings, and enhancing them with implants, bioengineering and drugs, rendering the incorporated technologies *cyborgs*, a combination of cybernetics and biology. The objective is the creation of an advanced human, or superhuman, with the defeat of human limitations and ultimately the defeat of death.

This sounds like a resurgence of eugenics. Francis Galton coined the term eugenics in 1883 to describe his *science* of human improvement. The Nazi regime's racial hygiene policies were arguably the most extreme form of eugenics, which included forced sterilisation, euthanasia and human *experiments* in concentration camps during World War II. Eugenics was based on the incorrect belief that most human activity, whether physical or mental, was determined by heredity. Therefore, if heredity could be controlled, the eugenicists believed they could improve future generations and the survival of the species.[7]

Good AI

Big data has become everyday language. It refers to massive datasets, often measured in terabytes or petabytes, too vast for traditional database tools to handle. Instead, these datasets are analysed using advanced software to discover patterns, trends and insights, specifically about human behaviour and their interactions.[8]

Our capacity to create and handle big data has grown symbiotically with and become AI's food. In turn, AI may be viewed as a colossal structure of interconnected super computers which create meaning from big data and presents it to us for our benefit.

Reflect on the benefits of AI, starting with AI that replicates what humans do, but without making mistakes. For example, imagine the elimination of human error from air travel accidents. We all know we make more mistakes when we are tired, so AI can automate repetitive, boring tasks.

We have a finite capacity to handle large amounts of information, but AI smoothly handles big data with the potential for infinite capacity. AI can also facilitate super-fast decision making, way beyond human capability and it doesn't need rest breaks or is limited by a 40-hour week.

AI has brought us digital assistants such as Siri, Alexa and Google. We can measure their cost-effective support from a dimension unknown to previous generations. These digital assistants can penetrate places inaccessible or too dangerous for mankind. For example, conducting deep ocean exploration or rescue missions into earthquake ravaged situations that could kill human rescue personnel.

AI is vital in healthcare applications, improving workflow, extending capacity and speed in diagnoses, saving lives and costs of protracted medical interventions. The spread of top-quality healthcare into rural and remote locations and to populations trapped in poverty are AI revolutions waiting to happen.

AI has the capacity to surpass human intelligence and can perform tasks more accurately and efficiently. However, others say anything in excess is not good, and nothing can match the human brain.[9]

For Christians, Dustin Ryan[10] eulogises about the huge leap forward afforded by the speed and accuracy of being able to translate the Bible and other texts into every language under heaven. The potential for evangelism is enormous, and Christians should not miss this opportunity. Pastors can also mitigate their own burnout and become more effective at shepherding their flock if they take advantage of AI without selling their souls to the devil.[11]

Some Dangers of AI

AI has been hailed as revolutionary and world-changing, but it's not without drawbacks, says Mike Thomas (2024). I think his survey of *14 Risks and Dangers* is a helpful introduction.

> *'These things could get more intelligent than us and could decide to take over, and we need to worry now about how we prevent that*

happening,' said Geoffrey Hinton, known as the 'Godfather of AI' for his foundational work on machine learning and neural network algorithms. In 2023, Hinton left his position at Google so that he could 'talk about the dangers of AI,' noting a part of him even regrets his life's work.[12]

The fact that Geoffrey Hinton admits he does not understand how AI's deep learning models work is a major concern. Hinton believes humanity doesn't know what it's doing.[13] This lack of transparency and explainability begs the question for the need of regulation; but who will craft the regulations and how can regulations work if we don't know what we are doing?

Thomas highlights the top concern among companies, namely the privacy and security of their data. Yes, we live in an interconnected world, but we certainly don't have global government yet, whose policies are applied effectively across every nation. Nevertheless, it is becoming harder and harder to travel anywhere without surveillance cameras collecting our personal data for AI's insatiable appetite.

Social manipulation through AI algorithms is already a reality that governments rely on to ensure their narrative takes root. This can be called propaganda. Thomas quotes the story of Ferdinand Marcos Jr who used trolls to garner young Filipino votes in their 2022 election. Succeeding chapters will quote numerous examples of society's behaviours being *altered* by the powerful to further their agendas. If we know it is happening, we might be able to push back. If this is true now, what hope have we against AI in the future, especially if we are inherently less intelligent than AI?[13]

Deep fake videos abound, some purport to be of our politicians.[14] When they become more sophisticated, will we be able to pick the fake? Even if some of us can spot the fake, what about those who don't have the time or interest to dive deep enough to check them out, they will be duped. We already have a politically unstable world, isn't AI more likely to tip us into anarchy?

AI algorithms are already trading on stock exchanges around the world at speeds impossible for human traders to match, but they don't respond to human *trust* and *fear*. Further, if the human investor sees the AI selling off thousands of trades, they could be scared into doing the same thing, triggering an unnecessary financial meltdown.

If a stock market crash is averted and AI brings smiles to their handlers, I doubt they will redistribute wealth to the less fortunate, it will only deepen socioeconomic inequality while the rich get richer, and the poor get poorer. Some may ague more wealth must be created for the philanthropists to distribute. However, this is simply giving the poor a fish, it doesn't teach them how to fish and to invest in fish farming.

Yuval Harari, arguably the most influential advisor to the World Economic Forum, unashamedly admits the flood of extremely useful devices, tools and structures will make no allowance for the *freewill* of the individual human.[15] He argues that democracy, the free market and human rights will not survive this flood:

> *Humans will lose their economic and military usefulness; hence, the economic and political system will stop attaching much value to them.*
> *The system will continue to find value in humans collectively, not in unique individuals.*
> *The system will still find value in some unique individuals, but these will constitute a new elite of upgraded superhumans, rather than the mass of the population.* (p. 356)

Harari asks, what to do with the superfluous people? He goes on to say:

> *...we might witness the creation of a massive new unworking class, people devoid of any economic, political or even artistic value, who contribute nothing to the prosperity, power and glory of society. This 'useless class,' will not be merely unemployed, they will be unemployable.* (p. 379)

You might respond; such a dystopian future seems too far-fetched to warrant serious consideration. But these ideas are from the same man who is excited about transhumanism. He argues the case that God is dead, and therefore mankind must put away all myths relating to the supernatural and replace Him with the 'man god' (Homo Deus).[15] He suggests establishing man as the supreme authority even with the ability to defeat death, bringing in the potential for immortality for *superhumans*, those whose biology has been augmented technologically.

Illustrating a further danger of AI; consider the pagers and walkie-talkie attack by Israel's IDF on Iran's Hezbollah terrorists in Lebanon in September 2024.[16] In this event little pocket devices were distributed to Hezbollah terrorist leadership and simultaneously, remotely detonated, inflicting untold physical and psychological harm on the enemy. Many regarded this event as the major turning point in the war that was launched by Hamas from Gaza, 7th October 2023.

No, this wasn't an AI operation, but it illustrates one of the deadly potentials for AI, namely the mobilisation of autonomous weapons. Putting aside the ethical consideration of being able to kill while being in no personal danger; surely it won't be long before AI is analysing the data and selecting the target for its own weapons. While autonomous weapons in *good hands* could be seen as safe, what if they get into criminal or terrorist hands? What if AI decides that their operators are in fact the *bad guys*?

According to Pastors Jay Kim and Gavin Ortlund most of us have been duped into believing that AI tools are benign with no hidden agendas.[17] But the creators admit these tools are incentivised to manipulate our behaviour for their profit. They describe this as the dehumanising potential, because while we believe we are operating in the realm of freewill, we are in fact being controlled. We think we are using technology, but technology is using us!

What does God say?

We might be excited about the good from AI or we might be paralysed by fear of calamity. We don't know the future, but God does. I don't believe He has ever been worried by AI as He has always known 'the end from the beginning' (Isaiah 46:10). Therefore, it seems to me scripture might give us a benchmark from which to construct our response to AI.

John Lennox, Professor of Mathematics at Oxford University (Emeritus), an internationally renowned speaker, has written a series of books exploring the relationship between science and Christianity.[18] One of his books most pertinent to our topic is *2084: Artificial Intelligence and the Future of Humanity*.[4] He quotes at length from the book of Revelation (my emphasis):

And I saw a beast rising up out of the sea, having seven heads and ten horns, and on his horns ten crowns, and on his heads a blasphemous name. Now the beast which I saw was like a leopard, his feet were like the feet of a bear, and his mouth like the mouth of a lion. <u>The dragon gave him his power, his throne, and great authority.</u> And I saw one of his heads as if it had been mortally wounded, and his deadly wound was healed. <u>And all the world marvelled and followed the beast. So, they worshiped the dragon who gave authority to the beast; and they worshiped the beast, saying, 'Who is like the beast?</u> Who is able to make war with him?' And he was given a mouth <u>speaking great things and blasphemies,</u> and he was given authority to continue for forty-two months. Then he opened his mouth <u>in blasphemy against God,</u> <u>to blaspheme His name, His tabernacle, and those who dwell in heaven.</u> It was granted to him to make war with the saints and to overcome them. <u>And authority was given him over every tribe, tongue, and nation. All who dwell on the earth will worship him,</u> whose names have not been written in the Book of Life of the Lamb slain from the foundation of the world. (Revelation 13:1-8)

Then I saw another beast coming up out of the earth, and he had two horns like a lamb and spoke like a dragon. And <u>he exercises all the authority of the first beast</u> in his presence and causes the earth and those who dwell in it to worship the first beast, whose deadly wound was healed. <u>He performs great signs, so that he even makes fire come down from heaven on the earth in the sight of men.</u> And <u>he deceives those who dwell on the earth</u> by those signs which he was granted to do in the sight of the beast, telling those who dwell on the earth to make an image to the beast who was wounded by the sword and lived. <u>He was granted power to give breath to the image of the beast, that the image of the beast should both speak and cause as many as would not worship the image of the beast to be killed.</u> He causes all, both small and great, rich and poor, free and slave, <u>to receive a mark on their right hand or on their foreheads,</u> and that <u>no one may buy or sell except one who has the mark or the name of the beast, or the number of his name.</u> (Revelation 13:11-17)

With this scripture as backdrop, Lennox describes the Omega Project as depicted in Max Tegmark's book *Life 3.0*.[19] Here a leader will emerge to rule over the entire world with their global government that will control the global economy. Under their authority everyone will be required to wear a security bracelet that will monitor their health, their location and every conversation they have. Without this bracelet it will be impossible to buy or sell and anyone who attempts to remove or disable their device will receive a lethal injection into their forearm.

The parallels with the vision in Revelation are palpable. But in case we are not sure, Lennox goes on to quote from the Apostle Paul, in his second letter to the Thessalonians:

Let no one deceive you by any means; for that day will not come unless the falling away comes first, and the man of sin is revealed, the son of perdition, who opposes and exalts himself above all that is called God or that is worshiped, so that he sits as God in the temple of God, showing himself that he is God.

Do you not remember that when I was still with you, I told you these things? And now you know what is restraining, that he may be revealed in his own time. For the mystery of lawlessness is already at work; only He who now restrains will do so until he is taken out of the way. And then the lawless one will be revealed, whom the Lord will consume with the breath of His mouth and destroy with the brightness of His coming. The coming of the lawless one is according to the working of Satan, with all power, signs, and lying wonders, and with all unrighteous deception among those who perish, because they did not receive the love of the truth, that they might be saved. And for this reason, God will send them strong delusion, that they should believe the lie, that they all may be condemned who did not believe the truth but had pleasure in unrighteousness. (2 Thessalonians 2:3-12)

This passage is all about *deception*, the works of Satan in our world. Can we be sure that we are alert to the possibility of delusion? When was the last time you heard a sermon that unpacked deception?

Are we desensitised to *blasphemy*? Can we discern whose *authority* is in play within our burgeoning technologies? Are we sure we are only *worshiping* the one true God, and we have not been *deceived* by a *strong delusion*?[20] Have we thought through the implications of *receiving the mark*? Have we counted the cost of not receiving the mark? Are these parallels with the AI revolution a coincidence? What if the Bible is giving us a warning?

As God is not threatened by AI, neither should we be.[10] In contrast to transhumanism's dream to become a god; two thousand years ago, God became man. Why do we ignore what He has already done? God becoming human was His invitation to us to defeat death once and for all. Jesus promises eternal life, and it begins right now. Transhumanism's ideal bypasses the problem of evil. Man has already attempted this, with the Nazi program of eugenics and the Soviet dream. They both led to rivers of blood.[21]

Wearing our Christian faith firmly on our sleeve we can never confuse AI with God's creation. God has set *eternity* in our hearts,[4] as we are made in His image.[3]

> *It seems to me that a lot of needless debate could be avoided if AI researchers would admit that there are fundamental differences between machine intelligence and human intelligence - differences that cannot be overcome by any amount of research.* (Joseph Macrae Mellichamp, 1985)

So, what then can we do? Let's keep a forensic eye on AI developments, *discerning* the good intent from any intent or evil.[10] I love Balogh's phrase, we should cultivate *digital discernment*.[22] I acknowledge this is extremely difficult when most developments encompass technologies way beyond mortal understanding. Nonetheless I believe we can and should invite the Holy Spirit to protect us from deception (Colossians 2:8) and lead us into 'all truth' (John 16:13).

While the digital age offers the vision of inclusivity and connectedness, it is merely a mirage. Kim and Ortlund encourage us to intentionally pour our hearts into authentic relationships, recognising that God never imagined any of us would walk alone (Genesis 2:18, Psalm 68:6).[17]

Our generation may have already embraced a 'strong delusion' (2 Thessalonians 2:11). It is humbling and such a privilege that we live to see these days unfolding before our eyes. Let's not 'fall asleep' on our watch (Matthew 26:40-45).

Footnotes

[1] Elizabethton Star (2023). What is exactly meant by 'woke?' and what is 'woke culture.' *Elizabethton Star.* https://www.elizabethton.com/2023/02/14/what-is-exactly-meant-by-woke-and-what-is-woke-culture/

[2] United Nations General Assembly in Paris (1948). *Universal Declaration of Human Rights (UDHR).* https://www.un.org/en/about-us/universal-declaration-of-human-rights

[3] Driscoll, Stephen (2024). *Made in our image: God, artificial intelligence and you.* Matthias Media. https://matthiasmedia.com.au/products/made-in-our-image?srsltid=AfmBOorhdZ7mIxu0-qGgFzz7y2Senngc4ZHG6LIVAJ0szjHY1JcqBp5X

[4] Lennox, John (2020). *2084: Artificial Intelligence and the Future of Humanity.* HarperCollins Religious US. https://www.johnlennox.org/shop/24/2084-artificial-intelligence-and-the

[5] Medium (2024, June 4). Understanding Artificial General Intelligence (AGI): The Future of AI Technology. *Medium.* https://medium.com/@social_65128/understanding-artificial-general-intelligence-agi-the-future-of-ai-technology-356390900e52

[6] AI for Humans (2024, November 19). *What the Heck Is AGI? A Beginner's Guide to the Next Big Thing.* [Video]. YouTube. https://www.youtube.com/watch?v=APSli0XHvh0

[7] Turda, Marius (2021, July 26). Reflecting on the legacies of eugenics. *The Wiener Holocaust Library.* https://wienerholocaustlibrary.org/2021/07/26/reflecting-on-the-legacies-of-eugenics/

[8] Adobe Experience Cloud Team (2025, January 14). What is big data? *Adobe Business.* https://business.adobe.com/au/blog/basics/big-data

[9] Maheshwari, Rashi (2023, August 24). Advantages of Artificial Intelligence (AI) In 2025. *Forbes.* https://www.forbes.com/advisor/in/business/software/advantages-of-ai/

[10] Ryan, Dustin (2024, May 6). A Christian's Perspective on Artificial Intelligence. *Christ over all.* https://christoverall.com/article/longform/a-christians-perspective-on-artificial-intelligence/

[11] Reachright (2023, April 5). *6 ChatGPT Prompts for Churches That Will Save Pastors 15 hours a Week.* [Video]. YouTube. https://www.youtube.com/watch?v=f_kKO2sldio

[12] Thomas, Mike (2025, August 27). 15 Risks and Dangers of Artificial Intelligence (AI). *Builtin.* https://builtin.com/artificial-intelligence/risks-of-artificial-intelligence

[13] 60 Minutes (2023, October 9). *'Godfather of AI' Geoffrey Hinton.* [Video]. YouTube. https://www.youtube.com/watch?v=qrvK_KuIeJk

[14] CBC News (2024, January 18). *Can you spot the deepfake? How AI is threatening elections.* [Video]. YouTube. https://www.youtube.com/watch?v=B4jNttRvbpU&t=93s

[15] Harari, Yuval Noah (2017). *Homo Deus: A brief history of tomorrow.* Harper Collins. https://www.ynharari.com/book/homo-deus/

[16] Sabbagh, Dan et al (2024, September 19). Pager and walkie-talkie attacks on Hezbollah were audacious and carefully planned. *The Guardian.* https://www.theguardian.com/world/2024/sep/18/pager-and-walkie-talkie-attacks-on-hezbollah-were-audacious-and-carefully-planned

[17] Kim, Jay & Ortlund, Gavin (2024, March 21). *How Should Christians Think about Artificial Intelligence.* The Gospel Coalition. [Video]. YouTube. https://www.youtube.com/watch?v=9zSpDVMG5Bo&t=61s

[18] Lennox, John (2024, September 12). *Can we live with AI?* Oxford Centre for Christian Apologetics. [Video]. YouTube. https://www.youtube.com/watch?v=zZxd9aeskx8&t=1007s

[19] Tegmark, Max (2017). *Life 3.0: Being Human in the Age of Artificial Intelligence.* Knopf Publishing Group. https://www.amazon.com.au/Life-3-0-Being-Artificial-Intelligence/dp/1101946598

[20] Hibbs, Jack (2023, May 5). *Has Man Created His god? AI!* Real Life with Jack Hibbs. [Video]. YouTube. https://www.youtube.com/watch?v=0Mi-e1Jl318

[21] Jones, David Martin (2018). *Suicide of the West versus National Awakening.* Crown Forum. http://davidmartinjones.com/wp-content/uploads/2019/12/DM-Jones-on-Goldberg-and-Hazony.pdf

[22] Balogh, Akos (2023, May 12). As a Christian, I Went Down the AI Rabbit Hole. Here Are 12 Things I Discovered. *The Gospel Coalition.* https://au.thegospelcoalition.org/article/as-a-christian-i-went-down-the-ai-rabbit-hole-here-are-12-things-i-discovered/

CHAPTER 6 - HOMOSEXUALITY

Ratu (chief) Apenisa Rakuro's story

My name is Apenisa Rakuro, I live in Fiji. This is the story of my self-discovery. When I was five or six years old, I was sexually abused, and I believe that I transitioned from there. Just imagine a five-or six-year-old going through abuse from a biological uncle, who was trusted in our home, who walked into my room and abused me. I believe, as a result of that abuse, I began to experience trauma in my life. Men became an object of sex for me. This has shaped who I was, I did not know who I was. My sexual feelings were directed towards men.

I began to act like a woman, being a woman in my mind. I think I entertained it and sometimes our parents can accommodate this by giving us certain chores in the home. Parents are not equipped to handle a boy who is being raised at home who is acting like a girl. In our Fijian culture my parents treated me as a girl at home, cooking and cleaning, doing everything a woman would do. My parents felt they had to accept me for who I thought I was.

I later became sexually active and lived the life of a homosexual. A seed had been planted at a very young age. The best thing my mum and dad did for me was to take me to church. So even though I was living that life, I knew somehow deep inside of me, I knew this was bad, this was wrong. It wasn't just that I was living an unholy life, it also had consequences in Fijian culture when a guy is acting like a girl, it's a disgrace. It's a disgrace for the family, so the family would try to deny it. Sometimes my mum and dad would look at me as though they had a crippled child at home. I was viewed as weird.

I grew up knowing that I lived a weird life. I avoided going to family gatherings in case people would see me and tell my mum and dad. It was embarrassing and shameful. So, I was growing up fighting my sexuality and fighting my culture. I was also wrestling with the embarrassment of my family. Today people are open about this but when I was growing up it was not acceptable.

When my parents got divorced, the hurt became even greater. I was about 23-years-old. The only place I felt needed or could relax was in church. My mum was in the choir; my dad was the preacher. That was where I came to know an assurance, even though I did not believe, as I was only going to church because of an obligation at that stage.

I was saying to God, maybe He has something to say concerning the situation of my parents' divorce. I was calling out to God concerning my parents, but it was not until God encountered me and I encountered God that my life changed.

At this time, I was responsible for my siblings. I was in a relationship. It came down to choices. It was not until I had to make a choice about who was going to look after my siblings. Somebody better rise up! Somebody better go to God for my family and for my family's restoration.

I was going to God for my mum and dad to get back together. I had grown up when they were always in church and when I went astray, I did not know what my identity was. I started searching. I went to Bible studies. I knew there were answers in church. I knew my relationship could lead to other things, it could have led to alcohol, or worse; it was not a safe future.

I thought, if I go to church, if I hear the Word, at least that outcome would give me good results. I rose up and I took both my siblings to God. I would take them to Bible studies. There were times when I would take them both up to the mountains and I would pray in the mountains with them.

While growing up I had seen miracles. For example, we would not have food at home, and we would pray for food and food would come. There was a consistency of God in our home, so I knew that God would meet us. I remember my mum said to my dad, 'There is no food and there is no money.' I remember my dad pointing up to the heavens, and as soon as he did that, there was a car parked outside that brought food and supplies for everything we needed. God has always been consistent in my family.

However, I had not come to Him personally for me, even though I had always known there was a God. In the process of getting my home restored,

I got my identity restored. Every time I would go to church, I was not there for me, I was there for my parents. I loved them so much. There was so much brokenness, I did not want my mum to cry anymore. I wanted my dad to return to her.

I would go to God, saying 'my family, my family, my mum, my dad,' until my prayer changed one day, and I said, 'I am here, it's me.' I knew then that God was tapping me on the shoulder and saying, 'I want you.'

There was a prayer warrior who came to me and said, 'You're praying for the wrong thing, God is in the process of making you.' I was praying for my friend who married my dad, I was praying for her removal. The prophet said to me, 'You are praying for her to be removed, but God has allowed her to come in to deal with you because there is an anointing upon your life, and God has to process you. God has allowed this for the goodness of you. You will one day be a voice of hope.'

I didn't understand this. How can a God of love allow such a thing? But today when I counsel someone from a broken family, I understand the wait, I understand how deeply I should pray. I understand the weight and heaviness inside of him or her. I don't just hear words to deal with a situation, but I am able to walk alongside them in their journey.

When people step on grapes to produce wine it takes the feet to crush the grapes. The feet have so much power they crush the grapes but do not crush the seed. The Lord showed me, while watching a video of people crushing grapes, they were dancing, they had music. It was the traditional thing to do. Then the Lord said, 'It is my pleasure to crush you, because it doesn't kill the seed, it processes you. The outcome, the wine that comes out of the grapes is my focus. The crushing is not my focus; the wine is my focus. The grape is cheap, but the wine is much more valuable.'

I went to God for my parents' restoration, but I did not know God was working on me. One thing I would advise the church, is maybe we can stop telling people who they are not, and maybe we tell them who they are.

We say, 'You are homosexual, you are this, you are that.' They are not that, they are created in the image and likeness of God! What healed me was when I found who I was, the fake-self started to disappear. I was mentored under a pastor who constantly told us who we are in the Kingdom, our position in the Kingdom, our identity in the Kingdom, our inheritance in the Kingdom. He preached to me who I am.

The ministration of the Word was telling me who I was, not who I was not. There is no issue with mankind, created in God's likeness. If there is a problem with man, there is a no problem with God. The only thing wrong is that men have been taught wrongly. They have lived in an environment that has taught them wrongly. It's the environment that men and women have lived in that has educated them that they are this or that, that they belong to LGBT or whatever.

I came to God regarding my condition and God said, 'Deny yourself.' I said, 'I have feelings for boys.' God said, 'Deny.' You have to crucify yourself on the cross. Just because you feel it, does not mean it's the absolute truth. Just because a young boy feels he's a cat, that doesn't make him a cat. The Bible says, 'You shall know the truth and the truth shall set you free.' The truth is not a feeling. I had to choose truth over feelings. It didn't happen overnight.

For me it was not until I met a man of God who fathered me and mentored me that I changed. The focus is sometimes that we are meant to be *straight*, but it should be we are to be *transformed* into the image of God. I have to be *transformed*.

In Fiji, I struggled to be a man, because here men play rugby! The other thing here in Fiji that as a man you have to have three or four girlfriends, and then you have to have two wives. There's a joke here, 'He's on his third wife, that's a man!' Society has defined men in a very wrong way.

But I turn to Scripture, and God says, 'Let's make man to look like us.' How far we have fallen away from the truth. Some try to behave like a man instead of allowing God to change them from within. They may be in a strong community, they drop the dresses, the walk, the lipstick but the work must begin from the inside.

I had a friend who came to the Lord about the same time as me. He was changing the way he talked, walked, his dress code, to seek to be accepted by the church. But for me, I asked God to change me from within, change my mind, and my heart. My friend who was trying to change himself from the outside, he ended up going back to the world.

I am not married, yet. I have been too busy, I do discipleship. I have raised young men and sons of God. I have raised missionaries, pastors, and doctors. I have become a father to many sons. Next month I will turn 40 years old and all my sons, even those with families overseas, are coming home to celebrate with me. I have raised families, fathers, mothers. In my home right now, I am raising five sons, the lowest number that I have raised. Normally there might be 15 or 25 even. I would be feeding them, sending them to school, equipping them, discipling them. Any young man that leaves my home knows how to cook, bake, how to clean a house and is grounded in the Word. The lifestyle I have lived has somehow contributed to the kingdom.

My house is called 'Mataniwai,' the *source of living water*. I remember when my mum was talking to my dad she said, 'You had better talk to your son because he is acting like a girl and may be one day he will bring a boyfriend in the house.' My dad would always point to heaven and say we will pray. I remember when we were sleeping, our parents would come and pray for us. I believe I am here today because of mum and dad's prayers.

My advice to parents, don't give up on your child, even if they are behaving and acting not the way you raised them. Don't give up, because God doesn't know what it means to give up.

Love has the anointing, and the anointing breaks the yoke that is on them. The time my pastor came to speak into my life, it was not just the words it was the anointing that had the ability to break the yoke I was carrying from a very young age, being raped placed a yoke on me. Eventually I came to a place where I knew I was free, but not until I came to the Lord which was in 2008. I have been on mission 17 years now! I was ordained in 2011 and had my first mission trip that year when I went to Micronesia. In 2012 I started being a missionary in America, and by now I will have travelled to nearly 50 nations. I train, speak to churches and minister. I have spoken to the LGBT community; I carry the message of the gospel of the Kingdom of God.

In 2018 I co-founded Kingdom International Discipleship where I am a senior pastor. Every Tuesday I go to a region of our city to speak with prostitutes and do Bible studies. Some of them forgo going to the streets to prostitute because I am there. I am glad to be the voice of God to these people, I just plant the seed of the Word, God brings the change.

❋   ❋   ❋

How did we get here?

I think most Christians have come face to face with the homosexuality question, either in their own circle of family and friends or with frustration and confusion about how their church has been handling the issue. Consequently, I suspect you will have found Pastor Rakuro's story eye opening as it is uncommon to hear of a former homosexual leading such a fruitful life for the gospel.

Waking up to the homosexuality question is big. One small chapter cannot do the topic justice, so I have elected to focus on three uplifting testimonies followed by an unambiguous survey of the Scriptures. I think this is the only way. I don't think an intellectual argument helps. If you know someone who would like to break free, my encouragement to you is to focus them on positive testimonies and prayer.

But how did we get here? Consider this extract from the introduction to Kirk and Madsen's 1989 book, *After the Ball: How America Will Conquer Its Fear and Hatred of Gays in the 90s:*[1,2]

Gay Suicide and the Big Lie: Under these conditions, too many desperate gays do, in fact, take their own lives. Hated and attacked, less thick-skinned gays despair, and—as the Biblical proverb has it—'fold their arms and eat their own flesh' (Ecclesiastes 4:5). *The resulting suicide takes many forms: some escape into drunkenness and drug addiction, others into camouflage marriages or the priesthood. Some martyr themselves to their work or don the robes of the bachelor-scholar and disappear forever into musty library catacombs. Many gays sever old ties, opt out of the wider world, and exile themselves to gay ghettos. Still others, desperately seeking an ersatz approval from a naive public, contrive assumed identities as 'straight' politicians, pop artists, and entertainers, and hit the campaign trail or the stages of Las Vegas, looking for love.*

What a tragic spectre; look at the emotional response it triggers in us. Thankfully we don't hear this narrative too often now (unless we are living under a repressive Islamic regime, that still sees homosexuals as criminals). Why have they gone quiet? They haven't, they have changed tack. Kirk and Madsen's strategies shifted from their earlier attempt to tap into our empathy, to psychological warfare on our minds, which has been a resounding success in the West.

From the late 1980s the same sex activists rolled out a three-phase strategy to manipulate our minds, feelings and behaviours:

Strategy 1 Desensitisation: 'To desensitise straights to gays and gayness, inundate them in a continuous flood of gay-related advertising, presented in the least offensive fashion possible. If straights can't shut off the shower, they may at least eventually get used to being wet.'

Isn't that the truth. As a member of an older generation, I still turn away even from the least offensive material, but I know that younger generations no longer bat an eyelid.

Phase 2 Jamming: 'Make the bigot believe he will be shamed and ostracised for rejecting homosexuals.'

The term 'jamming' was intended to simulate what we would do to the gears on a car if we wanted to stop it without using the brakes. No one wants to *be shamed and ostracised* but arguably to be labelled a *bigot* would be the only way to take a stand against psychological manipulation.

Phase 3 Conversion '...ironically, by conversion we actually mean something far more profoundly threatening to the American Way of Life, without which no truly sweeping social change can occur. We mean conversion of the average American's emotions, mind, and will, through a planned psychological attack, in the form of propaganda fed to the nation via the media.'

There you have it; propaganda, meticulously planned, and executed through academia, corporations, governments, and mass media. We have been brain-washed. To find a TV show, or Hollywood movie, without the planted gay narrative is now rare.

The homosexuality activists have been unwavering in their devotion to their cause. Look back to Chapter 1, Marriage, the synergy with the Same

Sex Marriage Act; Chapter 3, Education, where we unpacked the introduction of The Long March Through the Institutions and the Safe Schools Program; and Chapter 4, Screen Addiction and the investment in the pornography industry.

While We Were Sleeping, we have a lot to answer for. Have you noticed that in each of these three theatres of war, the enemy has created opposing sides: dividing, conquering, and paralyzing?

Rashad Vermé's Story

Personal testimony puts the lie to the propaganda avalanche. Building on Pastor Rakuro's experience I commend to you Rashad.[3]

When he was about eight, he went to one of his family member's homes. He was standing in their living room, and they had RuPaul's Drag Race playing on the TV. One of the elders, in his church, who was there at the time, saw the situation and said, 'Turn that TV show off, or this little boy will decide to do the same things when he is older.' This was exactly what happened.

At elementary school Rashad was bullied as he began to act effeminate, and he chose to hang with the girls more than boys. When he was 13 years old two of his close friends introduced him to pornography and he discovered gay porn. At 17 he got into a homosexual relationship with two males, who later planned to transition to females. What a familiar story.

However, at the start of 2021 he had a thought come to him. He had tried all the gay sex stuff, and it just resulted in anxiety and depression; why not try Jesus? He had grown up in a Christian home with a prayer-warrior mother, but he had never made a personal confession of faith in Jesus. So, now he did. He had some terrible songs he would listen to in his car which he trashed, but he had one song from Hillsong, 'Still,'[4] that he kept as it made a huge impact on him at this time.

He felt convicted to tell his mum the whole story, of his homosexuality and his subsequent conversion to Christ. When he did, he felt the spirit of homosexuality lift off him. He was delivered, but the process of deliverance was a battle. He just wanted to please the Lord, and he could now boast in Him, that he hasn't gone back to homosexuality or pornography.

Rashard met his wife-to-be in February 2022, and they were married in June. A year later they had a son. He now has a powerful Christian ministry that includes seeing his sister break free from lesbianism and follow the Lord.

It was clear that the trajectory he had been on led him into depression, and the likely next step would have been to follow his friends into transgenderism (Chapter 7, Transgenderism). I would argue his upbringing in a Christian home and his mum's intercession had securely planted a seed of God's identity that germinated just at the right time. His deliverance was no result from a changed external environment rather his new birth and deliverance were from within, echoing Pastor Rakuro's story exactly.

Rosaria Butterfield's Story

Former committed LGBTQ+ activist and a committed feminist, Rosaria finds Jesus.[5]

I believed that people were inherently good and if we are just allowed to flourish in the things that we want to do, we would have capacity to do such great things in the world...I was eventually fed up with dating men and began falling in love with girls.

I was writing a book, trying to work out how the religious right hated the person I was trying to be. I couldn't figure out why they wouldn't leave consenting adults alone. I started reading the Bible and it got me so mad. It said I needed to repent of my sin, and I thought, how can I repent of a sin that's me? I did not realise that sin was treason against a Holy God and condemnable to death and hell.

Fortunately, two of Rosaria's friends were a Christian couple who stuck by her through her personal battle. They regularly had her over for meals and they would study the Bible together as Rosaria was researching material for her book.

Rosaria began to understand that she had been carrying a false identity and began questioning whether her lesbianism was *true*. The clincher came from Romans 7 when she saw that hating sin was not the same as hating herself. She understood this because she saw she could not hate herself because God loved her with unconditional love and His love would never give up on her (again echoes from Pastor Rakuro's story).

When Rosaria committed her life to Jesus, John 8:31-32 was pivotal:

> *Then Jesus said to those Jews who believed Him, 'If you abide in My word, you are My disciples indeed. And you shall know the truth, and the truth shall make you free.'*

Repentance leads to sanctification and sanctification is where you grow to be more like Jesus. I know this is very hard, nobody flipped a switch in her, she didn't wake up one day and all her bad desires were gone.

The Christian life is rugged, it's real, but Jesus is the only way to faith and life, to joy, to meaning, to purpose, and to grace.

What does God say?

For this section I am indebted to Pastor Ryan Visconti, Generation Church, Arizona.[6] (He also introduced me to *After the Ball*).[1]
I Corinthians 6:9-10 (my emphasis).

> *Do you not know that the unrighteous will not inherit the kingdom of God? Do not be deceived. Neither fornicators, nor idolaters, <u>nor adulterers, nor homosexuals, nor sodomites</u>, nor thieves, nor covetous, nor drunkards, nor revellers, nor extortioners will inherit the kingdom of God.*

We all know this is no exclusive list of sins, but notice how sins are not graded, but *While We Were Sleeping*, the world has erased some.
Romans 1:24-27.

> *Therefore, God also gave them up to uncleanness, <u>in the lusts of their hearts</u>, to dishonour their bodies among themselves, who exchanged the truth of God for the lie, and worshiped and served the creature rather than the Creator, who is blessed forever. Amen<u>. For this reason God gave them up to vile passions. For even their</u>*

women exchanged the natural use for what is against nature. Likewise also the men, leaving the natural use of the woman, burned in their lust for one another, men with men committing what is shameful, and receiving in themselves the penalty of their error which was due.

Perhaps the most brutal text on homosexuality. This passage cannot be described as *love*, quite clearly it describes *lust*.

God created man in His own image; in the image of God He created him; male and female He created them. (Genesis 1:27)

You shall not lie with a male as with a woman. It is an abomination. (Leviticus 18:22)

God's command to mankind was to *be fruitful and multiply and fill the earth* (Genesis 1:28; 9:7). Homosexual or lesbian sex cannot fulfil this command.

...knowing this: that the law is not made for a righteous person, but for the lawless and insubordinate, for the ungodly and for sinners, for the unholy and profane, for murderers of fathers and murderers of mothers, for manslayers, for fornicators, for sodomites, for kidnappers, for liars, for perjurers, and if there is any other thing that is contrary to sound doctrine.
(1 Timothy 1:9-10)

This is only a sample of what God says. Some argue that Jesus never condemned homosexuality, and they quote Jesus's response to the women caught in adultery as support, though He did say to her, 'Go and sin no more' (John 8:1-11). But Jesus does address this if we read His words carefully:

And He answered and said to them, "Have you not read that He who made them at the beginning 'made them male and female,' and said, 'For this reason a man shall leave his father and mother and be joined to his wife, and the two shall become one flesh'? So they are no longer two, but one flesh. Therefore what God has joined together, let no one separate." (Matthew 19:4-6)

This is God's design for sexuality, one man and one woman. With no exception, homosexuality is always a sin in God's eyes.

If someone says that homosexuality is their *identity,* it's in their DNA, they were born with it, that is blasphemy, they are placing the guilt for their sin on God. If homosexuality is sin, it can't be made in God's image.

Let no one say when he is tempted, 'I am tempted by God;' for God cannot be tempted by evil, nor does He Himself tempt anyone. But each one is tempted when he is drawn away by his own desires and enticed. Then, when desire has conceived, it gives birth to sin; and sin, when it is full-grown, brings forth death. (James 1:13-15)

To deny sin is to make Christ's death on the cross null-and-void, and to deny the gospel. You can't be a Christian and a homosexual, comfortable with your homosexual desires and behaviours.[7] Our *true identity* is in Christ (Galatians 3:28).

Footnotes

[1] Kirk, Marshall & Madsen, Hunter (1989). *After the Ball: How America Will Conquer Its Fear and Hatred of Gays in the 90s.* Doubleday. https://catalogue.nla.gov.au/catalog/622167

[2] Internet Archive (2022). *Marshall Kirk & Hunter Madsen - After the Ball: How America Will Conquer Its Fear And Hatred of Gays in the 90s.* https://archive.org/details/marshall-kirk-hunter-madsen-after-the-ball-how-america-will-conquer-its-fear-hat/page/n25/mode/2up

[3] Vermé, Rashad (2025, January 24). *Former Gay Man Speaks Out!* Delafé Testimonies. [Video]. YouTube. https://www.youtube.com/watch?v=8WAHe91ZbEY

[4] Hillsong Worship (2014, October 8). *Still.* Hillsong Music & Resources LLC (Hybrid). [Video]. YouTube. https://www.youtube.com/watch?v=LYUhNboM3Hg

[5] Butterfield, Rosaria (2025, March 14). *Former Lesbian Finds Jesus Set Free Story.* Decision Point. [Video]. YouTube.
https://www.youtube.com/watch?v=cJc0McjBo3o

[6] Visconti, Ryan (2024, April 16). *What Does the Bible Say About Homosexuality? Corinthians.* Generation Church. [Video]. YouTube.
https://www.youtube.com/watch?v=blKRywVZLc4

[7] Keller, Tim (2015). The Bible and same sex relationships: A review article. *Redeemer Churches and Ministries.*
https://www.redeemer.com/redeemer-report/article/the_bible_and_same_sex_relationships_a_review_article

CHAPTER 7 - TRANSGENDERISM

Kirralie Smith's Story

I am the national spokeswoman for Binary, an organisation that is dedicated to dealing with gender ideology, and all the negative aspects of it. We primarily focus on women's sex-based rights, parental rights, and child safeguarding.

I am married 27 years, with three almost adult children and three foster children, and our first foster grandchild; that's where my heart is. I am a Christian. I have a Bachelor of Theology. I feel like we have to be really good stewards of what God has given us. For the last 15 years I have been an accidental activist, in terms of exposing the rorts concerning the Halal certification schemes (designed to ensuring relevant services comply with Islamic principles), speaking out through the same-sex marriage campaign and now with Binary. I have been given a large public platform, with my being a wife, a mother, and a Christian, it's really important for me to speak about those things.

While running Halal Choices, an internet-based organisation exposing rorts in Australia, I became politically involved with Cory Bernardi's Australian Conservatives. Then during the same-sex marriage debate I warned that if we redefined words such as marriage, we would end up redefining other words. I did advocate for full legal rights for any adult relationship they might chose, same sex or heterosexual, but I do not believe we should have changed the meaning of marriage, as marriage has always meant a union, in most cultures, between one man and one woman, for life.

This redefinition of words has come to pass so quickly with the reconceptualisation of 'women' so that a man can now be a woman and children are now being called 'mature minors,' as we are told that they can consent to unimaginable things like 'changing their sex,' which is a lie because no one can change their sex.

I ended up in Binary, pretty much accidentally, but intentionally and deliberately, I have never compromised on the truth. To me the truth is not a concept or idea, the truth is a person, and that person is Jesus. So, I will stick to the truth, and I will not compromise on that in any shape or form.

It probably all started for me because of my husband. He has always been into Middle Eastern politics and Israel, going to conferences all the time. I never had the time with little children in tow. Then, in 2011, we had the Rev Mark Durie, an amazing Australian reverend, come to our local area and do a weekend on Israel and the Middle East. He said, almost incidentally, that Halal Certification can fund mosques and Islamic organisations that are one hundred per cent against Christianity and Western values.

So, I just had the thought, I do the shopping, I just wouldn't buy Halal certified foods! So, I went looking for a list. There was no list! I went to a Halal certifier, several in fact, and it was confirmed to me that there were rorts going on.

Over the next nine years, I was in meetings with politicians advocating for companies that didn't pay their Halal fees. We ended up with a full senate inquiry in the Malcom Turnbull days. We developed nine brilliant recommendations. Sam Dastyari was the chair of the committee. He is Muslim himself but even so, he agreed to these nine recommendations, designed to get rid of these rorts and the manipulation going on at the time in Australia, and I believe is still going on. However, Malcom Turnbull simply swept it all under the carpet, so our nine recommendations were never implemented.

During the same sex-marriage debate I was never a formal part of the Marriage Alliance with their leader Lyle Shelton (Chapter 1), but I did use my platform with tens of thousands of followers here in Australia. I did several videos that got two million views, warning that if we redefine marriage it was going to lead to all sorts of problems, for example, that kids will be forced to submit to the updates in sex education that happens in schools.

After those videos went viral and when the campaign was lost, the Marriage Alliance Group approached me and asked if I would like to be the spokesperson for Binary, which is dealing with the fallout from the debate and that's what I have been doing ever since.

We started it as an extension of the marriage campaign. In 2013, Julia Gillard, as one of her final acts as Prime Minister with her government, removed protections for sexes in the sex discrimination act. They removed the definitions of male and female, well before the marriage campaign. I don't know if she saw what was coming, but some people thought she did. But once the same-sex marriage campaign was successful in Australia, it opened the flood gates for the Sex Discrimination Act to be used, against women particularly, but for anyone who stands up for biological sex.

We have seen this accelerated push to sexualise children and to erase women from law in Australia. I have had nine court cases brought against me, because I identified males in female sport, and said they shouldn't be in female sport.

Late last year, Sal Grover was taken to court. She had developed an ap called 'Giggle for Girls,' for females only. Trans identified men challenged that, and as a result, a judge in Australia, said sex is changeable, which is absolute nonsense. Nobody can change their sex.

We now have this incredible situation in Australia, where the law, the courts and the politicians have all agreed to this falsehood that people can change their sex. They can't, there is no evidence for that. There are no facts to support this. So, a decade later, all these things have come together in a co-ordinated way, that we are now all reaping the consequences.

First and foremost, Binary exists to get the definitions of male and female back into the Sex Discrimination Act. We lobby governments and we campaign. We are a registered third-party political campaign organisation so that we can take part in elections and really educate and raise awareness to inform Australians about what is going on. We lobby politicians personally, we hold events to educate them, we have just written our own book, *Devastated: How gender ideology is tearing Australian families* apart.[1] That's our primary mission; we also advocate for women, parents and children who are impacted by gender ideology.

Binary has been going since 2019. We were pretty much a lone voice in Australia at that time but there were others around the world who were strongly advocating for this cause as well, for example Helen Joyce in the

UK.[2] I am so thankful for those voices in the UK and some in the USA as well because the Australian media have been so reluctant to address any of these issues, but now that others around the world are raising them, especially President Trump in the US, they can no longer ignore it. So, this has helped our movement a great deal, we have been silenced, we have been gagged, we have not been given any airtime, we are ignored in so many ways. But the more this happens around the world, like the Cass Review in the UK; the UK have now banned or paused puberty blockers.[3,13] The Nordic Countries have done the same, New Zealand are considering it. But what about Australia? They are trying to ignore it, but I don't think they will be successful for much longer.

For example, it's just come out in Queensland, that 42 minors were put on puberty blockers and cross sex hormones without their parents' knowledge or consent in the Cairns Gender Clinic. The media is now a bit more emboldened to report on these things. This has also emboldened more politicians and medical practitioners. People like Dr Jillian Spencer[4] and Dr Dylan Wilson[5] are speaking out, they have the authority to do so because they work in this space. Professor Dianna Kenny,[6] Professor John Whitehall,[7] there are quite a few now, who have been speaking out and will continue to do so. I believe Dr Jillian and others got about 200 doctors to sign an open letter about their concerns about gender clinic practices in Australia.

I think it's a matter of when, not if. It's happening, but we are slow. As I said, our laws are so draconian and we are all threatened by them, and it's held over our heads that if we talk about these things we will be dragged into court. But Jillian and others, like me, say, give us more impetus to talk about it, because as soon as it's on the court record, the media will have to report it. There's a high cost to be paid in the meantime. I know that our book is making an impact with politicians and medical practitioners. It has emboldened them to speak out because the stories are just horrific. It's the failure of the political system, the medical system and the education system that have all worked together to destroy these families. It'll probably feel like a long slow march for a little while, then it'll just go. Unlike America we don't have executive orders so we can't have what Trump did, nevertheless it will all fall apart, it will all be exposed, but at what cost. How many kids will have to be irreversibly harmed in the process.

Here in Binary, we put people in touch with support groups. These groups can't be too public or out there, they do cop harassment, and they do cop abuse. There are parental support groups and there are de-transitioning support groups. If people contact Binary looking for that kind of support, we direct them to where is most appropriate. Tess Hacket has been in this space for more than eight years, she would be a great first point of contact, she is a parent of a daughter that transitioned, with whom she's had no contact since.[8] She is definitely the authority with supporting parents.

For me, looking into Islam (Chapter 14) as an ideology and now gender as an ideology, to me as a Christian, it is obvious that what we are dealing with is Satanic, it is part of the evil system that's anti-Christ, anti-God, anti-truth, and anti-family. It's against all those things that God has instituted. As I said, truth is not a concept it's a person. So, whenever we are dealing with gender ideology that is based on lies and deception, it's immediately obvious, that it is anti-truth, and anti-Christ.

That being said, Binary is not a Christian organisation, we are secular. However, everyone knows I am Christian, but we look at the issues from a biological, reality and scientific basis: men can't be women and women can't be men. It's that simple! Scripture came up with this first, God created us that way!

When I looked into the Fabian Society, Marxism and Communism, their aim has always been to have a large government that the people are dependent upon and to dismantle the family. That's been called The Long Slow March (Chapter 3), which has been going on for more than half a century. It's been intentional that first there could be a no-fault divorce, so people could easily get divorced, then came abortion, same-sex marriage and now transgenderism. They are all about separating the family because the family is the strongest unit we have in a civil society. If we can break apart the family, then the government has more control and can have that level of manipulation over our lives.

I don't think this is a conspiracy as such where there is one evil person, but man's heart is inclined to wickedness. We don't want to take responsibility for our own actions, so it's very appealing to blame the government. In the last twenty years or so, especially with the internet, the globe has shrunk. In the past I didn't know what was going on in America half the time, but now we know what's happening in real time. There is a lot of division and chaos, all these ideologies come back to anti-truth, anti-family and their goal is that we should be people who no longer take personal responsibility.

There are three major platforms for Binary:

1. Women's sex-based rights, e.g. A big campaign for women in sport. We look at female prisons, rape crisis shelters, women's bathrooms, any space or service that needs to be female only.
2. Parental rights are being usurped as these things are happening without parents' knowledge or consent.
3. Child safeguarding is a very important issue to us. Children are being sexualised at a very young age. We are being told children can consent to changing their sex knowing that the ultimate goal is that they want to tell children that they can consent to having sex.

That is absolutely unacceptable, and we will fight to make sure that doesn't happen. These children are being exposed to irreversible harm by taking experimental drugs. These health practices are absolutely appalling. We are working hard to make sure this policy is exposed and changed in this space.

The real victims in this are the families, and writing our book *Devastated* was absolutely devastating for me, though I am personally not impacted. The stories in the book are friends, and some are people I have met through the process. These are simply parents doing all the right things, the best things they can think of for their children, but government policies, and laws are totally betraying them and causing such harm to kids. It's a very fragile space that I work in. But it's so important that we do it and that we are a voice for the voiceless.

The truth is not an idea or a concept; the truth a person and his name is Jesus. And He said, He is 'the way, the truth, and the life. No one comes to the Father except through Me' (John 14:6), and 'you shall know the truth, and the truth shall make you free' (John 8:32).

The church has to get back to the truth. I hear, heartbreakingly, so many testimonies from people in churches saying their pastors won't talk about it and all they say is that we have to 'love' these people. Some have allowed transgender identified men into their female toilets, they don't challenge, they simply say we have to accept them. But this does not set these people free. It doesn't bring healing; it doesn't bring wholeness. I would say to churches, come back, sit at the feet of Jesus, the truth is kind and loving. It's not kind and loving to deceive people or to enter into their deception and not challenge them. As Christians we must challenge deception while still accepting the people. The father of lies hates us, he wants to steal, kill, and destroy. Jesus wants to give us life and give it in abundance.

❀   ❀   ❀

Transgender Ideology

Is transgenderism a reality that some have to accept and the rest of us support? Or is transgenderism *a belief*, an attitude, held consciously or *unconsciously*, which shapes understandings or *misconceptions* of the social and political world. In other words, is it an ideology?[9,16]

This section is based on a discussion between John Anderson (Chapter 10) and Helen Joyce;[10] one-time British Editor at The Economist before she joined the gender-critical campaign group Sex Matters as a director.[11]

A trans ideologue will say:

All of us are men, women, male, female, boy, girl according to some innate feeling or identity that we are born with and that is not necessarily related to our bodies, and only we can say we really are a boy or a girl.

They teach children that biological sex is not important. They tell them that they will know whether they are a boy or a girl. Then they tell them that somehow, they are to align their body to this gender identity. We are not meant to ask questions and think; we are just meant to be accepting and go along with it.

What has happened in our culture that has allowed such thinking, or lack of thinking? I argue that it links back to 'The Slow March Through the Institutions' (Chapter 3) and the pandemic of 'screen addiction' (Chapter 4). It seems to be very much a Western phenomenon, and particularly the English-speaking part of the Western world. It's an

American contagion that went global. It's also a Democrat contagion, based particularly in the liberal coastal cities. The Republican states never bought into it and are fighting back. The origins of Transgenderism are discussed at length by Trinity Westlake if you want to unpack this in more depth.[12]

One of the early drivers of transgender ideology were gay men who thought they were really women. Some thought they would be happier if they were women. But some were heterosexual men, who were fixated on being a woman for erotic reasons. They did feel shame, so they needed a narrative to explain their sexual preferences, and this evolved into - they were born in the wrong body. Then there were doctors who got a saviour complex and later they didn't want to admit that they were wrong.

The clinics have been so overrun with demand, and blinded by their own ideology, so much so they have done no meaningful follow up of their patients. They don't know the regret rate of those they have treated. Often surveys are only done online, and any survey done online means nothing as, by definition, it creates a biased sample, even if it's a million people. One of the oft quoted studies, excluded de-transitioners, as you have to identify as trans to be eligible to participate! All de-transitioners are treated as apostates, as if this were a religion. Yes, it is a religion, a godless, new religion that has believers, converts and now apostates. Helen remarked:

It's the most disgusting thing I have seen from the medical profession to tell parents they must do the transition, or their child will kill themselves, when there is no supportive evidence whatever and in fact there is clear evidence that their 'treatment' has no effect on suicide rates.

She went on to describe how any girl going on puberty blockers, say at ten years old and then goes on testosterone will be sterile. That is not infertile, as such but simply incapable of producing any eggs. It also means that their uterus and vagina will degrade, cause pain, bleeding, and atrophy, and they will have to have a hysterectomy before they are twenty. The activists don't publicise this.

The excuse given for this shattering intervention is that these girls could come off puberty blockers at say 14 for six months or so, to allow their ovaries to mature enough, go through a cycle or two of IVF, collect and freeze the eggs. This is a dystopian fiction. Nobody is going to do this. It's a miserable experience getting eggs harvested. In any case, the girls will have no uterus, so who's going to have their baby? This is the fantasy they don't even bother informing the 10-year-olds.

Once people get this central idea wrong that a girl can be a boy, it breaks everything. It breaks safeguarding, it breaks logic, it breaks common sense, it breaks medicine, it breaks education, it breaks government, and it breaks institutions. And all of them start acting in ways that are antithetical to the ways they are supposed to act. Teachers are harming girls. They didn't realise that, but they are doing things that are against safeguarding the child.

Many parents that follow through with this narrative, as they love their child, see no alternative. But they then become the strongest activists for the lie, as they cannot ever admit they made a mistake. These people are going to become a massive roadblock to cleaning up the chaos.

Helen's advice to parents who want to do the right thing by their troubled kids:

Do what you can to pre-empt it. That means being really clear with your child that sex change is not possible. That's not you being mean, it's simply describing the human condition, such as the fact that everybody dies. A boy who wants to be girlish can be and a girl who wants to do boy things can. These things are fine. This way you can inoculate your child before they ever hear it. Make sure you have strong relationships with your kids, very open relationships with your kids.

Parents have to be careful about what their kids are seeing online (Chapter 4). Pornography online is a big part of why the girls are going for this. Families must get out more, away from screens, into the real world, helping other people rather than focusing on themselves. This is part of a wider mental health crisis, that children are being taught to be fragile instead of strong.

Helen's advice concludes:

You should be really careful about what is happening in your children's schools. We can't fix this family by family; we have to

fix this at a societal level. Get informed about what your children are being taught at school, try to get elected to the school board. Do all of this before it comes to your child if you possibly can.
If you are one of the families it hasn't touched, then it's up to you to act, as those that have experienced the trans, can't act.
If you have been touched by this crisis, try to stay calm, work on your parenting as best you can. Try to keep them away from anything permanent.

Kirrilie Smith's 2024 book *Devastated* is a must read for those determined to break free from trans dogma.[1] It's real-life family testimonies that give families signposts to watch for from the impact of this insidious ideology.

Bill Muehlenberg's *The Utter Devastation Caused by the Trans Agenda,* gives a great review of Kirrilie's book for those who want a shorter, less psychologically confronting introduction.[14]

What does God say?

Most schools have at least one trans student, including Christian schools, so this issue can't be ignored by any of us. We are called to love everyone and hate the sin, but that doesn't mean we close our eyes to sin's fruit. I am indebted to Kurt Mahlburg for referencing many of these Scriptures.[15]

God created man in His own image; in the image of God He created him; male and female He created them. (Genesis 1:27)

So, the biological differences and complementary of sex are God's design and creation, not our whim or desire. Jesus endorses this in the New Testament with His very clear understanding of the issue:

Have you not read that He who made them at the beginning 'made them male and female,' and said, 'For this reason a man shall leave his father and mother and be joined to his wife, and the two shall become one flesh?' (Matthew 19:4-5)

It is understandable for some of those with no faith in God, to *feel* dissatisfied with the cards they have been dealt. But God knit us together in our mother's womb (Psalm 139:13) and:

Will the thing formed say to Him who formed it, 'Why have you made me like this?' Does not the potter have power over the clay, from the same lump to make one vessel for honour and another for dishonour. (Romans 9:20-21)

It's generally accepted that we are designed to live in community, so how does God want us to demonstrate love to our fellow man? We can ignore him and pass by on the other side of the road, or we can stop, stoop down, pick up the beaten-up outcast and support their rehabilitation (Luke 10:25-37). This cares for the person and treats the condition. I think that to support and affirm their lie, is not love at all, it's sentencing them to eternal trauma.

If we buy the lie, that trans is written into the genes, we deny it's a sin, we deny there can be deliverance and we deny they can be forgiven, healed, and saved. Whatever our past or struggles, the gospel offers cleansing, healing, and transformation through Christ, no exceptions.

But God, who is rich in mercy, because of His great love with which He loved us, even when we were dead in trespasses, made us alive together with Christ (by grace you have been saved). (Ephesians 2:4-5)

Let me conclude with some words from Kirralie Smith in her book *Devastated:*

These families have suffered needlessly as a result of politicians legislating lies and appeasing a small minority. The impact has been catastrophic and pervasive. Thousands of young people have been lied to. It will take decades to reverse the dreadful consequences.[1]

We have let this happen. Jesus said, 'Assuredly, I say to you, inasmuch as you did not do it to one of the least of these, you did not do it to Me'

(Matthew 25:45). I believe that politicians and the legislature should be *downstream* from society. However, we have let politicians and the legislature become the driving force in society, they are now *upstream* of society, *While We Were Sleeping.*

Our individual actions could not have stopped the tsunami of transgenderism, but our collective inaction cleared the stage for the lie. So, foreshadowing Chapter 13 Spiritual Warfare, I believe we need to confess *our sin* and the sin of *our nation* and call on God for the healing of our land (2 Chronicles 7:14).

Footnotes

[1] Smith, Kirralie (2024). *Devastated: How gender ideology is tearing Australian families apart.* Binary. https://www.binary.org.au/devastated

[2] John Anderson Media (2024, April 23). *Transgender Ideology, The Cass Review, and Stopping Child Harm Helen Joyce.* [Video]. YouTube. https://www.youtube.com/watch?v=vbY-g9hnL14

[3] The National Archives (2024, April). *The Cass Review: Independent review of gender identity services for children and young people: Final report.* https://webarchive.nationalarchives.gov.uk/ukgwa/20250310143933/https ://cass.independent-review.uk/home/publications/final-report/

[4] Rachael Wong (2024, December 2). Last year, Australian child psychiatrist Dr Jillian Spencer raised concerns about the use of puberty blockers without appropriate mental health counselling. *Facebook.* https://www.facebook.com/watch/?v=3727306227598707

[5] 7NEWS Spotlight Wilson (2023, September 3). *De-Transitioning: Dr Dylan Wilson extended interview.* [Video]. YouTube. https://www.youtube.com/watch?v=nTHw6a8bbLE

[6] Kenny, Dianna T. (n.d.). *On the WarPATH against WPATH.* Professor Dianna Kenny. Retrieved October 20, 2025, from https://diannakenny.com.au/on-the-warpath-against-wpath/

[7] Whitehall, John (n.d.). The teenage brain and decision making #139. *International Christian Medical and Dental Association.* Retrieved October 22, 2025, from https://icmda.net/wbnr139/

[8] In Defence of Children (2024, April 8). *Tess's Story Betrayed by the System Rape, Gender Transition, and a Family's Heartbreak.* [Video]. YouTube. https://www.youtube.com/watch?v=m20bE-y77ik

[9] Routledge Encyclopedia of Philosophy (n.d.). *Ideology.* Retrieved October 20, 2025, from https://www.rep.routledge.com/articles/thematic/ideology/v-1

[10] John Anderson Media (2024, April 24). *Transgender Ideology, The Cass Review, and Stopping Child Harm - Helen Joyce.* [Video]. YouTube. https://www.youtube.com/watch?v=vbY-g9hnL14&t=15s

[11] Sex Matters (n.d.). *Helen Joyce, Director of Advocacy.* Retrieved October 20, 2025, from https://sex-matters.org/about-us/team/helen-joyce/

[12] Westlake, Trinity (2024, May 28). Transgenderism: The Origins of this Subversive Ideology. *Daily Declaration.* https://dailydeclaration.org.au/2024/05/28/transgenderism-the-origins-of-this-subversive-ideology/

[13] Do no harm staff (2024, April 14). The Cass Report Is Out—An Early Analysis of Findings and Recommendations. *Do No Harm.* https://donoharmmedicine.org/2024/04/11/cass-report-slams-gender-affirming-care-model/?gad_source=1&gclid=CjwKCAiAnKi8BhB0EiwA58DA4SzZ3m4aOKkVv7z4O1zP8hiUAsViTurL-pRDZpVT2OtAdslcFKVy1xoCK8oQAvD_BwE

[14] Muehlenberg, Bill (2025, January 7). The Utter Devastation Caused by the Trans Agenda. *Daily Declaration.* https://dailydeclaration.org.au/2025/01/07/devastation-trans-agenda/#comment-35811

[15] Mahlburg, Kurt (2025, April 23). A Christian Response to Transgenderism: 10 Biblical Truths You Need to Know. *Daily Declaration.* https://dailydeclaration.org.au/2025/04/23/christian-response-to-transgenderism/

[16] Mahlburg, Kurt (2023, July 28). The Must-See 12-Minute Documentary on the Transgender Movement. *Daily Declaration.* https://dailydeclaration.org.au/2023/07/28/documentary-transgender-movement/

CHAPTER 8 - ABORTION

Jodie Pickard's Story

Jodie Pickard is the Founding Director of Love Australia, a leading prolife organisation that first began as Love Adelaide. Love Australia's latest endeavour is the introduction of the House of Refuge ministry to Australia, in partnership with Love Life America. This mission is to equip churches across Australia to be safe havens—where those experiencing an unplanned or crisis pregnancy have no need to seek an abortion clinic and where those who have been hurt by abortion can find healing.

Jodie picks up the narrative:

I am honoured to be asked to speak on behalf of the pro-life movement in Australia. I am one voice among thousands, if not tens of thousands. There have been faithful churches, individuals and pro-life organisations across Australia since 1969 who have never stopped fighting for life— many names we won't know this side of eternity. I wish for this chapter of the book to reflect this current and past collective effort, and I especially want to express my gratitude to the Love Australia Board, Love Sydney Committee, House of Refuge Team, House of Refuge churches and the hundreds of dedicated volunteers who make the Walk for Life events possible. Every conversation we have had over the past fifty-six years has been the weapon of truth defending against the torrent of deception. Ultimately, we are not fighting against people. God loves all people, but

He does not love all ideas—this is a spiritual battle (Chapter 13 Spiritual Warfare).

In my life, it all started with the greatest tragedy of our lives. In 1999, our second child was delivered stillborn—a heartbreaking crisis that forced us to look beyond ourselves. I knew our boy was in heaven, but I did wonder what that meant for me. 'Will I ever get to see him again?' I asked. Many years into this time of grief, I met two Christian women—and what I witnessed confounded me. These women possessed a peace, amid their own traumatic situations, that I did not understand. How was that kind of peace possible? I loved to be around them, and I began to ask questions. They soon became dear friends, and their testimony started me on my journey to salvation.

On 30 July 2006, while we were on holiday in Queensland, my husband and I had the gospel preached to us, we understood, and surrendered our lives to Jesus. We were baptised in the ocean at Hayman Island. We often comment that we 'went away as two people and came back as two other people.' The impact of this decision changed absolutely everything about our lives—and eventually, it led to my deep engagement on the issue of abortion.

A Christian friend from our children's school was volunteering at Genesis Pregnancy Support as a part of their sex and relationship education. She suggested that I would make a great presenter to these high schoolers. After being shown the contents of the program, I signed up on the spot! I wish someone had shared this information with me as a teenager. We were all completely lost—with no guidance about what a respectful relationship looked like. I also joined the executive board of Genesis Pregnancy Support,[1] volunteering with them for thirteen years—the last four as chairman.

Presenter training included learning about the four different abortion procedures, so that we could respond factually to children's questions. We watched the Dr Anthony Levatino's extremely confronting Abortion Procedure videos.[2] The first time I watched the explainers, I don't think I slept for two nights. Having delivered a lifeless child, myself, the impact was still more significant. How could this be happening in an apparently civilised society like Australia?

Over this same period, I was blessed to attend two Heartbeat International Conferences in the United States. The first was in Chicago in 2016. The keynote speakers were twin brothers David and Jason Benham—pro-life advocates, ex-professional baseball players, and now business entrepreneurs.[3] Their genuine love for the Lord and His people captured my attention. I bought their books and went on to follow their podcast. This led to me finding out that they were from Charlotte, North Carolina. As it would happen, our son had gained a college baseball scholarship in—you guessed it—Charlotte! While visiting the States in 2019, I reached out to Love Life after hearing the Benham Brothers speak about how they took their friend Justin Reeder to pray outside an abortion clinic, and how the Lord broke his heart with what he witnessed. Justin went on to start Love Life.[4,5]

Love Life invited me to go out with one of their teams to the abortion clinic in Charlotte. I was there to pray and watch what was going on. These side-walk counsellors were offering hope and help—calling out, 'Young mum, anything you need right now, we are here to help you. Please know you don't have to walk into that clinic.' Very occasionally, somebody would turn away choosing life for their baby. I saw three women change their mind that day! Two of them drove away in their cars letting the side-walk counsellors know of their decision and one entered the counselling RV bus. On board was an ultrasound machine and a private lounge area to counsel, run by a pregnancy help centre. The young woman I saw go on the bus was offered a free ultrasound and she chose life! What an impact this had on my involvement!

Love Life also engaged churches to prayer-walk around abortion clinics. After attending one in Charlotte, I imported this idea back to Australia. The first Love Adelaide prayer-walk was held in August 2019. With two other ladies, we made nearly 500 phone calls, inviting churches to come to this prayer-walk. Meeting at a park opposite the abortion clinic in Adelaide, 230 faithful people worshipped, prayed together, and prayer-walked around the clinic.

I started going to our abortion clinic and offering help. Unfortunately, it was short-lived. Less than a year later (in 2020) the South Australian Parliament legislated a 150-metre exclusion zone, which outlawed any communication related to abortion around a facility that performs them. It also prohibited praying. What has become of our nation when praying is made illegal?

Within six months of our prayer-walk, South Australia was facing an up-to-birth abortion bill. Comparable legislation had already passed in Victoria, the Australian Capital Territory, Tasmania, Queensland, and New South Wales. It was sweeping across the nation. As a result, everyone who was involved in South Australia's pro-life movement gathered at the home of Christopher Brohier, South Australia's Australian Christian Lobby director. It was decided we would bring the prayer-walk into the city and do all we could to bring awareness of this brutal bill. The first Love Adelaide Walk for Life was held on 8 February 2020, which was also the day our son celebrated his twenty-first birthday in heaven. The Lord's grace is overwhelming, isn't it? We gathered with 3000 people that day to defend life and have gone on to make it an annual event.[6,7] We have now held six Walk for Life events in Adelaide and three in Sydney. Our collective efforts have not been in vain. South Australia has the most amendments to the Termination of Pregnancy Act in Australia and politicians at the time reported that they received more correspondence, calls and meeting requests than at any point in their careers. Tragically, they did not care what their constituents were saying and passed the bill against their requests.

During another visit to the US, in 2022, while helping the sidewalk counselling with Pastor Flip Benham (father of David and Jason), he shared with me the new ministry Love Life had launched—the House of Refuge. I was shown the statement that every church that becomes a House of Refuge reads out to their congregation and was told about a survey that revealed that 40 per cent of women and 50 per cent of men at the time of their first abortion were attending church in the month prior. From that moment, the journey for House of Refuge to come to Australia began. The statement used by House of Refuge Churches reads:[8,9]

[Your church name] is a House of Refuge:
A place of refuge and safety for anyone dealing with an unplanned/crisis pregnancy. Whether you are a member of this church, a visitor, or it's someone you know, we are here to help. If you find yourself in an unplanned pregnancy, please know that being pregnant is not a sin and the child you carry is not a punishment, this child is a blessing.

God is creating this child in your womb. Whatever the circumstances that led to this pregnancy, we want you to know that you are loved and we will do whatever it takes to help you carry and care for this precious child before and after birth. We will never encourage a woman to have an abortion, because the child you carry is made in the image of God and is intrinsically valuable and loved by Him. You need to know how we will respond.

Here is what we won't do:
Please know that this church family will never gossip about you, shame you, or abandon you. This is a House of Refuge, and we will not allow the family of God to harm one another with words or actions contrary to the love of God as revealed in the Bible.

Here is what we will do:
Please know that we will do everything in our power to remove whatever obstacles that stand in the way of you having this child. There are people in this church ready to support and mentor you, connect you with resources inside and outside of our church. We will also encourage men to become great fathers who protect women and children.

Finally, we know that there may be women and men here who were at a stage in their lives when they needed a House of Refuge. You may now live with regret—maybe shame or heartache—over a choice made to terminate your pregnancy. You are not alone. There is refuge available for you as well. We can direct you to individuals who understand and can walk alongside you as you heal. If you need this help, please speak with us or you can confidentially contact Pregnancy Help Australia. https://pregnancyhelpaustralia.org.au 1300 139 313

Love Australia facilitates this ministry initiative. At the time of writing (October 2025), there are twenty-two House of Refuge Churches in Australia across five states—spanning Western Australia, South Australia, the Northern Territory, Queensland, and New South Wales.[9] Training for individuals is also about to commence in Tasmania, with churches keen to know more. We also have another thirty individuals who have been equipped with the House of Refuge training, faithfully serving in their churches and praying that they will also officially become a House of Refuge. We are all pioneering this together and the impact has started. Imagine what Australia would look like if every church was a House of Refuge!

In recent months, across Australia, the House of Refuge volunteers have been on the ground, engaging like first responders—loving their neighbours and meeting single parents and expecting parents in their need. Often, these connections happen through divine appointments or a friendly smile at community groups, workplaces, or church connect groups.

We have been able to reach and embrace a range of people: unexpected fathers cared for through prayer and settling wise words, young single mothers raising children, pregnant migrants, and mothers and fathers of larger families. Post-abortion bible study groups have been formed, leading those who have carried the weight and pain of a past abortion sometimes for thirty to forty years—finding healing, forgiveness and freedom in the gospel of Jesus Christ. Prayer groups across the nation uphold the many challenging situations—with testimonies of the faithfulness of God flowing from His grateful people.

Recently (August 2025), I visited the United States again and was blessed to be able to attend the Care Net conference. There were 1800 people in attendance, women and men who are dedicated to the support of those facing an unexpected pregnancy or have been hurt by abortion. It is always such an encouragement to be with so many pro-life people!

I heard the CEO Rowland Warren speak and met him at the bookstore when I bought his book, *The Alternative to Abortion: Why We Must Be Pro Abundant Life*.[10] The next four paragraphs are quotes from this powerful book. Roland's book reminds us that Jesus' goal was not just life for the here and now, but life for eternity. It's not just about heartbeats, but about 'heartbeats that are heaven bound.' He looked closely at John 10:10 in the Greek.

The word 'abundantly' comes from perisson (περισσός), which means superabundant in terms of quantity, but it also means superior in terms of quality. The kind of life Jesus advocated for was the abundant life where we live in close relationship with Him in terms of both quality and quantity. Jesus sacrificed his physical life on the cross so we can have eternal life. Without a vision for and model of God's design for the family, the pro-life movement lacks the power to break the cycle. If we save babies without transforming lives, we're missing the mission Jesus set before us: God's design for family and God's call to discipleship.

God's design for marriage and family stands diametrically opposed to the goals of the sexual revolution and abortion culture. Abortion is not just an attack on the sanctity of life but also the sanctity of marriage and family that God designed. The disconnection between conception and fatherhood is ingrained in our society. Even from a legal perspective, motherhood begins at conception, but fatherhood begins at birth. The thought that you are not yet a mother or a father when a baby is conceived is one of the greatest lies, with many thinking they get to decide if they want to be a parent when they already are one. It is the responsibility of the church to uphold this high ideal.

When the pro-life movement leaves marriage and fatherhood out of the conversation, we help create situations that we have spent decades trying to reduce: the intergenerational cycle of abortion, unwed childbearing, father absence and the breakdown of the family. Life decisions need the support that the church is uniquely positioned and called to provide. Pregnancy support centres are the critical short-term care, but the long-term care of bringing children up within the safety of a Christian church cannot be outsourced. The church is the only organisation structurally capable and biblically aligned to offer long-term support, guidance and discipleship. This is the outworking of a life ministry; this is a House of Refuge!

Our goal first and foremost must be to get Christians to stop having abortions. We can't be naive to think this is only happening in the US. This is the log in our eye, and there is an urgent need to overturn the desire for abortions in our own churches. This is why we are asking you to join us in praying and helping spread the word for churches to be equipped with this life ministry.

We need to offer clear, biblical teaching on why choosing life is not just necessary but is essential; or we will continue to lose ground. The abortion issue is divinely woven into our two most fundamental mandates from Christ, namely the Great Commandment and the Great Commission.

'And you shall love the Lord your God with all your heart, with all your soul, with all your mind, and with all your strength.' This is the first commandment. And the second, like it, is this: 'You shall love your neighbour as yourself.' There is no other commandment greater than these. (Mark 12:30-31)

...'All authority has been given to Me in heaven and on earth. Go therefore and make disciples of all the nations, baptising them in the name of the Father and of the Son and of the Holy Spirit, teaching them to observe all things that I have commanded you; and lo, I am with you always, even to the end of the age.' Amen. (Matthew 28:18-20)

The Great Commandment rests on three loves: Love of God, Love of Neighbour and Love of Self. All conflicts in the family and society happen because there is a failure to love God, love your neighbour, or love yourself.

As Christ-followers, we should care for our cultural orphans and widows—single mothers and their children. It is critical that we recognise that abortion is not a women-only issue. For every post-abortive mother there is a post-abortive father. We can also help bring fathers back to life. We don't just aim to save babies; we do what Christ asks, and we share the gospel to save souls. Our first thought should be that they need to be a disciple of Jesus Christ, in answer to the Great Commission.

In conclusion, this is a message I learnt from David and Jason Benham—about being *bold and broken*. They explain it through the example of Peter.

Boldness apart from *brokenness* makes us a *bully*. The example of this is Peter cutting the servant's ear off in the Garden of Gethsemane. He had good intentions to defend, but Jesus had to restore the result of his aggression.

Brokenness apart from *boldness* makes us a *bystander*. The example of this is when Peter was in the courtyard and denied the Lord three times.

The Lord wants to get us to a place of *boldness* on the foundation of *brokenness* which then makes us a *bridge* connecting heaven to earth. This was Peter with the Holy Spirit, boldly proclaiming the gospel.

The Lord is calling us to be the bridge between heaven and earth, to connect Jesus with broken people. And the answer is always *love*. That is why we have called our organisation Love Australia—Love Adelaide and Love Sydney and coming soon Love Tasmania! True sacrificial love cannot be defeated.

And now these three remain: faith, hope and love. But the greatest of these is love. (1 Corinthians 13:13)

❀   ❀   ❀

How did we get to abortion on demand?[11]

Early in 2025, Jenny Hagger asked this piercing question in The Daily Declaration. Her article covered key political moves starting with the 4 December 1969, when the South Australian Parliament passed the *Criminal Law Consolidation Act Amendment Bill (Abortion);* where she quoted MP Mr A Burdon (Labor, Mt Gambier), who gave this solemn warning in the debate:

We are probably discussing one of the most important social measures ever to come before any Australian Parliament… This is the commencement of a backward slide in civilisation. Once we take the first step here, it will become easier because gradually the moral standards of the community will decline, <u>which in turn will bring about abortion virtually on demand.</u> (Jenny's emphasis)

The God-fearing born again, are taught to expect the best, to give people the benefit of the doubt and to love their neighbours as themselves. Admirable, but what about Jesus' directive, 'I send you out as sheep in the midst of wolves. Therefore, be wise as serpents and harmless as doves' (Matthew 10:16).

Jesus' disciples were sent out amongst *wolves* two thousand years ago, and they haven't transformed into *scared rabbits* today! Rather I would argue the enemy today is more formidable with sophisticated communications and has had centuries to plan and execute their agenda.

How did we get to abortion on demand? *While We Were Sleeping.* Jodie Pickard woke up early through her own tragedy, and ever since she has led an inspiring crusade against *the slaughter of the innocents.*[12]

Remember, when Adam and Eve first sinned (Genesis 3:6-7), they *hid* themselves from God. I believe it is instinctive, to hide our perceived mistakes. Abortion has always been shrouded in secrecy, or privacy as we refer to it today, and we now instinctively seek to protect the rights of the woman, while completely disregarding the rights of the unborn child.

The result, we have respectfully kept our distance and as Jodie points out; *brokenness* apart from *boldness* has made us *bystanders.*

What can we do?

Every year in Australia, 88,000 babies are lost to abortion. As Proverbs 31:8-9 urges us, we must speak up for those who cannot speak for themselves and help those in trouble. Unborn babies are the most vulnerable in our society, we must be their voice.[13]

Love Life,[4] began in Charlotte, North Carolina, in 2016, and has now spread across the whole of the USA. Despite the anguish of the topic, they celebrate this testimony on their website:

> *Because of supporters like you, in 2023 Love Life was able to be present at 44 abortion centers across the nation with over 1000 partnering Churches and 306 House of Refuge Churches poised and equipped to help the moms that chose life. A watershed moment occurred in 2023 when we saw the 5,000[th] baby saved from abortion.*
>
> *Let that number sink in. 5,000 babies who were scheduled to die, with the permission of their own parents, are alive today. God used you to help bring about this miracle. Because of you responding to God's call to be a voice for the voiceless, Love Life was able to have trained people interceding at the darkest places in our cities.*

Thankfully there are many pro-life groups, all with their unique part to play. My goal in this chapter is to spotlight Jodie's initiative as an example. My prayer is that each one of us, who wakes up, will take a step forward in God's call to be a voice for the voiceless, in whatever group best suits our circumstances.

Looking back, at the battles lost, can be paralysing if we are not careful. But as Winston Churchill said, 'Those that fail to learn from history are doomed to repeat it.' Let's wake up to the enemy's strategy.

In the famous *Roe v. Wade*, legal case the U.S. Supreme Court ruled on 22 January 1973, that unduly restrictive state regulation of abortion was unconstitutional, effectively banning individual state legislatures from restricting abortion.[14] But the U.S. Supreme Court overturned *Row v. Wade* on 24 June 2022. Ginna Cross, paediatric nurse,[15] who had been working towards this her entire adult life, told Megan Basham:[16]

> *I mean, this was something that was strived for and prayed for by Christians for half a century, so when the decision came down it was surreal. Like, is this actually happening? All of us (working in pregnancy centres) felt like we never really expected it in our lifetimes, but the Lord is so good to us that this happened kind of against all odds.*

However, Basham was shocked to see many of the big-name evangelical leaders, who you would have assumed to be pro-life, use the fall of *Roe* as an opportunity to argue for *bigger government*, offering more childcare, and to support the pro-abortion narrative that Christians only care about babies before they are born.

Therefore, we must not assume our church leadership, or our denomination are unequivocally pro-life; sadly, many are not, and fall into the *bystander* category. Individually, we need to step up, ask questions, research, and intercede (Chapter 13 Spiritual Warfare).

We can *lead* conversions and, in that way, explore our network and community and, all being well, become connected with others who share our newly awakened perspective. I can assure you that anyone who taps into *Love Australia*,[6] will be connected and empowered with practical next steps for their journey. Don't forget Peter (Acts 12:5-17), standing at the door, when we are having our prayer meeting for his release! God can do and does do miraculous things, witness the overturning of *Roe v. Wade* in 2022.

Perhaps the best thing we can do, on the back of prayer, is to campaign for our church to sign up to become a *House of Refuge* and if they are not yet ready to join remember you can be equipped as an individual. Tell this vision to all who will hear, gather a core group in your church, pray against *the slaughter of the innocents*,[12] and arrange a meeting with your church eldership or leadership. Wouldn't it be great if this chapter can *birth* new *House of Refuge Churches* across our nation.[9]

What does God say?

For You formed my inward parts; you covered me in my mother's womb. I will praise You, for I am fearfully and wonderfully made; marvellous are Your works, and that my soul knows very well. My frame was not hidden from You, when I was made in secret...(Psalm 139:13-15a)

God sculptured my bones and all my bodily organs. Believing this, disproves the lie that some of us were accidents. I love the phrases *fearfully and wonderfully made* and, *when I was made in secret,* by our loving heavenly Father. Babies in the womb are not random cell collections that suddenly become a human being when they are born and start breathing air. They are the pinnacle of God's creation from conception.

Let this scripture be the anchor for our soul, as we seek to love *all* men and women, boys and girls; like Christ who gave his life so that *whosoever* believes in him, would not perish but have everlasting life (John 3:16).

Thus says the Lord: 'Execute judgment and righteousness and deliver the plundered out of the hand of the oppressor. Do no wrong and do no violence to the stranger, the fatherless, or the widow, nor shed innocent blood in this place.' (Jeremiah 22:3)

'Woe to those who call evil good, and good evil' (Isaiah 5:20). So many judicial systems are corrupted around the world, putting Christians in the cross hairs if we dare to raise God's standard, particularly in the defence of *innocent blood*. But with God nothing is impossible. We can turn this around if each and every one of us commit to prayer and boldly taking a stand.

Footnotes

[1] Genesis Pregnancy Support (n.d.). *Men*. Retrieved October 20, 2025, from https://www.genesispregnancysupport.org.au/men

[2] Live Action (2016, February 24). *Abortion Procedures: 1st, 2nd, and 3rd Trimesters*. [Video]. YouTube. https://youtu.be/CFZDhM5Gwhk?si=3MeYpyNpzYxJZECg

[3] Benham Brothers (n.d.). *Own Every Area Of Your Life, whatever the cost: We Can Help You Do It!* Retrieved October 20, 2025, from https://benhambrothers.com/

[4] Love Life (n.d.). *Love Life's Story*. Retrieved October 20, 2025, from https://lovelife.org/about-us/

[5] Perkins, Tony (2022, July 6). *Flip Benham on the Work Needed to Protect the Unborn Now That Abortion Issues Returns to the States*. Tony Perkins. [Video]. YouTube. https://www.youtube.com/watch?v=AyqpiyDg3Ho

[6] Love Australia (n.d.). *Love Them Both*. Retrieved October 20, 2025, from https://www.loveaustralia.org.au/

[7] Mahlburg, Kurt (2024, February 20). The Promising Growth of Pro-Life Movement 'Love Australia.' *Daily Declaration*. https://dailydeclaration.org.au/2024/02/20/the-promising-growth-of-pro-life-movement-love-australia/

[8] Love Life (n.d.). *Pastor's agreement to become a House of Refuge church*. Retrieved October 20, 2025, from https://link.lovelife.org/widget/survey/iMveqGr2jpKktoMl3gLT

[9] House of Refuge Church (n.d.). *About House of Refuge*. Retrieved October 20, 2025, from https://www.houseofrefuge.org.au/home

[10] Warren, Rowland, C. (2024). *The Alternative to Abortion: Why We Must be Pro Abundant Life* Care Net. https://www.amazon.com/Alternative-Abortion-Must-Abundant-Life/dp/0997228539

[11] Hagger, Jenny (2025, January 22). Day 4 – How Did We Get to Abortion on Demand? *Daily Declaration.* https://dailydeclaration.org.au/2025/01/22/day-4-abortion-on-demand/

[12] Zahnd, Brian (2018, December 28). The Slaughter of the Innocents: The Dark Side of Christmas. *Word of Life Church.* https://brianzahnd.com/2018/12/slaughter-innocents-dark-side-christmas/

[13] Australian Christian Lobby (ACL) (n.d.). *Abortion.* Retrieved October 20, 2025, from https://www.acl.org.au/abortion/

[14] Britannica (n.d.). *Roe v. Wade.* Retrieved October 20, 2025, from https://www.britannica.com/event/Roe-v-Wade

[15] Alliance Family Services (n.d.). *About Us.* Retrieved October 20, 2025, from https://www.alliancefamilyservices.org/about-us

[16] Basham, Megan (2024). *Shepherds for Sale: How Evangelical Leaders Traded the Truth for a Leftist Agenda, (Chapter 3, Hijacking the Prolife Movement).* Harper Collins US. https://www.amazon.com.au/Shepherds-Sale-Evangelical-Leaders-Leftist/dp/0063413442

CHAPTER 9 - EUTHANASIA

Leonie Robson's Story

Leonie and her husband Ivan live in Swansea, New South Wales, Australia. They became Christians in 1983 through a chronic illness of their third child. A neighbour came round to see them, saying they were heartbroken to see the suffering of their little one and asked if she might pray for them. The result of this encounter was Leonie and Ivan's radical rebirth and the healing of their son.[1]

Leonie and Ivan are now songwriters, worship leaders, parents and grandparents. They have operated in lay ministry in cross denominational settings for many years. They are now pastoring a Pentecostal Church on the NSW Central Coast. Leonie writes poetry and lyrics and is an artist of great repute, according to her granddaughter, at least!

Leonie tells her story:

I woke up to the battle for euthanasia gradually. I always saw there was a pressure on those growing old. I saw this with my grandmother when she went into full time care around 1975. It was pretty evident back then that this was simply a holding pattern.

At the time, I had an uncle, designated next of kin, who said to me. 'Do you remember when Nana had all those skin cancers removed off her face?' She had a couple of big grafts on her face, and they were terribly painful. 'Well, the doctor, her GP, got her transported to the Mater last week to get some more removed! They didn't tell me that this was going to happen.' So, I asked him, 'How did your find out?'

He said, he visited Nana, and she was crying and saying, 'don't let them do to my face what they did last time.' She had actually refused the doctor in the Mater and made him so mad!

By this stage I was 17 years old, and I just gotten into nursing. So, I said to my uncle, 'give me the telephone.' I rang the GP, and he said to me, 'who do you think you are?' I said, 'I'm her granddaughter, I have my uncle here and I am telling you right now, that if you lay one hand on my grandmother, we will sue you!' I had no idea what I was talking about. But he didn't do it, and a few months later she passed away. You have to wonder, what was in it for him? One has to put two and two together and say dollars!

You start to think that there is something radically wrong with this system. There were friends in our church, who had a family member die of bone cancer. He was in a lot of pain, but he stayed at home, where they kept him as comfortable as possible. This is understandable, you don't want people suffering. The step further that we are seeing now is an escalation from this, and it's been happening for years.

When my mum went into care, it happened very suddenly. She only lived a few streets from us; I saw her virtually every day. But suddenly, she hit a psychological wall, she had a nervous breakdown. So, we had to go through the medical system.

We got her to the hospital, and they said it's all because she has swelling on her knee. That was true, but this was minor beside what was really going on with her mental health. The doctors insisted that the only problem was the fluid. They drained the fluid and kept her in.

The next conversation with the doctors was that she did not think she could go home as she wasn't coping. So, we said to Mum. 'What do you want to do? Let's look at some options, we can get meals on wheels for example.'

She came home, but she was home for less than 24 hours. She just became catatonic again. We had to call the ambulance and take her back. She went through the process of the social worker talking with her. She said, she did not want to be at home anymore.

My mum had always said, 'don't put me in a nursing home, I saw my mum die there.' I said, 'don't worry, darling, we will keep you home as long as we possibly can.' They transferred mum into a low care facility. She was there for less than a year. But in that year, she was just dreadful. It was as if my mum had decided I don't want to do a thing again as long as I live except breath and eat. She wanted to be waited on. She desperately wanted everything to be done for her.

She started to self-harm. Here's this lady aged 85, getting little ornaments to try and cut her wrists. She would get herself out of the chair and fall on her head on purpose to get her head to bleed, because this would get her to the hospital. Once she was in the hospital, she lay in bed, and everyone did everything for her. I kept telling the doctors, she needs help with this mental condition.

Eventually she got admitted to the mental health unit in the Mater Hospital, Newcastle. My mum was a Christian; my mum was saved. My dad was drowned when I was 15, we never found his body. That blew up our family as you can imagine. My mum was then pushed into another marriage and that was a disaster from the beginning.

Eventually my mum was happy to get out of the mental health unit, and she agreed to go into a high care facility.

We were told point blank; you get one shot at this. If we say 'no' to the one they recommend, they say, 'we will put you in the next available place, no questions asked.' That could be anywhere up the NSW coast!

So, Ivan and I got proactive. We found one place, quite close, we were very happy with it, and they happened to have a spot for mum.

Meanwhile mum had a scan, and they found cancer in her stomach the size of a rock melon. When I was about 12, mum had had a total hysterectomy except one ovary. That one ovary had now become cancerous. This was instrumental in her dramatic behaviour and character change.

This high care facility was much more sanitary than some we had seen. We thought, this is good, we can do this. They took us to see the palliative care unit. There was a lovely lady in charge. She said, this is where we bring our residents at 'end of life.' There is music available, and we even feed them ice cream if they would like it. We had a picture painted that it was going to be gentle for mum.

But nothing prepared us for the pointy end when she couldn't eat any longer. She couldn't pass urine either because of the size of the mass. She was in distress. So, they rang me and said we are taking your mum down to the unit, they said she was very close to the end.

But when we saw her, she was still talking. She was still engaged. She kept saying 'I don't want to go to that room, I know what happens in that room!'

Within half an hour of being put into that bed, they came along with their needles. They said it was only to keep her calm. This was euthanasia. Mum died in there in 2016. There was nothing of palliative care about it at all.

Mum drifted off for a bit but then came round. She was agitated again, and I would sing to her and read Psalms, and we would be praying with her. Then she would drift off again. But the next time she would wake up with such a start that she would sit up in bed. She would be screaming out 'No, no, I don't want to do this. I don't want to go.'

You can imagine how we felt. The nurse would come in again and give her more injections. It was Midazolam and Morphine. It was horrible, you could see the fight in mum's face.

We got a phone call about three the next morning that she had gone. But it struck me so deeply that what we witnessed was ungodly. It was absolute evil. It wasn't gentle. It wasn't letting nature take its course. The nursing home business has someone waiting the next day to get into that room.

When we went back the next day, the lady in charge of the facility was there. She said to me, 'You know Leonie, did she put up a fight! We gave her enough to kill three people!' I thought to myself, you don't know what you're saying. You don't know what you're admitting.

I came home and had to process so much guilt; it took me years to process. It was the deception that injured us and made sure that she didn't go peacefully. She went completely drugged out and euthanised. We did everything we could, then it was out of our hands. We had documented that we don't want her to be resuscitated, but to let her go peacefully. But her passing was far from peaceful.

A massive part of the medical profession has denied their Hippocratic Oath. I think it has been attacked over many years. It's the cultural Marxism marching through the institutions (Chapter 3 Education). Anyone our age is saying, doesn't life mean more than this, than making sure that a baby doesn't get born, and making sure that old people are not a drag on society?

In Canada the drug cocktail they use in their euthanasia program is the same as the one used for executions over the border in the US. The MAiD (medical assistance in dying) system in Canada has been taking the supplies from the US so that executions in the US have had to be postponed![2]

The cocktail of drugs has a couple of steps to it. The first shot shuts down our airways, and we start to drown, a slow drowning, you can't yell, you're like a corpse, you're just breathing. It's like constant waterboarding, until your lungs fill with water and your die. Isn't that a gentle way of going![3]

❀   ❀   ❀

Approaches to the Euthanasia Question

Leonie's harrowing story raises far more questions than answers. We are not Leonie, and we have not travelled her journey, but we can honour the questions her story raises.

1. *Procedures.* In Chapter 8, we saw that being informed about the practical details of abortion was critical for Jodie's journey, for establishing the foundations for her thinking and actions. So, it behoves us, as lay people, to understand what is entailed in the procedures of euthanasia. In this regard, Leonie's experience is invaluable and her testimony at the end regarding the Canadian experience is eye opening.

2. *The Compassion Button.* I am sure that we are all wired to have compassion for the suffering, we wouldn't be human otherwise. When the sufferer is close to us, I am sure compassion goes into overdrive but then suggesting a way to end their suffering by premature death pulls different emotions. Suffice it to say, emotions triggered by compassion distort clear rational thought and cloud our vision of the truth.

3. *Who gets to decide?* The individual sufferer, if they can, their family and friends, the medical professionals, the medical ethics board, or our elected or self-appointed state government? Just as in a case of a trial by jury, can we be sure that the decision makers have all the evidence? Think of the Swiss cheese test, where we hypothetically cut half a dozen slices of Swiss cheese, mix them up, and only when we find all holes line up, can we pull the plug on the sufferer.[4]

4. *Playing God.* No human can ever claim to have created life, but some of us have ended life intentionally or inadvertently. In our approach to euthanasia, I suggest considering what God has to say, and seeking to do our best to follow the instructions in His Manuel. It is a terrible place to find ourselves 'playing God,' to voluntarily go there is a huge step to take, especially if we know God has said 'no.'

The few pages of this chapter can never do such a complex issue justice, I merely want to wake someone up to what happened *While We Were Sleeping* and perhaps to offer some fresh options.

The Hippocratic Oath

Hippocrates was born into a family of priest doctors in 460 BC in Kos, Greece.[5] He established the basics of medicine as it is practised today, developing medical terms, definitions, protocols, and guidelines for the classification of diseases. He is most well-known for The Hippocratic Oath, which medical professionals have pledged at the outset of their practice for over 2000 years.

The original Greek has been translated by many different scholars, so it is hard to be definitive about the exact wording, but the meaning is clear. Here are some extracts from the original version:[6]

With regard to healing the sick, I will devise and order for them the best diet, according to my judgment and means; and I will take care that they suffer no hurt or damage.

Nor shall any man's entreaty prevail upon me to administer poison to anyone; neither will I counsel any man to do so. Moreover, I will give no sort of medicine to any pregnant woman, with a view to destroy the child.

Whatsoever house I may enter, my visit shall be for the convenience and advantage of the patient; and I will willingly refrain from doing any injury or wrong from falsehood, and (in an especial manner) from acts of an amorous nature, whatever may be the rank of those who it may be my duty to cure, whether mistress or servant, bond or free. (my emphasis)

The Oath was rewritten in 1964 by Dr. Louis Lasagna, Academic Dean at Tufts University School of Medicine, Massachusetts, USA, and this revised form is widely accepted in today's medical schools. Here are some extracts:

I will apply, for the benefit of the sick, all measures [that] are required, avoiding those twin traps of overtreatment and therapeutic nihilism.
I will respect the privacy of my patients, for their problems are not disclosed to me that the world may know.
Most especially must I tread with care in matters of life and death. If it is given me to save a life, all thanks. But it may also be within my power to take a life; this awesome responsibility must be faced with great humbleness and awareness of my own frailty. Above all, I must not play at God. (my emphasis)

The differences are stark. The intent of the original text is clearly the pledge to 'do no harm' to the patient, or their child if a lady is pregnant. Contrasted with the revised version that covers 'over or under' treatment and 'privacy' not mentioned in the original. There is no longer a pledge to 'do no harm' while opening the door to the possibility of 'taking the life of their patient' and if called to do so to take the responsibility with humility. Ironically, then it also instructs that the medical practitioner not 'play God'!

Some websites covering The Hippocratic Oath claim that the phrase; 'First, do no harm,' attributed to the ancient Greek physician Hippocrates, 'isn't a part of the Hippocratic Oath at all' (Harvard Health);[7] and 'it is generally believed that the famous phrase, 'first do no harm' is contained in the original Hippocratic Oath but it was not' (National Institute of Health (NIH)).[8]

It is unsurprising that the oath has been changed over the centuries but consider where we have come from and where we are today. The original oath was, 'first do no harm,' now it is 'within my power to take a life.'

An Overview of Voluntary Assisted Dying

Voluntary assisted dying (VAD) is lawful in all Australian States. VAD has also been passed in the Australian Capital Territory (ACT) and is due to commence on 3 November 2025. VAD is illegal in the Northern Territory. Health professionals can conscientiously object to participating in VAD, and medical practitioners, nurses and allied health professionals working in aged and home care can decide whether or not to participate in VAD.[9]

Globally, there has been a significant increase in the number of people choosing VAD in recent years. However, finding credible statistics for comparison across jurisdictions is extremely difficult, but it is fair to say Canada leads the world in euthanasia, closely followed by The Netherlands and then Belgium.[10]

The rise in people electing VAD springs from the evolution of the Hippocratic Oath and mirrors the rise in the availability of abortion (Chapter 8), the diminishing respect for human life and the increasing push for culling the world's population to preserve the planet (Chapter 12).

The Euthanising Process

Leonie has given us a window into euthanasia within the palliative care system in Australia, asserting that it has been going on long before it has become officially legal and voluntary (VAD). She ended with a commentary on the recent Canadian situation.

This has been corroborated by Kelsi Sheren's testimony during an interview with Jordan Peterson.[11] Jordan speculated that when the transgender (Chapter 7) furore dies down, in the next three or four years, if the MAiD (medical assistance in dying) people have their way, there will be the push for romanticised death encounters for the young.

The mechanism for the procedure, Kelsie reported, includes Sodium Thiopental, made in Italy, used by anaesthesiologists. The USA have been using this drug for death penalty executions. A study of those deceased showed that 85 per cent of them had twice as much water in the lungs than normal. This drug was causing drowning akin to dying by waterboarding.

So, the reason those who are dying under MAiD[12] in Canada seem peaceful is because they are given a paralytic injection first and they start drowning to death and are unable to scream out for help. Veterans are being offered MAiD by their government, so they don't have to pay out compensation for them.

In 2021 alone, the Canadian government saved C\$ 86.9 million from their palliative care budget because of the take up of MAiD. Kelsie said, 'I am not going crazy, I am screaming at the top of my lungs, we are killing innocent people, and children are next on the chopping block… If anyone is a God-fearing individual right now, all I ask is stop lying. If you want to kill people to save money, say so. Stop dancing around saying you are doing this out of empathy.'

Legitimate Responses

Compounding the euthanasia question have been the burgeoning medical treatments for prolonging life, such as cardiopulmonary resuscitation (CPR), tube feeding and dialysis.[13] Now we have the tension between the potential of extending life or the capability of prematurely cutting it short. This question is heightened when we seek to apply God's will, as revealed in Scripture, when none of these interventions were available.

Young's study of patients' views on end-of-life practices that hasten death, found most viewed current palliative care practices, such as pain relief with opioids and symptom management with Palliative Sedation (PS), as hastening death, in contrast to some medical research which asserts that proportional therapeutic doses do not hasten death.[14] Some in the study did not agree with the 'doctrine of double effect' ('DDE') and saw such practices as 'slow euthanasia' and 'covert euthanasia,' and implied these procedures were performed without patient consent, though they fell short of calling it murder. The assertion *there is no hastening of death* cannot dispel the *perception* of the contrary.

'HOPE' is a coalition of groups and individuals who oppose the legalisation of euthanasia and assisted suicide and support measures that will make euthanasia and assisted suicide unthinkable. They respect all political or personal ideologies and religious beliefs and practices. Their aims are to:[15]

1. *Build networks with like-minded people across Australia who support our aims.*

2. *Present a united voice in presentations to governments or other organisations with respect to issues related to euthanasia and assisted suicide.*
3. *Network and exchange information between supporters and concerned people.*
4. *Develop an educational and media strategy for educating the public on issues related to euthanasia and assisted suicide.*
5. *Build a research team for collecting and assessing information.*
6. *Organise events and promote quality speakers who can address issues related to euthanasia, assisted suicide, and hospice/palliative care.*
7. *Encourage people from all walks of life to engage in the public debate and to raise such matters with their political representatives.*
8. *Create the opportunity for informative debate.*

In contrast, some Christian's legitimate response is to demonstrate love and compassion to those with a terminal or hopeless illness and that they should have the option of a pain-free, peaceful and dignified death with legal voluntary assisted dying. Those in 'Go Gentle Australia' also state that conservative Christians who opposed marriage equality (Chapter 1) and discussion on sexual orientation (Chapters 6 and 7) are wrong.[16] They claim to represent 75 per cent of Christians in Australia, including three out of four Catholics, who, they say, according to Vote Compass 2019, support VAD as an end-of-life choice, showing true empathy, love and compassion for a dying person who is needlessly suffering.

What does God say?

Christians can sometimes be persuaded into supporting assisted suicide and euthanasia, believing that it is the compassionate thing to do, but what does the Bible say? The following is partly adapted from a booklet, *Euthanasia and Assisted Suicide*, by Tim Dieppe.[17]

We are not one of the animals, the sanctity of human life sets us apart. 'Whoever sheds man's blood, by man his blood shall be shed; for in the image of God He made man' (Genesis 9:6). Our value, and so our claim for protection, comes not from our *quality of life* or gifts and abilities, but from our status as being made in God's image. Therefore, we all have special intrinsic value regardless of how young, old, able-bodied, or disabled that life might be. God expands on this:

He who strikes a man so that he dies shall surely be put to death. However, if he did not lie in wait, but God delivered him into his hand, then I will appoint for you a place where he may flee. But if a man acts with premeditation against his neighbour, to kill him by treachery, you shall take him from My altar, that he may die. (Exodus 21:12-24)

The deliberate act of murder, a violation of the sixth commandment, is stepping in front of God, who gives life and takes life away (Job 1:21). The intentional destruction of someone who has been created in the image of God is therefore a deliberate act of rebellion against God. This is a very blunt statement but when all the caveats are stripped away, 'The Lord kills and makes alive; He brings down to the grave and brings up' (1 Samuel 2:6).

When we believe we are faced with a decision to take a life or let one live, on account of terrible suffering or a medical diagnosis of no hope; if we choose to euthanise, we are denying God's power to heal and to raise the dead. So far in this chapter we have not discussed the power of prayer for the alleviation of suffering or for complete healing, but why not? We regularly pray for the sick; why exclude the terminally ill, and take it upon ourselves to number their days?

The Bible directly addresses euthanasia. In 1 Samuel 31, when the Philistines fought against Israel and the battle went badly for them, the men fled but were killed on Mount Gilboa.

Then the Philistines followed hard after Saul and his sons. And the Philistines killed Jonathan, Abinadab, and Malchishua, Saul's sons. The battle became fierce against Saul. The archers hit him, and he was severely wounded by the archers. Then Saul said to his armorbearer, 'Draw your sword, and thrust me through with it, lest these uncircumcised men come and thrust me through and abuse me.' But his armorbearer would not, for he was greatly afraid. Therefore, Saul took a sword and fell on it. And when his armorbearer saw that Saul was dead, he also fell on his sword, and died with him. (1 Samuel 31:2-5) (my emphasis)

This passage is clearly opposed to euthanasia and doesn't condone suicide. The armour bearer had refused to comply with King Saul's request, even though the King had authority over him.

However, a little later, severely wounded Saul called to a stranger and requested he finish him off, and this time the man obliged. He then ran to David to report that he had complied with King Saul's request. After a day of mourning, David's response was to order that the man be killed because he should not have killed the Lord's anointed (2 Samuel 1:1-16).

The Bible teaches that suffering is not necessarily something that should be avoided at all costs (see Rod's story, Chapter 12 Climate Change). Romans 5:3 teaches us to 'glory in tribulations, knowing that tribulation produces perseverance.' Similarly, James teaches: 'Count it all joy when you fall into various trials, knowing that the testing of your faith produces patience. But let patience have its perfect work, that you may be perfect and complete, lacking nothing' (James 1:2-4).[18]

Society has come to expect relief from suffering and hardship, yet the Bible is full of examples where He allows suffering to build faith and to develop character. I would rather bring my loved one into the Lord's hands in prayer and hold their hand in their suffering. A huge sacrifice on our part I know, but at least we are humbly kneeling at His feet as we commit our loved one into His hands.

All our days are numbered by the Lord, says Job (Job 14:5); and Moses calls on God to teach him how to number his days, so that he can apply his heart to wisdom (Psalm 90:12-14). To put our hand out to limit those days is flagrant *playing God*, that is commanded that we should not do, even by the 1960s revision of the Hippocratic Oath.

I argue that withholding life-saving treatment from a dying individual is not euthanasia when there is no intent to cause death, even if that is the ultimate result.[18] Rather it is a form of generosity or the preventing of harm to a person. Examples include removing a ventilator from a grandmother with no hope of recovery or choosing to refrain from potentially fruitless chemotherapy. In this scenario, no lethal or potentially lethal drugs are administered and in prayer we are bringing our loved one into the Lord's hands from where He can bring down to the grave or bring up with renewed health (1 Samuel 2:6).

Footnotes

[1] The Latter Rain - Leonie and Ivan Robson (2023, November 7). *Interview for 'Song of Songs Chapter 2' used with the kind permission of www.firstfruits.com.* [Video]. YouTube. https://www.youtube.com/watch?v=JNwoSk-KV4E&t=442s

[2] Mahlburg, Kurt (2023, August 11). Oh, Canada: 10 Tragic Facts About Canada's Euthanasia Regime. *Daily Declaration.* https://dailydeclaration.org.au/2023/08/11/oh-canada-10-tragic-facts-about-canadas-euthanasia-regime/

[3] Robson, Leonie (2022, February 25). Euthanasia: Darkness on the Far Side of Midnight. *Daily Declaration.* https://dailydeclaration.org.au/2022/02/25/vad-darkness-on-the-far-side-of-midnight/

[4] Clinical Leadership Solutions Ltd (2019, March 15). *Reasons Swiss Cheese Model.* [Video]. YouTube. https://www.youtube.com/watch?v=MfWpMrEOlJ8

[5] Szasz, George (2024, June 13). The father of medicine. *BCMJ, Doctors of BC Publication.* https://bcmj.org/blog/father-medicine

[6] MIT Education (n.d.). *Hippocratic Oath (ca. 400 BCE) Translated by Francis Adams.* Retrieved October 21, 2025, from https://classics.mit.edu/Hippocrates/hippooath.html

[7] Shmerling, Robert H. (2020, June 22). First do no harm. *Harvard Health Publishing, Harvard Medical School.* https://www.health.harvard.edu/blog/first-do-no-harm-201510138421

[8] Hajar, Rachel (2017). The Physician's Oath: Historical Perspectives. *Heart Views, Oct-Dec, 18*(4),154–159. doi: 10.4103/HEARTVIEWS.HEARTVIEWS_131_17

[9] End of Life Directions for Aged Care (ELDAC) (n.d.). *Overview of Voluntary Assisted Dying, Our Toolkits.* Retrieved October 21, 2025, from https://www.eldac.com.au/Our-Toolkits/End-of-Life-Law/Voluntary-Assisted-Dying/Overview

[10] Buchholz, Katharina (2022, August 31). Where Most People Die by Assisted Suicide. *Statista.* https://www.statista.com/chart/28130/assisted-suicide-numbers/

[11] Jordan B Peterson Clips (2024, May 23). *The Horrifying Truth Behind MAiD They Aren't Telling You Interview with Kelsi Sheren.* [Video]. YouTube. https://www.youtube.com/watch?v=3YYxOfwrsrU

[12] Dying with Dignity Canada (2024, May 24). Clarification about the medications used in a MAID provision. *Dying with Dignity Canada.* https://www.dyingwithdignity.ca/blog/clarification-about-the-medications-used-in-a-maid-provision/

[13] Advanced Care Planning Australia. (n.d.). *Advance care planning gives you the opportunity to plan your future health care and medical treatment while you're healthy and can make decisions yourself.* ACPA, An Australian Government Initiative. Retrieved October 21, 2025, from https://www.advancecareplanning.org.au/understand-advance-care-planning/life-prolonging-treatments

[14] Young, Jessica E. et al (2021). Patients' views on end-of-life practices that hasten death: a qualitative study exploring ethical distinctions. *Annals of Palliative Medicine, 10*(3), March 31. doi: 10.21037/apm-20-621. https://apm.amegroups.org/article/view/45543/html

[15] HOPE (n.d.). *HOPE - Preventing Euthanasia & Assisted Suicide.* Retrieved October 21, 2025, from https://www.facebook.com/NOEuthanasia/

[16] Go Gentle Australia (2020, October 14). A Christian Response to 'No Euthanasia Day.' *Go Gentle Australia.* https://www.gogentleaustralia.org.au/a_christian_response_to_no_euthanasia_day

[17] Christian Concern (2024, June 12). What does the Bible say about euthanasia and assisted suicide? *Christian Concern.* https://christianconcern.com/resource/what-does-the-bible-say-about-euthanasia-and-assisted-suicide/

[18] Wurster, Mary (2018, July 27). What does the Bible teach about euthanasia and physician assisted suicide? *The Ethics and Religious Liberty Commission of the Southern Baptist Convention.* https://erlc.com/resource/what-does-the-bible-teach-about-euthanasia-and-physician-assisted-suicide/

CHAPTER 10 - POLITICS

John Anderson's Story

John is a sixth-generation farmer and grazier from New South Wales, who spent 19 years from 1989, in the Australian Parliament. He served as a senior Cabinet Minister in the reformist government led by John Howard (1996 to 2005), one of the most successful governments in Australian parliamentary history. This included six years as Leader of the National Party and Deputy Prime Minister.

John picks up the narrative:

As a young person I had more than a passing interest in good public policy. In 1974, my last year at the King's School, Parramatta, during the Whitlam Labor Government era, I was standing on the parade ground for our passing-out parade beside one of the busiest roads in Sydney and only one or two cars went past while I was on the parade ground for about an hour. There was a petrol strike.

I remember getting mail that was two or three weeks late because the Redfern Mail Exchange was on strike. I remember, with great regularity the airline industry would be crippled by strikes at the beginning of school holidays. As a son of a serviceman who almost lost his life in WWII while doing something he didn't want to do, fighting against the Germans; thinking to myself, it really hurt that the Prime Minister of Singapore, Lee Kuan Yew, warned that Australia was in danger of becoming the 'poor white trash of Asia.'[1] That pricked my pride a bit. Here we were, an incredibly fortunate country, and nothing seemed to be working properly.

Against this backdrop, I went to university but played no role in student politics. When I left university to return to the farm, I did what everyone did in those days, I joined the local branch of the National Party. It was a small branch but active. Somewhat to my dismay, I turned up late for the AGM, only to discover that the retiring secretary was nominating me to take his place. A great many folks, that I highly respected, insisted I do it.

So, at the age of 25, I was duly elected secretary, and I remember going home that night with all the books of minutes and reading through them till one o'clock in the morning to make sure everything was recorded properly!

In 1983 I attended our electorate's council meeting for the National Party. The retiring member, Frank O'Keefe was disparaging of the recent election of the Hawke government. In old bushman style, who liked to do things properly, he talked about somebody or other who came into the chamber with an open necktie, and somebody else who was an intellectual and of no use, and someone else who didn't look like he had showered for a while.

Well, I couldn't help it! I stood up at the end of his remarks and said, 'As somebody with a university degree, who is wearing a tie, and did have a shower this morning…' And for some reason it resonated, the house broke up! And to my utter amazement, only a couple of months later, Frank asked if I could see him.

I was working on the farm, so I agreed to see him after dark. On entering his office, he said, 'You can't tell anyone, but I am going to resign at the next federal election, and I want you to run in my place.' 'You want me to do what, sir?' I said, never having contemplated the idea. It had never crossed my mind, even though I had an interest in good public policy.

I said, 'I don't think I could, I am a Christian, I don't think people like Christians.' Frank said, 'I am a Christian, I belong to the Parliamentary Christian Fellowship; my wife's a Christian; that's no barrier, that's a plus!' He said, 'I won't take 'no' for an answer, you have eight days before I have to make an announcement, and I would love to announce that you're my preferred successor.'

My father, horrified, was totally opposed to the idea. I was only 27. It was precocious of me to even think about it; however, I did ask three people I respected, one being Peter Chiswell, then Bishop of Armidale. They all said go for it!

I was always impressed with the ability some people have to move people. There was a part of me that wanted to be an orator, and I don't think I have ever become one! But Tony Abbott said, on my leaving parliament that in fact, 'I could move a crowd.'

Another advantage for a life in politics was my love of driving, because the electorate I eventually became member for was the size of England! There were five of us who ran for preselection, I was the youngest. So, I made a point of referencing the Labor party who made a virtue of enlisting young people, stating the National Party should do the same. The argument cut through, and I won pre-selection!

But the party pre-selected me on provisional boundaries during a redistribution, and my constituency, Paterson, was abolished two weeks later! I was no longer a pre-selected candidate as my electorate had gone!

I got married and started a family. Then about three years later, in 1988, the member for Guider, Ralph Hunt, rang me, and said, 'Are you ready?' I blurted out, 'Ready for what?' I had assumed, that as a Christian, God had his purposes, and I could get on as a husband and as a dad.

Ralph said, 'I am now retiring, and I want you to run in my place.' I said, 'I think the time has gone Ralph. I have a wife and young kid, and I am not sure this is the right move, taking on a seat this size.'

Anyway, he asked my wife and I to see him for a weekend. He preyed on my sense of responsibility. My father-in-law, a retired Rear Admiral, said, 'You will never get another opportunity like this, have a go.' At that time there were 10 or 12 standing for pre-selection and the campaign was vicious. There is nothing worse than an ugly pre-selection, as you are fighting your own. So, I entered parliament in a by-election, in April 1989, in opposition until February of 1996, when we won government.

You ask, should Christians be involved in politics? I would say with Broughton Knox, former principal of Moore College, 'You should be asking yourself, why would I not join the political party of my choice?' He and I see politics as very important. Paul told Timothy to pray that they may live a peaceful and quiet life in all godliness and dignity, for the advancement of the gospel.

Christians have a huge stake in democracy, because it is the product of the Christian worldview. It was Christians, who struggled for concepts of dignity, worth, fairness, justice, and how to accord each individual recognition as unique, dignified human beings, made in the image of God, but flawed by sin. It was Christians who came up with democracy, more so, in my view, than the legacy of the Greeks. They have championed the idea of the equality of all souls in the eyes of heaven.

Our longest serving Prime Minister, Robert Menzies, actually used those words in 1942:

Democracy is more than a machine; it is a spirit. It is based upon the Christian conception that there is in every human soul a spark of the divine; that, with all their inequalities of mind and body, the souls of men stand equal in the sight of God.[2]

How do you give every person, worth? How do you give them a say in who will lead them and shape where their culture will go? At the same time, how do you balance the dangers of democracy?

The American Forefathers, particularly Alexander Hamilton, understood this. The danger is mob rule, the lynch mob. People losing their sense of perspective, being persuaded to do mad and stupid things that are not fair and trample on the rights of the small and the minorities.

John Fairfax, the founder of what became the Sydney Morning Herald, was a Congregationalist and an evangelical. He had reservations about universal suffrage for the same reason that Alexander Hamilton grappled with it so deeply. How do you protect the interest of the minority against mob rule? How do you stop the misuse of democratic rights that can squeeze out the marginalised?

Our forefathers found ways of limiting power, of countering the drift towards pride and megalomania, which grips so many people who achieve a certain status. How do you change governments that have become tired or proud, at the point of a pencil rather than the point of a gun? How do you enshrine the concept of *common law* and the *common man*? So that everyone should face the law equally whether you are poor or a prime minister. These are all concepts from the Christian worldview. I suspect today most Christians haven't thought this through, and that really distresses me.

If we are concerned for our fellow man, if we want to love our neighbour as ourselves; if we want to recognise that Jesus plainly cared for the poor and the marginalised, (Jesus was not only focused on the next world), but we ought also to be engaged. We ought to use the tools we have to try to ensure a society in which people can flourish, in which children are valued, in which our neighbour is loved as ourselves. Politics is only a part of this. The way we interact with our family, our community is *upstream* of how we act corporately.

We have taken God out of our society and culture, and government has become our god. And this ultimately disappoints us as it's only human government. Pride gets in the way. Gamesmanship is now played by so many people in public life that it threatens the very fabric of our society. There are honourable exceptions.

I would say to Christians, 'Wake up, get behind people who are seeking to serve and are not seeking to be served. You've got a responsibility, they need you, so they can be strengthened and emboldened to carry on the battle.'

Sometimes I hear from good politicians, who say to me, 'John, this is just hopeless, I am going to give it away and go back to private life.' Then I say, 'That's the very reason you're needed, because things are not going well, you are person of good intent and sound moral principles.'

Governments should not be *over* us. This is the whole point the American Founding Fathers championed, the essential freedoms and rights of the individual, that trump elective rights. We only give up our rights, freedom of conscience and religion, freedom of speech, freedom of assembly and the freedom to own property to the extent necessary to do the things we can't best do for ourselves. We should accept responsibility to do what we can for ourselves and for our neighbours. And our neighbours should accept responsibility for what they can do for us and our communities.

Our freedoms are vested in us as individuals. Government does not grant us freedom. We give government the right to restrict some of our freedoms for the common good when necessary. Government's job is to defend the freedoms of the individual against its own interests and its own desire to increase its own power. We have lost the plot on this. We desperately need Christians who understand that politics should be *downstream* of culture. Culture is *downstream* of values and values are *downstream* of beliefs.

Here in Australia, the conservative right has moved so far left, there is now only one big *uniparty* in the middle. It is ineffectively opposed by a plethora of competing right wing conservative parties that mainstream media ignore. This is the perfect case for why good men and women of sound Christian conscience and wisdom are desperately needed in public life.

A young man once said to me, 'I want to get involved in politics.' Normally I try to discourage people because it's a unique set of giftings, but he plainly had something to offer. So, I said, 'Go and join the political party of your choice and, start attending meetings.' Then he would call me up and say, 'Why do you want me to get involved with this bunch, they're all playing games, they are all playing social misfit roles, no one seems interested in better policy and better outcomes for the country, it's all about winning the latest factional game.' So, I said, 'You've just seen why you should get involved.' He eventually became quite senior with a position where he could make a difference.

We are at a civilizational moment. There have been many powerful civilisations down through the ages. A civilization arises when a set of ideas are embraced by enough people for a long enough time to earn the right to be called a civilization. Most collapse. The fuel that powers these civilizations starts to run low. At that point, you have to refuel the machine with high quality fuel of the sort you started with, or you need to find a substitute.

We have sought to find alternatives, such as *progressivism*, which centres on the idea that it's all about *me*.[3] I will be god over my own life, even though that's a tragedy because we are not up to the task, and we see the unhappiness it produces. Other facets of progressivism are leading to collapse, such as 'all wisdom resides in the present,' so we can't learn anything from history, and 'all cultures are the same,' so don't be judgemental about good and bad cultures.

We are running out of fuel - the results are there to see. Our wealth is declining. We are crippled by debt. We are crippling our children's future. We are depressed. We are anxious. We have mental health epidemics, and we have external enemies. This is what progressivism has given us.

In addition, the enlightenment has also failed us. It has not proven to be a fuel that we can run on, neither has postmodernism. Wokeism is a term we use to describe progressivism but it's a superficial term.

Christians hold the key. They have a secure hope, and they can point to reality. They can demonstrate the need to love and to sacrifice and to put others first, and to invest in their children. Or they can *sit on the fence* and hope it all goes away, but one day we will all be called to account.

❀   ❀   ❀

Western Christians Sitting on the Fence

All Christians are naturally distraught when we look at the society we occupy and feel powerless to change anything. But consider how we got here, a combination of ingredients that we failed to see, *While We Were Sleeping,* it's not too late to wake up.

Paul encouraged his disciples in Romans 12:2, not to let the world squeeze them into its mould.[4] A great example of this is how many parents (as well as church and other community leaders) are now hesitant to draw a clear distinction between what is right and wrong as this is deemed judgemental now that society has an excuse for every transgression (Genesis 3:4).[5]

The church has been most effective at training its own leadership but singularly lacking in equipping its people for works of service in the wider community, the political realm.[6]

It seems to me that churches have a responsibility to give wise biblical teaching, explaining exactly how the teachings of the Bible apply to situations in life, and that should certainly include instruction around government policy matters that contravene God's law even if they have passed into civil society as legitimate and legal.[7]

> *As Christians, we need to remember that the entire world is locked in a tremendous spiritual battle. There are demonic forces, forces of Satan, that seek to oppose God's purposes and bring evil and destruction to every human being that God created in his own image, and also bring destruction to every human society and every nation.* (Grudem)[7]

The result, according to Muehlenberg, is that countless millions of Christians in the West take absolutely no interest whatsoever in politics, meaning that they allow any and every evil and godless government to rule. 'Ignorance of political matters is not a virtue – it is in fact a sin.'[8]

If believers do not snap out of their sinful slumber and apathy real soon, they will simply find that it is too late. Bible-believing churches will be closed down, the proclamation of the gospel will be greatly restricted, and Bibles may well be burned in the streets. I kid you not! That is exactly where we are headed today in the West. Yet most believers are blissfully unaware of all this and couldn't give a rip.[8]

Then there is the misunderstood phrase 'separation of Church and State' which some believe came from the American founding documents but didn't. The phrase 'building a wall of the separation of church and state' was penned by President Jefferson in 1802 in a letter he wrote to a Baptist Association in Connecticut, assuring them that the First Amendment, regarding religious freedom, ensured that government interference or overreach was kept *out* of the church. It was never drafted to keep the church *out* of government. Tragically many have bought the lie that Christians should keep *out* of government.[9]

Michael Jensen (2024) sought to grapple with the Christian's role in politics and lands effectively *sitting on the fence*. He fails to call Christians to take action against corrupt and demonic acts of governments; rather we should hold our head high, doing good while ever we can (John 9:4).[6,9,10,11]

The Call to Action

John Anderson's story is a call to action. But we must acknowledge that we are engaging in a spiritual battle, not a human debate where we trade well founded arguments. It's not a time to be nice and hope that people like us.[4] There is a liberal progressive agenda, influenced by spiritual forces of evil, that if allowed to progress any further, will be the demise of democracy.[9]

Count the cost. Our peaceful slumbers have deceived us into believing that we are called to have church as usual; exciting, uplifting and seeker friendly. When we come down from *the fence*, most will lose family and friends, some will come up against the authorities, some will be sent to jail, some will lose everything, and some may lose their life.[12]

Everyone is not called to frontline political service; John made that crystal clear. His own entry into politics was on the invitation and encouragement of others. Perhaps our calling is to encourage another. Nonetheless, I believe we must all engage in politics, understand the political landscape, and don't allow ourselves to be deceived by the government's propaganda arm, legacy media.

Let's do all we can to keep politicians as honest as possible. Let's seek to inject as many God-fearing men and women of courage and conviction into our parliaments. Let's listen, extremely carefully to the language of those seeking election. Are they selling themselves to ungodly agendas under the guise that they might get elected, any means justifying the end?[13]

Gary Hamrick regularly exhorts his church, and online followers, to be politically active.[9] On one occasion he quoted from Erwin Lutzer's book, *When a nation forgets God, seven lessons we must learn from Nazi Germany*.[14] Here is a quote from a German eyewitness on the *apathy and indifference* of the church during WWII:

> *I lived in Germany during Nazi Holocaust. I considered myself a Christian. We heard stories of what was happening to the Jews but we tried to distance ourselves from it, because what could anyone do to stop it. A railroad track ran behind our church and each Sunday morning we could hear the whistle in the distance, and then the wheels coming over the tracks. We became disturbed when we heard the cries coming from the train as it passed by. We realised it was carrying Jews like cattle in the cars. Week after week the whistle would blow. We dreaded to hear the sound of those wheels because soon we would hear the cries of the Jews on route to their deathcamp. Their screams tormented us. We knew the time the train was coming and when we heard the whistle blow, we began singing hymns. By the time the train passed our church, we were singing at the top of our voices. If we heard the screams we sang more loudly and soon we heard them no more. Years have passed, and no one talks about it anymore. But I still hear that train whistle in my sleep. God forgive me. Forgive all of us who call ourselves Christians and yet did nothing to intervene.[14]*

What does God say?

About 600 BC Daniel and his friends were part of the first deportation of Jews into Babylon, under the pagan rule of Nebuchadnezzar. Daniel's friends, Shadrach, Meshach, and Abed-Nego were hauled into court for not serving Nebuchadnezzar's gods nor worshiping his image. They were threatened with the burning fiery furnace.

> *Shadrach, Meshach, and Abed-Nego answered and said to the king, 'O Nebuchadnezzar, we have no need to answer you in this matter. If that is the case, our God whom we serve is able to deliver us from the burning fiery furnace, and He will deliver us from your hand, O king. But if not, let it be known to you, O king, that we do not serve your gods, nor will we worship the gold image which you have set up.'* (Daniel 3:16-18)

There was no compromise. They were prepared to die for their faith. Do we disciple new converts to count the cost of following Jesus? Unless we do, we set them up for *sitting on the fence.*

Later, now under the reign of Darius, the Mede, Daniel is proclaimed third ruler in the land. But because of the excellent spirit within him, Darius was minded to set him over the whole kingdom (Daniel 5:29 – 6:4). A God-fearing, God-worshiping man to be elected to Prime Minister, just under the king. You can imagine the opposition! The trap was set:

> *All the governors of the kingdom, the administrators and satraps, the counsellors, and advisors, have consulted together to establish a royal statute and to make a firm decree, that whoever petitions any god or man for thirty days, except you, O king, shall be cast into the den of lions. Now, O king, establish the decree and sign the writing, so that it cannot be changed, according to the law of the Medes and Persians, which does not alter." Therefore King Darius signed the written decree.* (Daniel 6:7-9)

Daniel's response was unshakable:

Now when Daniel knew that the writing was signed, he went home. And in his upper room, with his windows open toward Jerusalem, he knelt down on his knees three times that day, and prayed and gave thanks before his God, as was his custom since early days. (Daniel 6:10)

He could have worshipped and prayed behind closed doors and windows, but he was a man of impeccable integrity, this was no politician keeping his faith a *private* matter.

We know what happened. Daniel was thrown into the lion's den. The mouths of the lions were shut up by an angel sent to Daniel's aid (Daniel 6:21-22). The outcome was tremendous; Darius came to worship Daniel's God and made this extraordinary proclamation:

I make a decree that in every dominion of my kingdom men must tremble and fear before the God of Daniel. For He is the living God, and steadfast forever; His kingdom is the one which shall not be destroyed, and His dominion shall endure to the end.
He delivers and rescues, and He works signs and wonders in heaven and on earth, who has delivered Daniel from the power of the lions.
So, this Daniel prospered in the reign of Darius and in the reign of Cyrus the Persian. (Daniel 6:26-28)

We may be praying for revival to sweep away all the evil in our land, and to rescue multitudes into the Kingdom, but if we are not taking a stand, if we are not counting the cost, if *we are sitting on the fence* will God heal our land?

Footnotes

[1] Kerin, John (2015, March 24). The poor white trash of Asia: a phrase that changed an economy. *Australian Financial Review.* https://www.afr.com/politics/the-poor-white-trash-of-asia-a-phrase-that-changed-an-economy-20150323-1m5mzm

[2] Mahlburg, Kurt (2021). Sir Robert Menzies: Twenty Quotes on Faith and Freedom. *Daily Declaration.* https://dailydeclaration.org.au/2021/06/24/sir-robert-menzies-twenty-quotes-on-faith-and-freedom/

[3] The Ethics Centre (2017, November 17). Progressivism is a political ideology based on the possibility of moral progress. In practice, this looks like an optimism about the future of humanity. *The Ethics Centre.* https://ethics.org.au/ethics-explainer-progressivism/

[4] Durie, Mark (2019, July 23). *Christianity in Politics.* Australian Christian Lobby, Not Ashamed Conference. [Video]. YouTube. https://www.youtube.com/watch?v=na2SXLJhfaQ&t=36s

[5] Bernardi, Cory (2013). *The Conservative Revolution.* Connor Court Publishing. ISBN 9781922168962 https://www.amazon.com.au/dp/1922168963?ref_=mr_referred_us_au_au

[6] Baba, Eliazar, Daila. (2022). The Church and Politics. *International Journal of Humanities Social Sciences and Education, 9*(4), 162-168. https://doi.org/10.20431/2349-0381.0904014

[7] Grudem, Wayne (2013). Why Christians Should Seek to Influence Government for Good. *Family Research Council.* https://downloads.frc.org/EF/EF13D76.pdf

[8] Muehlenberg, Bill (2018). Why Christians should be involved in Politics? *Australian Christians.* https://australianchristians.org.au/wp-content/uploads/2020/09/Why-Involved-By-Bill-M-2018.pdf

[9] Hamrick, Gary (2020, October 19). *Church in America, Wake Up! Jeremiah 6:16-19.* Cornerstone Chapel – Leesburg, VA. [Video]. YouTube. https://www.youtube.com/watch?v=10HRwSKTUiU&t=338s

[10] Jensen, P. Michael (2024). *Subjects and Citizens: The Politics of the gospel, lessons from Romans 12-15.* Matthiasmedia. https://matthiasmedia.com.au/products/subjects-and-citizens?srsltid=AfmBOoqYMIdKdkyss9koRXu0Zcfd-w_uFlGXNx_Yi9ZjjStTqUxFarDe

[11] Lawson, Joshua (2020, June 11). You Can Be A Christian, You Can Be A Marxist, But You Can't Be Both. *The Federalist.* https://thefederalist.com/2020/06/11/you-can-be-christian-you-can-be-marxist-but-you-cant-be-both/

[12] Panahi, Rita (2025, May 7). *'Absolutely atrocious': AEC official silences Family First candidate.* Sky News Australia. [Video]. YouTube. https://www.youtube.com/watch?v=3-NtMyfPRxk

[13] Twelves, Jim (2023, October 9). It's a Mad World! – Part 1: Politics. *Daily Declaration.* https://dailydeclaration.org.au/2023/10/09/its-a-mad-world-part-1-politics-globalists/

[14] Lutzer, Edwin W. (2016). *When a nation forgets God, seven lessons we must learn from Nazi Germany.* Moody Bible Church, Chicago. https://www.amazon.com.au/When-Nation-Forgets-God-Lessons/dp/0802413285

CHAPTER 11 - HEALTH

Dr My Le Trinh's Story

My Le Trinh was a true immigrant success story, until her hard-won new life in Australia fell apart during the pandemic. After 27 years of practicing as a GP, Trinh fell foul of the medical regulator's strict rules around Covid treatment, leading to the suspension of her medical registration. Trinh is now fighting to have her registration restored and for the 'Covid lies' to be properly investigated.[1,2,3]

My Le takes up the narrative:

I grew up in Cambodia and couldn't speak a word of English when I arrived in Australia. I was in Cambodia till about five and a half years old when my mother decided to send six of her children to Vietnam for safety away from the Khmer Rouge. I was one of the six.

I came to Australia in the early 1970s when I was 12 with my auntie because three years after arriving in Vietnam, the south fell to communism. You couldn't talk; you couldn't criticise the government. If you upset your neighbour, you got dobbed in. So, everyone kept to themselves. For a time, Australia fulfilled the promise of freedom. But over the past four years, I've watched in despair as the Australia I loved seemed to erode before my eyes. Policies enacted under the guise of public health now appear to destroy lives with a cold detachment. Leaders that lie, seem to ruin without remorse or accountability.

I am struck by the chilling realisation; this government, in its cold and calculated deeds, echoes the terror of Pol Pot regime in Cambodia. In some ways, it feels even more insidious, cloaked as it is in pretence. The facade of care has trapped so many in a web of deceit, a mirage of compassion masking their acts of destruction.

It's really hard to get into medicine, you have to be in the top one per cent; I did! I wouldn't have had that opportunity if I was still in Vietnam. I now have a family and a career. I also had a business; I managed my own medical centre for ten years; we had between six and eight doctors at any one time.

This achievement has given me the opportunity to help others. Since 2007 I have been back to Cambodia regularly working with a Christian organisation from Australia. We did medical mobile clinics in the villages. We would do one village a day. It was lots of fun. But when I first went back to Cambodia, after more than 36 years away, it was very emotional for me.

When Covid came, I knew early on, something serious was going on when they locked down Wuhan, China. I just thought something really big was going to happen. I spent a lot of time researching, as I knew the media was lying.

The year before, I was following Donald Trump's election campaign in 2019. I knew about the media lying then. I knew about the corruption in governments in the US. I knew that a lot of things were done to steal the election from Trump in 2020.

At that stage, I had sold my business and was only working part-time in the medical centre. I decided to take a bit of time off because I wanted to know what was going on. If I had spent a long time working, I knew I would not have had enough time to study and research. Also, I had a brother who was unwell. I felt I needed to know what's going on so that I could protect my family.

Through my research I realised that Covid was a scam. I knew that the virus was being leaked from the lab. There was an interview with Professor Francis Boyle who knew a lot about gain-a-function research in America and the involvement of the National Institutes of Health (NIH). So, the next step for me was to find out how serious was this virus, and as a doctor, what's the best treatment.

I followed America, as the virus hit them first. By May 2021, I knew that Ivermectin worked, that it was a highly effective medication. I knew that the virus could be treated, and no one need die. I knew what I needed to do, in the middle of a pandemic, as a doctor, I knew what I was called to do and that was to treat the sick.

If I knew a treatment that worked, how could I stay home? How could I not tell people that it worked? But at the time there was so much censorship, if I were to come out and tell people, they wouldn't believe me.

I was very aware of the censorship in both America and Australia. But I was not a public figure, and I was not on social media, so I didn't voice my opinion. I decided that I would not take that risk, it was better that I just help people that come to me. So, I decided to go back to work. I prayed to God, as I knew He wanted to use me. I knew the government was covering up the cure for Covid and there was also the ban on Hydroxychloroquine. The use of Ivermectin was not an approved treatment for Covid 19, but at that stage it wasn't banned, we could prescribe it as an alternative, I was not breaking the law.

However, I did know it was controversial and was prepared to deal with the consequences. It was my moral duty; I couldn't not tell people that there was a treatment available. I could not deny people a treatment that was *safe and effective*. Our moral duty is to do good for others. I guess some of us don't have the courage though. For me, if I go out and save a life and lose my licence, I am happy. I am a doctor; I can't allow people to die.

The authorities found out about what I was doing from a patient I was treating who sadly ended up in casualty for a different issue. There they found out about me as they knew that this patient had had Ivermectin from me.

I had been a GP for 27 years with no dramas. Then suddenly, within one day, I received two complaints resulting in my suspension! One was about the patient I had treated earlier, made by a junior doctor in a training hospital.

I wanted to know why they had made the complaint, as I had saved this patient's life by treating her; she was gravely ill and could have died from Covid unless I had intervened. She was really bad, she should have been in ICU, but she didn't want to go to hospital, so I gave her my best shot, using the Front Line Covid-19 Critical Care Alliance (FLCCC) protocol, a well backed up protocol developed by renowned physicians, a group that had come together to design a protocol to treat Covid. It worked, that's why she lived!

The complaint was not really about me but about Ivermectin. They had found a doctor who had prescribed it, and now they were going after me.

I called up to find out if my patient was OK, because from reading the report on me I couldn't tell. I rang the doctor who was making the complaint and as it turned out, she told me that she did not know why she made the complaint, she was just following orders from her superior. A week later, the Therapeutic Goods Administration (TGA) banned Ivermectin.[4]

The second complaint was from someone called 'John Smith.' I still don't know who John Smith is. He alleged he was a member of the community, and he said that I was an anti-vaxxer and that I had promoted Ivermectin in an online forum. He alleged that he had a friend, who was prescribed Ivermectin by me, he did not have worms but had been given Ivermectin and he was concerned about his friend's health. As a result of this, he reported me.

John Smith also alleged that I held community groups, treating people with Ivermectin. I looked for the patient's details, his friend. The name was redacted but the Medicare Number was not. I was able to trace that back, the prescription belonged to my brother! My brother has never known a John Smith, so how did he get hold of my brother's prescription?

I asked the Medical Council where John Smith got this prescription as it belonged to my brother. They wouldn't tell me, and they made me submit my brother's medical record and investigated as if it were a real case.

I had taken that prescription to the chemist myself for my brother. So, I went to the chemist to ask where my prescription was, they couldn't find it as they had had to hand over all Ivermectin prescriptions to the Australian Prudential Regulation Authority (APRA).

I appealed my suspension which was under emergency powers. To do this you had to deem that the person is a danger to the public. So evidently, I am deemed to be a danger to the public!

My challenge was meant to go to the tribunal however, two weeks before the date set for the hearing, the judgment of Dr Pridgen's case was released.[5] This was very important, as it states that the Medical Council does not have the power to suspend, and secondly, it states that the Medical Council must refer me to the tribunal for a proper hearing, and that the decision to suspend me was only an interim decision.

Therefore because of the Pridgen case, I decided to challenge the tribunal's authority. I effectively took the tribunal to court. I asked them if they had the authority to hear my case. My case was dismissed, and I am now waiting for a hearing in the Court of Appeal, which is at the highest level of the Supreme Court.

The fact that I have had to do what I have done is because the government lied. They lied to the people, they lied to the profession, and it's only a few people like me who would not put up with their lies, because I valued people's life more than my career, more than my licence.

There is nothing I have done that is illegal, there is nothing I have done wrong. The Medical Council and the Health Care Complaints Commission in New South Wales (HCCC) have nothing against me. For them to pursue me is very cowardly, they should be ashamed of themselves. They have not just wronged me they have wronged the public and the healthcare profession. No one should have to put up with what I have put up with in the last three years.

Many lives have been lost. Many families have been broken because of the Covid lie. Some people know the truth, and some don't. They have destroyed families and friends; they have destroyed society. They have destroyed everything. They have destroyed the healthcare profession.

If Ivermectin hadn't been banned there would have been no need for a vaccine, and all those lives and vaccine injuries would have been prevented. Once you get Covid you normally get long term immunity, if you don't there are *safe and effective* treatments.

❀   ❀   ❀

The Rape of Healthcare by Big Pharma and Government

The most telling claim from My Le's testimony was her assertion that:

> *There is nothing I have done that is illegal, there is nothing I have done wrong. The Medical Council and the Health Care Complaints Commission in New South Wales (HCCC) have nothing against me.*

Her declaration of innocence is against *her measure* of right and wrong, namely her pledge *to do no harm,* and above all, to save lives. The

149

authorities opposing her hold a different measure of justice, namely that Ivermectin and Hydroxychloroquine were not to be prescribed to Covid patients as they represented *a danger to the public* and that the new novel vaccines were the only *approved* protocol for treatment.

My Le's conflict with authority was not an isolated incident; tragically many excellent doctors were pulled from the frontline of healthcare during the Covid era because they put their patient's health before any compromise of their professionalism to governmentally approved protocols for treatment regimens.[6,7,8]

The Covid era challenged all of us, and as an academic, it gave me the opportunity to do my own research, and become a My Le supporter, fully recognising we might both be guilty of *confirmation bias* (the tendency to interpret new evidence as confirmation of our existing beliefs or theories). For background to the events that led to My Le's suspension, I recommend Topher Field's documentary *Battleground Melbourne*.[9]

I propose that healthcare systems, particularly in the West, have been slowly raped from as early as the 1980s. Their independence has been stolen and, in some cases, set adrift from their anchor, the *Hippocratic Oath* (to first do no harm) as discussed in Chapter 7 Transgenderism and Chapter 8 Abortion.

Big Pharma has been the perpetrator, aided and abetted by government regulation. In Australia, healthcare professionals, who want to retain their credentials, must abide by TGA and APHRA rules even if discussion with their patient would favour an alternative approach.[6,12]

An illustration from my own experience, starting in the 1980s. I witnessed the way pharmaceutical companies would approach doctors with their latest treatment protocols and would offer lavish, fully paid, conferences if the doctors 'pushed' their remedies on their patients. I knew this was their *modus operandi* from friends in healthcare. However, in those days the doctors had genuine autonomy to buy their spin or not. They had liberty to treat in the way they judged most effective. It was never a one-size-fits-all approach.

Pressure from Big Pharma was mounting. From the 1980s through into this century there was the OxyContin story that led to doctors across North America prescribing a painkiller that had about one and a half times the strength of morphine and resulted in untold death and misery because of its addictive side effects.[10]

Who wouldn't want to alleviate pain? I don't blame the doctors. In the beginning, the Sackler family who owned Purdue Pharma, honestly partnered with general practitioners who saw the need for a *safe and effective* drug that could bring people's pain under control and give them back their lives. However, whistleblowers were silenced who saw the effects of addiction. Far from being *safe and effective*, OxyContin destroyed careers, families and millions of lives were lost.

Purportedly, OxyContin reaped between $10 – $20 billion for the Sackler family. So, paying out around $4.3 billion in settlement for more than 3000 lawsuits against them, hardly touch them. Since 2000, more than one million people in the United States have died of drug overdoses, the majority were due to opioids. Law enforcement targeted the addicts, while the rich end of town, Big Pharma, were cushioned from responsibility by their government.[11]

Mikki Willis's 2023 documentary, *Plandemic III - The Great Awakening*,[12] unpacks the role of healthcare in the global threat of communism. He argues that the Covid era was not a random terrible accident but rather part of a global plan that started with *the long march through the institutions* (Chapter 3 Education). Willis opens the case against Anthony Fauci as the chief orchestrator of Big Pharma's strategies over five decades.[13]

State and indeed global control of healthcare make no sense for the patient when the autonomy and privacy of the relationship between doctor and patient is *violated*. I understand that the state needs to be involved with the administration of fees from taxes but when it dictates *what* the doctor can and cannot do, that is when patient care is compromised, and government *control* of their people becomes the primary objective. Here healthcare becomes *a tool of control* for government not *a responsibility*. This is when totalitarianism is crouching at the door.

Reading Up and Waking Up

Since 2021 I devoured many books as I sought to grapple with the current state of our world and specifically with healthcare. Six authors radically shaped my thinking, waking me up as if being hit by the paddles of a defibrillator! They were Engelbrecht's (2021) *Virus Mania*;[14] Kennedy's

(2021) *The Real Anthony Fauci*;[13] Williams and Bailey's (2022) *Terrain Therapy*;[15] Basham's (2024) *Shepherds for Sale*;[16] the Baileys' (2024) *The Final Pandemic*;[17] and Dodsworth's (2021) *A State of Fear*.[18]

These authors revolutionised my thinking. Together they have joined the dots, revealing a healthcare system I never imagined existed. They woke me up!

I don't anticipate many of you will share my perspective entirely, but I think all of you will find resonance with one or two aspects of my story. I would love for you to keep an open mind, and if I manage to pique your interest sufficiently, and you have the opportunity, follow some of my many references.

New Zealand doctors, Sam and Mark Bailey both left mainstream medicine. Mark left of his own freewill in 2016. In September 2020, his wife Sam was invited to join the authors of *Virus Mania* to contribute to their third edition, but *coincidentally* in the same month she was fired from her network TV role as a healthcare presenter as she refused to parrot the official Covid narrative on air.[14] Another New Zealander, Dr Ulric Williams a famous GP and surgeon way back in 1929, began to see flaws in his chosen profession and by 1933 he too left mainstream medicine and began to treat his patients without drugs or surgery, he became a Naturopath.[15]

My Le Trinh, Mark and Sam Bailey and many thousands more, challenged the establishment in the Covid era.[19] Were they mistaken? Science has never been about consensus; it's always been about discovery and challenging the status quo. In this chapter, I aim to explore healthcare from their perspective.

Experiments, by French chemist Louis Pasteur (1822-1895) developed *Germ Theory* supported by German microbiologist Robert Koch (1843-1910) who first proposed that specific *germs* cause specific diseases.[14,15,17] Paralleling their proposal were improvements in hygiene within medical practice and many environmental improvements, such as filtered drinking water, mechanically assisted sanitation systems in cities, and improved diet to name but a few.

Germ Theory forms the foundation of Western mainstream medicine today and has been the bedrock for the Covid era, namely that a specific virus, Covid 19 (SARS-CoV-2) infects patients with Covid.

In contrast *Terrain (or Miasma) theory* which emphasises the prevention of disease by strengthening the immune system through better nutrition and reduced exposure to environmental toxins, was the alternative healthcare philosophy at the time and was ousted by Germ Theory.[13,15]

Pasteur and Koch were bitter rivals of two French scientists named Antoine Béchamp (1816 – 1908) and Claude Bernard (1813 – 1878), who postulated that it wasn't the germs coming in and creating disease, but rather that diseased environments attracted and housed germs in the first place, allowing them to proliferate out of control and cause disease. They were arguing that germs themselves don't make us sick, but having a misaligned body that is damaged and functioning poorly does.[20]

Belief in Germ Theory led to the development of vaccines that would target specific germs. Hence the practice of taking or injecting them into the healthy to render immunity from attack.[13] However, Kennedy's work documents the prevalence of a whole range of diseases over time and shows that because of improvements in the environment (Terrain Theory), many of them were nearly eliminated. Then at, of near elimination, vaccines were fraudulently introduced for diseases, such as measles, pertussis, tuberculosis, scarlet fever, and polio; and mainstream medicine claimed their *efficacy* at dramatically curbing the prevalence of these diseases when the data demonstrates no such effect.[13,14,17] Terrain Theory proponents argued that vaccines were introducing poisons and toxins into healthy bodies, rendering more harm than good.[15]

Central to Germ Theory is the existence of *bacteria* and *viruses,* self-replicating, disease carrying, transmissible and infectious particles.[14,17,19] Bacteria can be easily isolated, and their self-replication can be demonstrated. However, Terrain Theorists, the Baileys, have been at the forefront of a campaign to show that *so-called viruses* can't be isolated and can't be shown to self-replicate, and therefore can't be transmissible, infectious particles. Their position is that there are no such entities as living viruses, that cause specific diseases.[14,17]

Further, Daniel Roytas, an Australian nutritional and naturopathic medicine university lecturer has published *Can you catch a cold?*[17,21] His work is supported by the *no virus* position, and thus the *no contagion* hypothesis regarding colds and influenza. He writes:

The idea that the common cold and influenza are spread via coughing, sneezing, and physical contact has been firmly implanted in our minds since childhood. However, the results of human experiments cast doubt on this theory. Researchers have failed to consistently demonstrate contagion by exposing healthy people directly to sick people or their bodily fluids. These findings suggest that our understanding of infectious disease is incomplete and challenges the long-held belief that a cold or flu can be 'caught.' [21]

If viruses don't exist, then the *so-called modern-day pandemics* have been faked. This is Robert F Kennedy Jn's view, writing about Anthony Fauci's global war on democracy and public health; lists Fauci's long list of contrived diseases that include smallpox, chickenpox, bird flu, Zika, hepatitis B, MERS, measles and Covid. [13]

To illustrate the ingenuous creation of phony epidemics Kennedy quotes that in 1906 infectious diseases caused 33 per cent of annual deaths in the US and by 1976 less than five per cent of deaths were from infectious diseases; hence the reason why the Centers for Disease Control and Prevention (CDC) and NIAID have been under extreme pressure to justify their taxpayer funded budgets. [13]

The Baileys document the government mandated slaughter of millions of animals to drive *fear* of the possibility of deadly diseases leaping from animals to humans. They list the 2003 Dutch Bird Flu 'crisis' resulting in 26 million chickens being euthanised in the Netherlands. And earlier, in the UK in 2001 during the alleged foot-and-mouth 'outbreak,' six million, mostly healthy cows and sheep were incinerated with the side effect of destroying untold livelihoods in rural communities. [17,18]

If viruses don't exist what about the Polymerase Chain Reaction (PCR) Test for the so-called Covid-19 virus? This test was not designed to detect viruses, but molecules that healthcare authorities have now claimed to come from specific viruses. The inventor of the test, Dr Kery Mullis had this to say about his PCR:

I don't think you can misuse the PCR. The results, the interpretation of it, yes... With the PCR, if you do it well, you can find about anything in anybody... If you can amplify one single molecule up to something you can really measure, which PCR can do. There are very few molecules, that you don't have at least one of, in your body. So that can be thought of as a misuse. PCR does not tell you if you are sick, and it does not tell you that the thing you have ended up with was really going to hurt you. (my emphasis)[22]

Dr Tom Cowan explained how the PCR Test was used in the Covid era.[23] A sample of RNA was collected, presumed to be RNA from the alleged virus. This sample, though, was so small that nothing could be detected, so the PCR Test 'amplified' the sample. This may have been done, say 25, 36 or even 45 times. Now, there was sufficient RNA to be sampled and compared to the 'so-called' standard that had been published from a sample from Wuhan, China.[18,22]

The 'case numbers' from the PCR were the key driver of *fear* that gave governments around the world the ammunition for their draconian measures to 'defeat the enemy,' 'Covid – 19.' All the technicians needed to do to *manufacture* cases in a specific locality, was to dial up the number of amplifications to achieve their desired case numbers.

Another flaw with the PCR as a measure of the spread of a so-called contagious disease, was the number of samples being collected. The mainstream media reported 'case numbers,' but this was naturally directly correlated with the sample size that wasn't reported. Sample sizes were massaged by the media reporting 'outbreaks' in particular suburbs that naturally resulted in more people coming forward for testing, which in turn boosted case numbers!

If viruses don't exist, and the modern-day pandemics are fake, then the vaccines are fake also. The first red flag for me was when I heard that governments round the world were giving immunity against liability for all vaccine manufacture thanks to Fauci's orchestration because he cut short the trials to minimise the potential for the documentation of vaccine injuries. The untimely speed of the vaccine role out was not to combat a virus but to justify his ban on alternative treatment protocols (such as FLCCC, outlined in Dr My Le Trinh's story).

The second red flag for me in the Covid era was the perfectly harmonious narrative between Western governments that reported the 'alleged virus lab leak,' the 'manufacture of cases' to create fear, and the 'vaccine, our only hope' of survival.

To illustrate the *orchestration*, consider the use of the drug Remdesivir in the US. Fauci won Federal Drug Administration (FDA) approval for the use of Remdesivir for Covid, despite it being a deadly poison and extremely expensive at US$ 3,000 per treatment. Its wholesale cost is roughly 1,000 times greater than that of hydroxychloroquine (HCQ) and ivermectin (IVM) (see My Le's case). Fauci had to outlaw both HCQ and IVM to give free reign to Remdesivir and later the vaccines.[13]

Fauci was aware of Remdesivir's toxicity when he orchestrated its approval for Covid. In its trial in the Ebola era (2013-2016), 54 per cent of patients died. It was only to be administered in hospitals to Covid patients, they were prevented from having any early treatment at home, they had to wait till they were so ill they needed to be admitted to hospital. Therefore, many of the needless excess deaths in the Covid era were on account of Remdesivir, though these numbers served Fauci's purpose beautifully in raising the level of *fear* in the community. The people simply saw the spike in 'Covid deaths.' Remdesivir, and the delayed treatment connection, were not being made.[13]

As early as the late 1930s Ulric Williams knew that the dollar was the primary driver of developments in medicine. He stated that the 'business of disease was the second largest in the world after finance.'[15]

If deadly viruses exist government-controlled healthcare, and Big Pharma, would not have needed *nudge theory* (a behavioural economics concept that uses soft interventions, called *nudges*, to influence people's choices while pretending to preserve their freedom of choice),[22] censorship, and propaganda to ensure their programs' success. If there was a genuine pandemic, there would have been no need for advertising like this:

> *George left the pub...and went home to kill his dad.*
> *Sasha had a great night out at her friend's house... and popped in to kill her nan on the way home.*
> *Once Ade's finished keeping fit... he'll go home to kill his mum over dinner. Stop.*
> *Horrified? Of course.*
> *But would you feel different if their weapon of choice was Covid-19?*

Coronavirus is killing people every day.
Not adhering to public health guidelines is a principal cause of the
spread of Coronavirus.
Covid kills. And you don't have to have symptoms to spread it. Protect
the lives of friends, family, neighbours, and the community.
Don't bring Covid home this Christmas.[18]

The behavioural science framework for *making* populations comply with lockdowns and all the other restrictions on our liberties, should have provided the opportunity for public debate. But there was none. There was none in our parliaments either, the *uniparty,* here in Australia, was born, where both left and right-wing parties sang from the same song sheet (Chapter 10 Politics, John Anderson's story). Nudge theory was developed in the UK and their services bought by governments throughout the Western world.[18,22]

Remember the catch phrase, 'trust the experts.' For authorities to demand this indicates that their people were not convinced by what they had seen and what they had experienced. If there had been robust scientific analysis of the facts before any manipulation, the people would not have been *required* to 'trust the experts.' The silencing by governments of expert doctors[19] who offered early treatments that would have competed with vaccines or who refused to accept with blind faith, Big Pharma's zero liability, shoddy testing and experimental vaccines being rolled out across the globe; was evidence of totalitarian dictatorship.[13]

Saddleback pastor Rick Warren has been a guest at the World Economic Forum (WEF), Davos, Switzerland, several times, where he urged world leaders to use the Christian church as a means of 'universal distribution' for various government programs because churches have a 'built in credibility with local residents.'[16]

Consequently, some Christian leaders were *bought* to sell the Covid narrative for the authorities. Their messaging was to urge followers to take the vaccine so that they could spread healing in their communities like Christ when He walked on earth. This was followed up with the slogan, 'Love your neighbour, get the shot, Luke 6:31,' endorsed by celebrated theologian N.T. Wright, bestselling author Philip Yancey, Christianity Today, and many more.[16]

Another example of manipulation to sell the government narrative was the Billy Graham Center's partnership with the Biden Administration to create a website, *Coronavirus, and the Church,* providing clergy with resources they should convey to their congregations.[16]

Mainstream Christianity didn't applaud churches that remained open during the Covid era, rather they were ostracised, marginalised, and labelled rebellious. Basham tells the story of Trinity Bible Chapel, Waterloo, Ontario, Canada that stayed open. There Jennifer Scott, a functional drug addict was *saved* by this church. Jennifer exclaimed that, 'I know for a fact that I'd be dead right now if God had not used this church in my life.'[16]

In retrospect, during the Covid era I would have expected the Christian church to have viewed health from a more wholistic and spiritual perspective as Ulric Williams had done. When he was leaving mainstream medicine, he came across a book called *The Light of the Sevens,* by Len Elliott Bassett (1929). Bassett opened his eyes to the spiritual, mental and physical paradoxes within medical science and practice. Williams reflected that:

> *Good health is an outward <u>expression</u> of a harmony within, and obedience to the spirit and law of life... God is positive, and evil (devil) is negative. Disease (ill health) is the negative of positive good health. Many people are sick because they are negative; and we are negative because we allow negative thoughts into our mind, and negative foods into our bodies. To be well we must become <u>positive</u>.* (Williams' emphasis)[15]

After all, we are all made in God's image (Genesis 1:27), so why wouldn't God make everything good? If our starting point is that we all need artificial supplements and vaccines to *protect* us, we are, by default, saying that God failed to do a good job when He made us.

When doctors pay insufficient attention to the divine Spirit and the *natural law* of His creation, they look *within* our bodies for the *cause* of sickness and never find it. The primary cause is never in the body, that's where effects appear. The cause will be found in the *mind* or in the *manner of our living.* Hence mainstream medicine's focus on the symptoms and treating the symptoms, rather than seeking to address the root cause or causes.[15]

Williams goes on to say, almost all drugs are poisonous, and many venomous, and only a few may be *temporally admissible*. Consequently, to imagine a world where we are required to stave off a deadly virus that has suddenly leapt from the animal kingdom to humans after all our forefathers lived with animals far more closely than we have without ill effect, is hard to accept.[15]

We have all seen the enormous advances in medical science. For example, the bionic ear invented by Professor Graeme Clark, and a host of other wonders.[24] So much so, particularly in the West, it has become natural for us to anticipate that medicine knows best and can fix us without turning to God.

The Covid era woke me up to the mainstream medicine agenda. I think there are three elephants in the room; Big Pharma with their enormous business interests; governments operating at the beck and call of Big Pharma; and globalist organisations like the World Health Organization and the World Economic Forum. These interests have come to dominate healthcare at great cost to our health and freedom.

All three mitigate against personal autonomy and personal responsibility. The Covid era has caused me to question everything and take back responsibility for my own health as a child of God seeking to fulfil His plans and purpose for my life.

What does God say?

The Word is teaming with references to our health. Here is a small sample (my emphasis):[25,26,27]

> *God said to the children of Israel during their exodus from Egypt:*
> *'You shall serve the Lord your God, and <u>He will bless your bread*
> *and your water. And I will take sickness away from the midst of*
> *you</u>'* (Exodus 23:25).

Referring to Jesus, from the Old Testament, Isaiah says:
> *Surely, He has borne our griefs and carried our sorrows; yet we*
> *esteemed Him stricken, smitten by God, and afflicted. But He was*

wounded for our transgressions, He was bruised for our iniquities; the chastisement for our peace was upon Him, <u>and by His stripes we are healed</u>. (Isaiah 53:4-5)

King Solomon exhorts us:

<u>A merry heart does good, like medicine</u>, but a broken spirit dries the bones. (Proverbs 17:22)

The prophet Jeremiah reports:

<u>For I will restore health to you and heal you of your wounds,</u> says the Lord, because they called you an outcast saying: This is Zion; No one seeks her. (Jeremiah 30:17)

Matthew's commentary about Jesus was that:

Jesus went about all Galilee, teaching in their synagogues, preaching the gospel of the kingdom, <u>and healing all kinds of sickness and all kinds of disease among the people</u>.
(Matthew 4:23)

The Apostle Paul exhorts us to:

<u>Be anxious for nothing</u>, but in everything by prayer and supplication, with thanksgiving, let your requests be made known to God; and the peace of God, which surpasses all understanding, <u>will guard your hearts and minds through</u> Christ Jesus.
(Philippians 4:6-7)

And the Apostle James asks:
<u>Is anyone among you sick?</u> Let him call for the elders of the church, and let them pray over him, anointing him with oil in the name of the Lord. <u>And the prayer of faith will save the sick</u>, and the <u>Lord will raise him up</u>. And if he has committed sins, he will be forgiven.' (James 5:14-15)

It seems to me that our natural response to a health challenge in the West is to tap into the physical healthcare system, be they nutritional supplements, the medicine cabinet, or our general practitioner. This is the way of the world, and I don't think God wants us to conform to the world (Romans 12:2). In the last few years, I have been challenged to first ask God about what the *cause* is, rather than how can I limit the *symptoms*. Next, I go to God in faith, and finally I go to healthcare providers if He says to do so. It's turning our automatic response on its head. Let's practice Dr Ulric Williams' *principle*, of the three-legged stool, *spirit, mind, and body*; all three in perfect harmony.[15]

God does use sickness for His purposes, but such circumstances are rare, for example Job and the Apostle Paul. Overwhelmingly, God's Word is full of promises for healing coupled closely with a right mind, heart, and forgiveness. *All* kinds of sickness and disease are His speciality but the key ingredient from us must always be *faith*.

Let's conclude with the story of the lady with an issue of blood who secretly approached Jesus:

> *Now a certain woman had a flow of blood for twelve years and had suffered many things from many physicians. She had spent all that she had and was no better but rather grew worse. When she heard about Jesus, she came behind Him in the crowd and touched His garment. For she said, 'If only I may touch His clothes, I shall be made well.'*
>
> *Immediately the fountain of her blood was dried up, and she felt in her body that she was healed of the affliction. And Jesus, immediately knowing in Himself that power had gone out of Him, turned around in the crowd and said, 'Who touched My clothes?'*
> (Mark 5:25-30)

Footnotes

[1] Café Locked Out (2023, June 15). *Interview with an Australian Giant, Dr My Le Trinh, From War To Peace To Here*. [Video]. Rumble. https://rumble.com/v2ubjhg-interview-with-an-australian-giant-dr-my-le-trinh-from-war-to-peace-to-here.html

[2] Barnett, Rebekah (2023, October 23). Refugee, GP, Renegade: Suspended doctor My Le Trinh. *Umbrella News.* https://umbrellanews.com.au/health/2023/10/refugee-gp-renegade-suspended-doctor-my-le-trinh/

[3] Trinh, My Le [@myletrinh123]. (2024, January 9). *Dr My Le Trinh (suspended).* X [Twitter Post] https://x.com/myletrinh123

[4] Therapeutic Goods Administration (TGA) (2021, September 10). New restrictions on prescribing ivermectin for COVID-19. *TGA.* https://www.tga.gov.au/news/media-releases/new-restrictions-prescribing-ivermectin-covid-19

[5] Chapman, Scott (2022, May 30). Pridgeon v Medical Council of NSW [2022] NSWCA 60 HWL. *Ebsworth Lawyers.* https://hwlebsworth.com.au/pridgeon-v-medical-council-of-new-south-wales-2022-nswca-60/

[6] Sladden, Julie (2025, June 3). The Silencing of Science: Censorship and the Collapse of Free Speech in Medicine. *Daily Declaration.* https://dailydeclaration.org.au/2025/06/03/free-speech-medicine/

[7] Lampard, Rod (2025, January 8). APHRA Targets Dr William Bay Again, Reigniting Battle for Free Speech. *Daily Declaration.* https://dailydeclaration.org.au/2025/01/08/aphra-targets-dr-william-bay-again/

[8] Barnett, Rebekah (2023, December 26). Australian Medical Regulator Finally Relaxes Covid Gag Order on Doctors. *Daily Declaration.* https://dailydeclaration.org.au/2023/12/26/australian-medical-regulator-finally-relaxes-covid-gag-order-on-doctors/

[9] Field, Topher (2022, January 13). *Go Watch the Official 4k Version of Battleground Melbourne Documentary: Link in Description.* [Video]. YouTube. https://www.youtube.com/watch?v=xzfJGC1_yPo

[10] Twelves, Jim (2023, September 22). The OxyContin Story: a Modern Parable. *Daily Declaration.* https://dailydeclaration.org.au/2023/09/22/the-oxycontin-story-a-modern-parable/

[11] Ferragamo, Mariel & Klobucista, Claire (2025, March 28). Fentanyl and the U.S. Opioid Epidemic. *Council on Foreign Relations.* https://www.cfr.org/backgrounder/fentanyl-and-us-opioid-epidemic

[12] Willis, Mikki (2023). *Plandemic III - The Great Awakening (2023) - COVID Vaccine Documentary*. CuresWanted. [Video]. Brighteon. https://www.brighteon.com/ccb0bafc-cc0d-4215-aaba-b0ab5d3002c5

[13] Kennedy, Robert F. Jr. (2021). *The Real Anthony Fauci: Bill Gates, Big Pharma's Global War on Democracy, Humanity, and Public Health.* Children's Health Defence. https://www.amazon.com.au/Real-Anthony-Fauci-Democracy-Humanity/dp/1510766804

[14] Engelbrecht, Torsten; Köhnlein, Claus; Bailey, Samantha & Scoglio, Stefano (2021). *Virus Mania: Corona/COVID-19, Measles, Swine Flu, Cervical Cancer, Avian Flu, SARS, BSE, Hepatitis C, AIDS, Polio, Spanish Flu. How the Medical Industry Continually Invents Epidemics, Making Billion-Dollar Profits At Our Expense.* BoD – Books on Demand. https://books.google.com.au/books/about/Virus_Mania.html?id=TaIXEA AAQBAJ&redir_esc=y

[15] Williams, Ulric & Bailey, Samantha (2022). *Terrain Therapy: How To Achieve Perfect Health Through Diet, Living Habits & Divine Thinking.* Samantha Bailey. https://drsambailey.com/terrain-therapy/

[16] Basham, Megan (2024). *Shepherds for Sale: How Evangelical Leaders Traded the Truth for a Leftist Agenda.* Broadside Books, An Imprint of HarperCollins. https://koorong.com/product/shepherds-for-sale-how-evangelical-leaders-traded-the_9780063413443?srsltid=AfmBOoqF9Ijnj4z-bIXwpkIr4DKQIiC_rTKhCINnlBvmpjkOI_q06vRQ

[17] Bailey, Mark & Bailey, Samantha (2024). *The Final Pandemic: An Antidote To Medical Tyranny.* Mark and Samantha Bailey, New Zealand. https://www.amazon.com.au/Final-Pandemic-Antidote-Medical-Tyranny-ebook/dp/B0CW1QXP31

[18] Dodsworth, Laura (2021). *A State of Fear: How the UK government weaponised fear during the Covid-19 pandemic.* Printer & Martin. https://www.amazon.com.au/State-Fear-government-weaponised-Covid-19/dp/1780667205

[19] Great Barrington Declaration (n.d.). *Signatures.* Retrieved October 22, 2025, from https://gbdeclaration.org/view-signatures/

[20] Alexander, Tudor (2024, May 14). A Tale of Two Theories (Germ & Terrain Theory). *Medium.* https://medium.com/@tudor.onutu/a-tale-of-two-theories-germ-terrain-theory-fb5d0d233e69

[21] Roytas Daniel (2024). *Can You Catch A Cold? Untold History & Human Experiments*. Daniel Roytas. https://www.amazon.com.au/Can-You-Catch-Cold-Experiments/dp/1763504409

[22] Twelves, Jim (2023, November 27). Our World Has Gone Mad! – Part 6: Medicine. *Daily Declaration.* https://dailydeclaration.org.au/2023/11/27/our-world-has-gone-mad-part-6-medicine/

[23] Cowan, Tom [@drtomcowan]. (2025, April 20). *The PCR Test Debate: What Are We Really Detecting?* X [Twitter Post]. https://x.com/drtomcowan/status/1913648216316240053

[24] Nguyen, Minh Hien (2022, October 7). 'I want to fix ears': Graeme Clark tells the tale of the invention of the multi-channel cochlear implant (bionic ear). *The University of Melbourne, Faculty of Engineering and Information Technology.* https://eng.unimelb.edu.au/ingenium/i-want-to-fix-ears-graeme-clark-tells-the-tale-of-the-invention-of-the-multi-channel-cochlear-implant-bionic-ear

[25] Bailey, Sam (2024, November 19). What docs the Bible say about Germs? *Dr Sam Bailey, Substack.* https://drsambailey.substack.com/p/what-does-the-bible-say-about-germs?utm_source=publication-search

[26] Bible Study Tools Staff (2024, April 26). Bible Verses about Health. Bible Study Tools. https://www.biblestudytools.com/topical-verses/bible-verses-about-health/

[27] Open Bible Info (n.d.). *Health Care*. Retrieved October 22, 2025, from https://www.openbible.info/topics/health_care

CHAPTER 12 - CLIMATE CHANGE

Rod Lampard's Story

Rod is a theologian and culture wars commentator. He and his wife Jonda, and their five kids are home-schooling veterans. He spent 12 years in management at Koorong, and is a Tabor Adelaide Alumni, where he earned a Bachelor's Degree in Ministry and Theology. Rod is also an independent journalist and writer for Caldron Pool,[1,2] The Daily Declaration, and a contributor to The Spectator Australia.

Rod takes up the narrative:

Talk about blessings. A lot of the Pentecostal churches talk about blessings as being, wealth, material gain, and comfort, and if you don't have those things, God's not there or you are living a life of sin. This was my background. I have encountered this many times. What we understand blessing to be is mixed up in our culture, especially in Australia. To be blessed may mean you will have some really difficult times, the blessing comes through the fruit that's produced, through righteousness, repentance, humility, and the spiritual disciplines that flow from that.

I say to the kids (my home-schooled children), blessing doesn't necessarily mean you will have an easy run. Mary was blessed above all women, but she suffered greatly, despite the great joy of being the mother of the Saviour of the world. Look at the Apostles, they were blessed by God, but they all died for their faith. Take Pilgrims Progress (1678), Bunyan was in prison when he wrote that, and his book has blessed millions.

I don't think I ever had a real awakening moment to the *climate change* hoax; but I have always been suspicious. When I really got involved was during the same sex marriage plebiscite in 2017 (Chapter 1 Marriage). That woke me up to the culture wars.

During my years managing one of Koorong's bookstores I was leaning into the Emerging Church,[3,4] and the New Apostolic Movement (NAR), a Christian movement in the late 20th century, advocating for a renewed emphasis on apostolic and prophetic leadership. It was characterised by its belief in direct revelation, spiritual warfare, and a vision for Christian dominion over various aspects of society, including politics and culture. However, these movements were left leaning, and at the time, I was comfortable with that, I resonated with the desire for reparations for victimhood.

My studies at Tabor College had focused on political theology; Jonathan Edwards (1703-1758),[5] Karl Barth (1886-1968),[6] and Dietrich Bonhoeffer (1906-1945).[7] I have a background in these writers and thinkers, Barth, and Bonhoeffer particularly. The left falsely sees them as unashamedly left leaning. Ironically what brought me out of the left and Liberal Theology (an emphasis on reason, experience, and social justice over traditional doctrines),[8] was my reading of Karl Barth on Liberation Theology.[9]

The theology of liberation is a combination of Marxist philosophy with certain biblical motifs. It argues that we should reconstruct the whole of Christian theology by seeing it through the 'axis of the oppressor and the oppressed.'

The majority of the people around me at the time said that Karl Barth was a Socialist and indeed a Marxist. But he wasn't, I had read his original material. This is important to *climate change* because one of Barth's principles was his rejection of Natural Theology (knowledge of God based on observed facts and experience apart from divine revelation).[10]

In 2016 I found myself defending a fellow Barth student who lived in Nagaland, India. He was a proud supporter of Donald Trump, and those in the Barth camp were hammering him for this. They were calling him a racist and he wasn't even white! I asked them, 'Why are you condemning him?' The result was that he and I were booted out of the leftist camp. This drew me into the culture wars. Nothing on the right had attracted me, it was merely my repugnance for what I had seen of the left.

I had been around the language of 'climate crisis,' 'climate justice,' 'reparations,' all part of Liberation Theology. I suppose I was left leaning; some may say progressive; even though I had been saved in 1996 and was a hundred per cent for God; I still preferred to sell Keith Green over Joel Osteen in my Koorong days!

I didn't really have an opinion about *climate change* until I was being told what Karl Barth said as opposed to what he actually said. Then there was the catalyst of 2016 with Trump and the hypocrisy of the left. I started to read more intently, particularly the works of Jean Bethke Elshtain (1941-2013)[11] a political scientist in the US, a Lutheran who was a huge influence on me. Her *Democracy on Trial (1993),*[12] and *Sovereignty: God, State, and Self (2006),*[13] were two books which helped me on my journey out of the left.

However, I have to credit God, through the Holy Spirit's leading. We can be acutely aware of His leading, but we need to *decide* to follow Him or not.

What made me aware of the *climate crisis* issue was their Marxist affiliation and their political language which is essentially Communism. It's a faith. They have you believe that man is in control of the five major climate types – tropical, arid, temperate, continental, and polar. But the earth is living and breathing, it's the way God designed it, the only habitable zone in our solar system. How can man be the sole cause of *climate change*?

I agree that pollution is bad, that doesn't mean I am an environmentalist in the sense that I am a Gaia worshiper, surrendering the sovereignty of God to man. We need to steward our environment; Biblical stewardship of the environment is similar to Biblical stewardship of the home. We need to look after the space around us and cultivate it as God commanded Adam and Eve. The *climate change* movement is all about crossing the line from worshiping God to worshiping the creature (Romans 1:25). Two American thinkers, Daryl Harrison and Virgil Walker's podcast *Biblical Theology of Climate Change* is spot on.[14] The *climate change* religion is the complete denial of the Creator as we are to believe we are the saviours of the planet rather than the stewards.

The start of my rejection of this religion was Barth's rejection of Natural Theology that was embracing the worship of the state in 1930s Germany. I think what happened in 2020, and on through the Covid excuse for Communism was confirmation for me (Chapter 11 Health). A catalyst had certainly been back in 2016 being labelled a racist or homophobic by my friends, when I wasn't. I was booted out by the left; the left left me. I didn't go hard right; I went rather further towards Christ.

I have seen the mistreatment of people like Judith A. Curry, Peter Ridd, Joanne Nova, Ian Plimer, and Steven E. Koonan. Koonan's book, *Unsettled?*[15] is a phenomenal window into true science as opposed to politicised science. By definition, science is never settled.

Koonan argues that science has been hijacked by activists and politicians and the legacy media, all of whom are part of a cabal fixated on controlling information and pushing a particular narrative. We are given information they think will be popular and right and good for their party. This is how the Australian Labor Party thinks and now also the Liberal Party. This partly explains why the National Party of Australia split from the Liberal Party after the Federal election in 2025.

Another influence for me has been Albert Camus (1913-1960)[16] who rejected the French Communists, particularly after the Soviets rolled their tanks into Hungary in 1956 when they killed pro-democracy demonstrators. Albert could not understand why the French Communists said nothing about this. He had a similar epiphany that I had when he saw the left's hypocrisy.

The church has bought the *climate change* narrative. Look at the Anglican Church's website. We have stopped talking about the Gospel, we are no longer talking about Christ, we are talking about Karl Marx. We are not talking about the Creator; we are talking about the creation without the Creator. We are steering more towards the idolatry of Natural Theology, the worship of the state and the worship of nature.

What we see with *climate change* is an ideology entering into our theology. This comes back to Barth; we are seeing theology surrender to ideology. Theology is being made a slave to serve the *climate change* movement, just like they did with same sex marriage (Chapter 1 Marriage).

If you follow the dots, you see the rhetoric, including Black Lives Matter, it's all the language of control. If they can control theological thinking and theological arguments through the use of language, they can change what Scripture says, *doing violence* to the text, as Barth would say, to present an argument in support of their political goals.

Theology should be separated from such arguments. God is God and we are not. God moves us, and God acts on us first, then we move towards

God. They use language such as 'if you don't have solar you are not saved; if you are not vaccinated you can't be a good Christian as you are not loving or practicing sacrificial love.'

Take 'climate justice,' what does this mean? 'Climate reparations,' this is all coming from Marxian Woke Critical Theory, Frankfurt School thinking. This is dangerous, it's not Biblical, it's not true Theology, it's actually a rejection of God's revelation, which is the essence of sin. It's making us the centre rather than God's saving grace through Jesus Christ being the centre.

If we are led by Christ, instead of the spirit of the age, we will be fine. If the temperatures are increasing, and the science suggest they are, I am sure we will adjust. The agenda's modelling, just like with Covid, is off the wall! You can see how all of that is being propagandised by the legacy media. For example, the Bureau of Meteorology has changed the colouring of their maps to red when they are only depicting moderate temperatures. This is blatant psychological manipulation designed to create fear. Ellul would say, this is manipulative propaganda.[17] The legacy media are the worst offenders in pushing misinformation and disinformation.

We should hold fast to Paul's words in his first letter to Peter, 'Be sober, be vigilant; because your adversary the devil walks about like a roaring lion, seeking whom he may devour' (1 Peter 5:8).

❀　　❀　　❀

The church has bought climate change

Rod has graciously taken us on his own journey of discovery into climate change and done so through his critical thinking, his living relationship with Jesus Christ and his courage to change his mind. He has given a clear rationale as to why much of the Western church has left leaning tendencies. No wonder, then, why much of the church *has bought climate change*, because it is steeped in leftist ideology.

Thank you, Rod, for unpacking so much Theology, not just relevant to this chapter alone but a firm foundation for many of the issues we are seeking to awaken in this book. To read more of Rod's work on climate change, I recommend, *Turning Activists into Prophets: Why the Climate*

Change Religion is Dangerously Authoritarian (2024),[18] and *Barack Obama's Mansion on the Magnum PI Estate is Peak 'Climate Crisis' Hypocrisy* (2024).[19]

Megan Basham's book *Shepherds for Sale: How Evangelical Leaders Traded The Truth for a Leftist Agenda,* opens with a chapter entitled *Climate Change.*[20] John MacArthur endorsed her book: 'This may just be the single most important book on modern evangelicalism in recent years. It is bold, clear, and very well researched.' This section seeks to capture Megan's key points on the *climate change agenda*.

Remember 2022, when 30 per cent of Sri Lankans were malnourished due to the imposition of green policies banning chemical fertilisers and pesticides. Eventually, protesters stormed government buildings, and the president fled the country. This was just one of many instances where the *climate change agenda* could be clearly seen.

The Evangelical Environmental Network (EEN) was founded in 1993, with its mission 'to win church goers over to the green agenda.' Over time, *Christianity Today,* the *National Association of Evangelicals* (NAE) and the *Southern Baptist Convention* (SBC) were all bought into the fold. By 2006, 14 members of the *Council of Christian Colleges and Universities* (Robert Andringa) launched their *Creation Care Initiative.*[21] This was endorsed by Rick Warren, Saddleback Church; W. Todd Bassett, Salvation Army; Richard Stearns, World Vision, and more. No climate scientists endorsed this initiative other than the Intergovernmental Panel on Climate Change (IPCC),[22] a subsidiary of the United Nations.

In opposition to this push, was Professor Cal Beisner founded *The Cornwall Alliance for the Stewardship of Creation.*[23] 66 people from the Roman Catholic, Jewish and Protestant communities, as well as other layman, pastors, scholars, and religious leaders, endorsed the declaration when it was first released in March 2000; and by the middle of that year there were over a thousand signatories. Evidently, not all Christians were buying the *climate change agenda*. This was a major pushback but it's not hard to see why so many Christians have been persuaded due to the influence of the Creation Care Initiative. Beiser commented:

I saw how so many of the environmental movement's favourite policies were really harmful to the poor by slowing, stopping, or removing economic development.

In contrast, Jonathan Merrit, president of the SBC in 2008, called for:

Southern Baptists to be unified on global warming demonstrated by active preaching, promoting, and practicing Creation Care in their churches.

Further, Jonathan Moo's support for the Creation Care agenda implied our need to cut the world's population, reduce our driving and flying, in order for creation to flourish.[24]

It is significant to consider the funding for the Creation Care Initiative. One of the biggest was the Annenberg Foundation, a left of centre body with their vision to reduce population through abortion (Chapter 8). Other funding organisations were vocal in their lobbying against any increase in nuclear power generation.[25,26]

Megan concludes her chapter with a critique of the production of cobalt for the lithium-ion batteries essential for electric cars and the storage of solar energy.[27] Perhaps the world's largest producer is the Democratic Republic of Congo (DRC), where it is dug out of the ground by slave labour including many children as young as four. They work 16-hour shifts, breathing in toxic fumes. Walls and tunnels frequently collapse, amputating the lucky, burying some alive.

Joining the dots of the *climate change agenda* reveals a hidden agenda most Christians and the *climate change narrative* never discuss. Dig deep, there are so many angles to be considered.

Weather or Climate

The *climate change* narrative conveniently ignores the fundamental difference between *weather* and *climate* but uses every example of extreme *weather* to push their *climate* change agenda.

Weather is defined as the state of the atmosphere at a given time and place, with respect to variables such as temperature, moisture, wind speed and direction, and barometric pressure.[28]

Climate on the other hand can be described as the *average weather* taken over a long period in a *particular region*, bigger than a specific place.

> *Climate is the general weather over a long period. This can include rainfall, temperature, snow or any other weather condition. We usually define a region's climate over a period of 30 years.*[29]

The Earth's climates are always changing

We are bombarded daily, with one element or other of the *climate change agenda*. The cost of living, the advertising for 'green' energy providers, or the marketing of subsidised electric vehicles, all justified by the so-called 'science.' Let's consider what true scientists have to say, the ones who have not been bought.

Professor Ian Plimer is perhaps Australia's best-known geologist. Emeritus Professor of Earth Sciences at The University of Melbourne, where he was Professor and Head of Earth Sciences (1991-2005), then Professor of Mining Geology at The University of Adelaide (2006-2012).[30,31] In 2022, he wrote:

> *If green activism achieves its aims, the Third World will remain in poverty. Western countries will become impoverished and even more reliant on China which uses climate change as a weapon against the West...The long march of the left through schools and universities has produced green activists and a generation that cannot write, read, calculate, think, solve problems, or look after themselves. They have no knowledge of the past, Western civilization, science and critical thinking and the brutalities of previous communist and socialist regimes.*[32] (Chapter 3 Education)

Plimer's book, *Green Murder*, details hundreds of pages of fully referenced evidence for climate change back through Earth's history, with a specific emphasis on ice ages and the fact that we are currently warming as we come out of the last one. Scientists do not dispute the evidence for this, but the current *climate change narrative* pays no attention.

In 2023 I wrote an essay exploring some of the reasons for climate changes that the popular narrative ignores.[33] Here are some of these causes:

In 1911 Serbian scientist Milutin Milankovitch (1879-1958), theorised that the long-term, collective effects of changes in Earth's position relative to the Sun were a strong driver of Earth's long-term climate and were responsible for triggering the beginning and ending of ice ages, by describing three cycles.[34]

Eccentricity. Earth's orbit round the Sun isn't a perfect circle. Over time, the gravitational pull from the two largest planets, Jupiter and Saturn, cause the shape of Earth's orbit to vary from nearly circular to slightly elliptical. Currently, Earth's *eccentricity* is near its least elliptical (most circular) and is very slowly decreasing, in a cycle that spans about 100,000 years. As a result, the amount of heat we receive from the sun increases and decreases accordingly.

Obliquity. The angle of the Earth's axis of rotation is tilted as it orbits around the Sun, known as *obliquity* and this explains our seasons, as the hemisphere facing the Sun has summer, the hemisphere tilted away has winter. But the obliquity varies between 22.1 and 24.5 degrees with respect to Earth's orbit. The greater the obliquity the more extreme our seasons. It is believed that periods of greater obliquity can trigger deglaciation after an ice age. These cycles span about 41,000 years.

Precession. As the Earth rotates about its axis, it wobbles slightly, much like an off-centred spinning top before it falls over. This wobble is believed to be due to tidal forces caused by the gravitational influences of the Sun and Moon that cause Earth to bulge at the equator, affecting its rotation. This cycle, known as *precession* spans about 25,770 years.

Another contributor to climate change is the *sunspot cycle* of 22 years. The comings and goings of sunspots have been shown to parallel changes in the Earth's climates and certainly the timing of the Little Ice Age (1450 to 1820) correlates well, when bonfire parties were held on the frozen River Thames in London.[35]

In addition to these *external* variables there are a number of *internal* influences on climate change. Volcanic activity emits huge amounts of greenhouse gases and water vapour, much more significant triggers for global warming change than anthropogenic carbon dioxide. Additionally, explosive volcanic eruptions can send ash into the stratosphere that can be distributed around the planet by jet streams shielding us from the Sun's rays.[36]

Then there is the distribution of continental masses around the globe resulting from *plate tectonics*.[37] Their distribution influences the proportion of the Sun's rays that are reflected back to space as land absorbs and oceans reflect heat.

Finally, the *theory* that the burning of fossil fuels, coal, oil and natural gas is creating climate change (anthropogenic warming), is the direct effect of man's activity. This focuses on the additional production of carbon dioxide (CO_2), one of the greenhouse gasses that traps the Sun's energy in the atmosphere as the radiation bounces off these molecules on their way back out to space, and as a result, are returned to earth creating the heating effect.

Our atmosphere is 78 per cent nitrogen, 21 per cent oxygen, 0.9 per cent argon, and 0.1 per cent other gases (including CO_2).[38] But CO_2 is essential for plant growth and as Jordan B Peterson has pointed out; the globe's food production from plants has increased thanks to the extra CO_2 produced by man and the deserts have begun to shrink![39,40]

(A word of caution. If you are not aware, or perhaps have forgotten, the internet is far from 'balanced' in the articles and websites sourced on a search. Generally, government websites (whatever the country), NASA, Wikipedia and National Geographic, to name but a few, all point their readers to the *doctrine* that climate change is an *inconvenient truth* with no room for discussion of alternative views).

What does God say?

There is no *climate crisis* but there is a *climate change agenda*. God is in control, and He certainly doesn't want us to be slaves to fear. In this context I commend to you the work of Warwick Marsh (Chapter 2) and Kurt Mahlburg from 2023, *10 Reasons to question climate alarmism*.[41,42]

Returning to some real scientist's *Cornwall Declaration on Environmental Stewardship*; a sample of their concerns that marries perfectly with our Christian worldview:[23]

> *Many people believe that 'nature knows best,' or that the earth—untouched by human hands—is the ideal. Such romanticism leads some to deify nature or oppose human dominion over creation. Our position, informed by revelation and confirmed by reason and experience, <u>views human stewardship that unlocks the potential in creation for all the earth's inhabitants as good</u>. Humanity alone of all the created order is capable of developing other resources and can thus enrich creation, so it can properly be said that the human person is the most valuable resource on earth. Human life, therefore, must be cherished and allowed to flourish. The alternative—denying the possibility of beneficial human management of the earth— removes all rationale for environmental stewardship.* (my emphasis)

And again, a selection, from their beliefs: 'Our common Judeo-Christian heritage teaches that the following theological and anthropological principles are the foundation of environmental stewardship:'

> *God, the Creator of all things, rules overall and deserves our worship and adoration.*

> *The earth, and with it all the cosmos, reveals its Creator's wisdom and is sustained and governed by His power and lovingkindness.*

> <u>*Men and women were created in the image of God, given a privileged place among creatures, and commanded to exercise stewardship over the earth. Human persons are moral agents for whom freedom is an essential condition of responsible action.*</u> *Sound environmental stewardship must attend both to the demands of human wellbeing and to a divine call for human beings to exercise caring dominion over the earth. It affirms that human*

wellbeing and the integrity of creation are not only compatible but also dynamically interdependent realities. (my emphasis)

The mighty hand of God runs throughout this chapter. Before earth was, there was God (Genesis 1:1, John 1:1). He created us and we inhabit His handywork. The Bible says, 'Then God blessed them (the pinnacle of creation, man and woman), and God said to them, "Be fruitful and multiply; fill the earth and subdue it; have dominion over the fish of the sea, over the birds of the air, and over every living thing that moves on the earth"' (Genesis 1:28).

Only a Godless agenda can see mankind as a plague or a pollutant on the planet, to be culled and confined, so that mother earth can flourish. That was never God's plan and purpose for His creation. However, if you regard your existence as happenstance, or the mere luck of random selection, then I can understand how fear might drive your agendas and behaviours. Rather, let's end on this magnificent promise from God:

> *While the earth remains,*
> *Seedtime and harvest,*
> *Cold and heat,*
> *Winter and summer,*
> *And day and night*
> *Shall not cease.* (Genesis 8:22)

Footnotes

[1] Caldron Pool (n.d.). *Rod Lampard.* Retrieved October 22, 2025, from https://caldronpool.com/?s=Rod+Lampard

[2] Rod Lampard (n.d.). *Rod Lampard.* Retrieved October 23, 2025, from https://rodlampard.com/

[3] Connor, Mark (2007, August 23). The Emerging Church. *Mark Connor.* https://markconner.com.au/the-emerging-ch/

[4] Piper, John (2008, March 12). What Is the 'Emerging Church'? *Desiring God.* https://www.desiringgod.org/interviews/what-is-the-emerging-church

[5] Britannica (n.d.). *Jonathan Edwards.* Retrieved October 23, 2025, from https://www.britannica.com/biography/Jonathan-Edwards

[6] Britannica (n.d.). *Karl Barth.* Retrieved October 23, 2025, from https://www.britannica.com/biography/Karl-Barth

[7] Britannica (n.d.). *Dietrich Bonhoeffer.* Retrieved October 23, 2025, from https://www.britannica.com/biography/Dietrich-Bonhoeffer

[8] Hoffecker, Andrew (n.d.). Liberal Theology. *The Gospel Coalition.* Retrieved October 23, 2025, from https://www.thegospelcoalition.org/essay/liberal-theology/

[9] Frame John M. (n.d.). Liberation Theology. *The Gospel Coalition.* Retrieved October 23, 2025, from https://www.thegospelcoalition.org/essay/liberation-theology/

[10] Muehlenberg, Bill (2024, February 26). On Natural Theology. *Culture Watch.* https://billmuehlenberg.com/2024/02/26/on-natural-theology/

[11] George, Robert P. (2013, August 15). Jean Bethke Elshtain: Gifted Thinker and Courageous Woman. *Public Discourse.* https://www.thepublicdiscourse.com/2013/08/10760/

[12] Elshtain, Jean B. (1993). *Democracy on Trial.* Basic Books. https://www.amazon.com.au/Democracy-Trial-Jean-Elshtain/dp/0465016170

[13] Institute for Faith and Learning – Baylor (2021, June 18). *Jean Bethke Elshtain - Genetic Fundamentalism and the Myth of the Sovereign Self.* [Video]. YouTube. https://www.youtube.com/watch?v=wvftXGxZmwA

[14] Harrison, Darrell & 1 Walker, Virgi (2023). Episode 124: Biblical Theology of Climate Change. *Just Thinking Ministries.* https://justthinking.me/ep-124-a-biblical-theology-of-climate-change/

[15] Koonan, Steven E. (2021). *Unsettled: What Climate Science Tells Us, What It Doesn't, and Why It Matters.* Ben Bella Books. https://www.amazon.com.au/Unsettled-Climate-Science-Doesnt-Matters/dp/1950665798

[16] Stanford Encyclopedia of Philosophy (2021, December 13). Albert Camus. In *Stanford Encyclopedia of Philosophy.* https://plato.stanford.edu/entries/camus/

[17] Ellul, Jacques (1988). *Jesus and Marx: From Gospel to Ideology.* Ethics & Public Policy Center Inc., U.S. https://www.amazon.com.au/Jesus-Marx-Ideology-Jacques-Ellul/dp/0802802974

[18] Lampard, Rod (2024, May 22). Turning Activists into Prophets: Why the Climate Change Religion is Dangerously Authoritarian. *Daily*

Declaration. https://dailydeclaration.org.au/2024/05/22/climate-change-religion/

[19] Lampard, Rod (2024, October 16). Barack Obama's Mansion on the Magnum PI Estate is Peak 'Climate Crisis' Hypocrisy. *Daily Declaration*. https://dailydeclaration.org.au/2024/10/16/obama-mansion-climate-crisis-hypocrisy/

[20] Basham, Megan (2024). *Shepherds for Sale: How Evangelical Leaders Traded the Truth for a Leftist Agenda*. Harper Collins US. https://www.amazon.com.au/Shepherds-Sale-Evangelical-Leaders-Leftist-ebook/dp/B0CRQGNLMY

[21] Evangelical Environmental Network (n.d.). *Creation Care Champions*. Retrieved October 23, 2025, from https://creationcare.org/what-we-do/initiatives-campaigns/overview.html

[22] IPCC-63 (n.d.). *The Intergovernmental Panel on Climate Change*. Retrieved October 23, 2025, from https://www.ipcc.ch/

[23] The Cornwall Alliance for the Stewardship of Creation (n.d.). *The Cornwall Declaration On Environmental Stewardship*. Retrieved October 23, 2025, from https://cornwallalliance.org/the-cornwall-declaration-on-environmental-stewardship/

[24] Dallas Theological Seminary (2021, May 6). *Theology and Creation Care - Jonathan Moo*. [Video]. YouTube. https://www.youtube.com/watch?v=1n5jmUbSOik

[25] Hilton, Zoe (2024, July 11). *Nuclear vs Renewables: What Will It Cost?* Centre for independent Studies. [Video]. YouTube. https://www.youtube.com/watch?v=Mw_AX9WaJ08

[26] Anderson, John (2025, May 2). *Power Bills Are Soaring - Zoe Hilton*. John Anderson Media. [Video]. YouTube. https://www.youtube.com/watch?v=F5ZSqT8lGbA

[27] Kara, Siddharth (2022, December 23). *The Disturbing Reality of Cobalt Mining for Rechargeable Batteries*. PowerfulJRE. [Video]. YouTube. https://www.youtube.com/watch?v=CIWvk3gJ_7E

[28] National Weather Service (n.d.). *Climate vs Weather*. Retrieved October 23, 2025, from https://www.weather.gov/climateservices/CvW

[29] Met Office UK (n.d.). *What is Climate?* Retrieved October 23, 2025, from https://weather.metoffice.gov.uk/climate/climate-explained/what-is-climate

[30] Connorcourt Publishing (n.d.). *Ian Plimmer*. Retrieved October 23, 2025, from https://www.connorcourtpublishing.com.au/Ian-Plimer_bymfg_1-0-1.html

[31] Plimer, Ian (2024, November 21). *Professor Ian Plimer Launches Climate Change: The Facts 2025*. Institute of Public Affairs. [Video]. YouTube. https://www.youtube.com/watch?v=KPJV4fPZ_oc

[32] Plimer, Ian (2022). *Green Murder: A life Sentence of net zero with no parole*. Connorcourt Publishing. https://www.amazon.com.au/dp/1922449822?ref_=mr_referred_us_au_au

[33] Twelves, Jim (2023, February 1). Keeping, or Losing, Our Faith in Climate Change. *Daily Declaration*. https://dailydeclaration.org.au/2023/02/01/keeping-or-losing-our-faith-in-climate-change/

[34] American Museum of Natural History (n.d.). *Milutin Milankovitch: Seeking the Cause of the Ice Ages*. Retrieved October 23, 2025, from https://www.amnh.org/learn-teach/curriculum-collections/earth-inside-and-out/milutin-milankovitch-seeking-the-cause-of-the-ice-ages

[35] Hessayon, Ariel (2025, January 12). The Little Ice Age and the River Thames frost fairs of the seventeenth century. *Ariel Hessayon*. https://arielhessayon.substack.com/p/the-little-ice-age-and-the-river-38f

[36] Astrum (2022, January 23). *Aftermath of the Biggest Volcano Eruption Ever Caught on Tape from Space – Tonga*. Astrum. [Video]. YouTube. https://www.youtube.com/watch?v=sZZVVwqZ0rs

[37] Pacific Northwest Seismic Network Plate Tectonics (n.d.). *Plate Tectonics*. Retrieved October 23, 2025, from https://pnsn.org/outreach/about-earthquakes/plate-tectonics

[38] Dobrijevic, Daisy & Sharp, Tim (2023, July 23). Earth's atmosphere: Facts about our planet's protective blanket. *Space.com*. https://www.space.com/17683-earth-atmosphere.html

[39] Peterson, Jordan, B. (2022, November 9). *Killing the Poor to Save the Planet: Dr Peterson and Bjørn Lomborg read their article most recently published in the Telegraph*. Jordan B. Peterson. [Video]. YouTube. https://www.youtube.com/watch?v=NIMLW2RundY&t=1283s

40 Phelan, Matthew (2024, July 8). Dr Jordan Peterson claims burning fossil fuels is GOOD for environment because it's making the planet 'greener.'.. what's the truth? *Daily Mail.* https://www.dailymail.co.uk/sciencetech/article-13604831/Dr-Jordan-Peterson-fossil-fuels-GOOD-climate-change-truth.html

41 Marsh, Warwick & Mahlburg, Kurt (2023, November 10). 10 Reasons to Question Climate Alarmism. *Daily Declaration.* https://dailydeclaration.org.au/2023/11/10/10-reasons-to-question-climate-alarmism/

42 Marsh, Warwick (2023, November 10). 10 Reasons to Question Climate Alarmism. *Canberra Declaration.* [Video]. YouTube. https://www.youtube.com/watch?v=cxMsjRFhukE&t=26s

CHAPTER 13 - SPIRITUAL WARFARE

Brian Pickering's Story

Brian was born on the Mid-North Coast of NSW, the son of a Methodist Minister.[1] He made a personal commitment to the Lord when his father died in his mid-twenties. He went into banking, working his way up to a senior management position nearly 40 years later, from the mail room to the board room, his gifting being in administration. He was retrenched from the bank along with many other senior people around the year 2000 when the banks changed from being a service industry to for-profit companies. Brian was running a prayer ministry while he was still in the bank. So, the golden handshake provided him with the resources to move into full time ministry without missing a beat. This was definitely God's provision, releasing him into his calling.

Brian picks up the narrative:

My story is not a story of my faith in Him, but of His faithfulness towards me. In my earlier years I would not have thought of myself as a diligent prayer. But as the years went by God led me into areas where I understood prayer more, where I could see the impact prayer could have in the lives of individuals, families, and nations.

Fifty-five years ago, my life turned dramatically, not once, but twice. It was shortly after the birth of the first of our three children, seemingly overnight I developed a crippling back condition which stopped me from being able to walk properly, stand up for any period of time, or even to sit without considerable pain. Initially it was thought I had pulled something out of place but after weeks of treatment without any improvement I was referred to a specialist for a more detailed examination, testing and diagnosis.

The diagnosis, in laymen's terms, was that I had premature ageing of my spinal discs. The normal ageing process was hitting me in my mid-twenties. The only treatment I was offered was the fusion of my spine which, if successful, and that was not guaranteed, would result in some loss of movement but a reasonably normal life. If it did not work, I was told I should prepare myself for life in a wheelchair with constant pain. This was at a stage in my life when we were just starting a family and I had a promising career in the bank.

This created a crisis of faith in my life. I had been a Christian all my life. I believed in the Bible as the Word of God. I believed the miracles of healing that Jesus performed throughout the New Testament. I believed He raised people from the dead and believed He still healed today. But there was one big 'but,' would He heal me in what was now my greatest hour of need. Whilst I believed He could heal others, I doubted that He could do that for me 'now' when I needed it. Rather than have an immediate operation I asked the doctor for twelve months to explore other avenues. So, I began a journey of placing myself in every position I could so that God could heal me. I was prayed over by dozens of faith-filled people. I attended prayer meetings and Church services, but nothing changed for me.

After nine months of searching, at a low point in my journey to conjure up faith, I had an encounter one morning in the kitchen of our home as I prepared breakfast for myself and the family. I sensed a presence in the room, and I heard an inner voice saying 'Brian, do you want to be healed?' I replied, 'Of course I do,' and the inner voice that I recognised to be that of Jesus said, 'Then reach out to me and I will heal you.' In what I can only describe as a momentary gift, a mustard seed of faith was given to me, and I accepted the invitation and reached out to Jesus who instantly healed me. It was not my faith that healed me, because I had none, but it was His faithfulness alone.

I look back on the years from the time of my healing to the next life changing time of my life as years of training. I was heavily involved with Church life in my local Church but also at State and National level within my denomination. But a restlessness set in around the age of 40, when I became dissatisfied with the mundaneness of my Christian life. Going to Church every Sunday, praying every day, and reading my Bible every day became a way of life, but it did not satisfy me. As I read my Bible, I began to wish I had been alive when Jesus was alive, to see him perform the miracles, such as the raising of Lazarus, and the many healings that Jesus performed throughout his ministry and the feeding of 5,000 people with just five loaves and two fish.

I wanted my expression of Christianity not to be routine, but life changing, not only for myself but for many others as well. I believe He answered my cry as I felt Him ask me for just two things. Not finance, not resources, not even my talents; but I believe He asked me to give Him my *total availability and my radical obedience.*

At the time I began this journey I was a banker. I had been trained up to handle money; to make money work for me, I knew how to use it to make more. But God knew that if I was to run a prayer network where only He was to provide the money needed, He needed to change the way I thought about finance. After some six years of training in going to country towns and meeting with people in those towns to encourage them to pray for their community He asked me to organise a 40 Hour Prayer Weekend. At the time that was not within my capacity to comprehend. Forty hours of prayer – I could hardly pray for 40 minutes let alone 40 hours. I believe He asked me to write to those I had been visiting over the previous six years and invite them to a country location in NSW to attend this 40-hour prayer weekend where He would teach us how to pray for cities and nations. My job was to arrange accommodation for them all and provide five meals from Saturday breakfast through to Sunday lunch and a neutral venue in which to meet.

I have a gift of facilitation so I went about preparing for the 100 guests I believed He had told me would attend. So, I did what every good banker would do. I costed 50 motel rooms for two nights, 500 meals and a neutral venue. Some 40 years ago when this story took place the total budget came to $6,000, maybe the equivalent of $30-40,000 today. So, I simply divided the 6000 by 100 and decided I would need to charge everyone $60.00 per head. At this point I heard that voice say, 'What is this business about charging?' So, I said, 'Well how am I going to pay for it all?' The inner voice said, 'I will' and I said, 'How are you going to do that?' His reply was that I could take up an offering from the people in the last session on the Sunday afternoon before they went home, and He would ensure there was sufficient in the offering to pay all the bills. This was the second great challenge to my faith after my healing and again I failed the test. I said that will not work. You may be God, but I am a banker and that will not work down here on earth. He said I thought you wanted to be *radically obedient* so you could see miracles, so I was caught over a barrel. Now at this point I could have been excused for believing this was all a figment of my own imagination. I have been told by my investment advisor that I have a high tolerance for risk. So, I thought, OK I will do it once and see what happens and if it fails, I will get a loan and pay it off over a number of years and never be so stupid again. I told my wife, and she agreed it would not work and was a stupid idea but to her credit she allowed me to pursue my 'dream.'

The weekend came, 100 people turned up, and it was a great weekend appreciated by all, especially the sit-down Saturday night restaurant meal paid for by me. Sunday morning came and one family asked me whether I minded if they left before lunch as they had 500 kilometres to travel home. I knew I couldn't ask for the offering till the last session which was to start at 2.00 pm but I resisted the urge to ask them to contribute to the cost of the weekend before they left so I waved them goodbye without them contributing nary a cent towards the cost!

The final session came, and people made their contributions towards the cost of the weekend as they felt able. We counted all the contributions, and it came to $6,600. $6,000 to cover the expenses and $600 to put down as a deposit on the next one. Now that is a good, but true, story but it was more than that because as God had provided it changed my whole attitude as to how we would run the ministry. As a result of that weekend, we made a decision to never charge but to rely on God moving the hearts of those who came. Again, I want to point out it was not my faith that achieved that result but His faithfulness. My contribution was not my faith but my Radical Obedience.

The prayer network started in New South Wales. I was invited by other ministry leaders to establish a national prayer network under the AD 2000 & Beyond Movement.[2] I was appointed National Co-ordinator of the Australian Prayer Network.[3] It began with about 200 names of people who had been to prayer conferences. Those names were given to me by a pastor from Brisbane who had been asked to start a network but being a pastor in a local church, he would not have had the time to do this himself, so he came to me, offering me the job. That network now has over 700 churches affiliated to it, a couple of thousand prayer groups and up to 100,000 people through those prayer groups now praying for our nation on a regular basis. It's nothing that I have done except to follow the Lord step by step.

Most people would say that prayer is a conversation we have with God. Prayer for most people is very personal, and in fact most Christians only ever pray for themselves, their friends and their family. God has challenged this mindset to see how prayer works in changing nations and changing cities and changing society. My focus is not so much on the personal, our ministry is to pray for the nation, the nations, and cities. We interact with governments and with the church. We do prayer projects in cities alongside churches. Prayer, to me is the conduit of power that flows from the throne room of God into the circumstances of our lives.

There is personal prayer when I talk with God, but there is also a power transaction with God as he uses ordinary people as a channel. This is intercessory prayer, it is what we do when we become an agent for God to use us to change the circumstances of others' lives, including the lives of cities and nations. I believe that God does call particular people to that ministry, but I also believe that all of us are called to be intercessors, allowing God to do in us what He wants to do in others.

The intercessory prayer principles also apply at the family level, just like the national. I am a father to my family, and I am also an intercessor for my family. In other words, I allow God to use me to impact the life of my family. And I do that in how I live my life in relationship to my God. Everything I do in relation to someone else's life is an intercession for that person.

The Western world has moved away from God. We have said we don't need God; we can look after ourselves. We are now finding that we can't look after ourselves. We need to realise we need God much more than we think we do.

There is nothing more exciting than working on the cutting edge of what God is doing in His world. Whilst many see prayer as an activity they undertake from time to time, real prayer from my perspective is an activity of God going on 24/7 in which I am invited to join Him and make myself *totally available and radically obedient* to the part He calls me to play in changing the world.

I trust this has encouraged you to try a different approach to your Christian walk. Not waiting for things to come to you but by making yourself *totally available* and taking the initiative in *radical obedience.*

Remember it is not our faith that determines how far we can go down a path to which He calls us but His faithfulness.

❀   ❀   ❀

Intercession the Sword of Spiritual Warfare

How do we respond to Brian's story? God broke into his life using the circumstances we might all face - injury, or retrenchment. The key was the way he responded which opened the door for God's faithfulness to break in.

Let's not put Brian on a pedestal and say that God only uses the special ones for *spiritual warfare*; most of us are simply called to prayer. Rather, I believe we are all called to spiritual warfare. Though Brian does not use the term, 'spiritual warfare,' it seems to me evident that what his ministry was all about, was building an army of *spiritual warfare warriors*, which he did remarkably well.

In 591BC, in Ezekiel 22, the people of Israel were in a terrible state, murder, idolatry, making profits from their neighbours by extortion, oppressing strangers, mistreating orphans and widows, taking bribes and committing adultery are just a few of their sins. This litany sounds similar to the issues addressed in earlier chapters of *While We Were Sleeping*.

God's anger burnt against the sins of His people, the Jews, and He looked for one righteous man to plead their cause, *to stand in the gap* for them. But He found none.

> *So, I sought for a man among them who would make a wall and stand in the gap before Me on behalf of the land, that I should not destroy it; but I found no one.* (Ezekiel 22:30)

It is tragic that 2,400 years ago God was looking for an *intercessor,* and He is still looking. I am praying He finds *you!*

Intercessory prayer is when we intercede on *another's behalf* and plead their cause. Intercession is a calling on all Christians. It has been described as *exposing oneself for the protection of another or something*. Meaning that we take up a position on the battlefield *in the place of a wounded* brother or sister in Christ or a cause or situation we are called to intercede for.[4]

This description of intercession illuminates two paths we should take. Firstly, perhaps most importantly, intercession is not about us and our needs and wants. This is prayer for *others*. Our needs are set aside because our *heart*, our *attention* and our *energy* are all focused on *someone* or *something* that will not directly benefit *us* at all. Intercession is as *selfless* as Christ's death, resurrection and His continual intercession for us.

Secondly, how do we know *what* we should be interceding for? Intercession demands a precursor, a time and place when we *look* with Christ's eyes and *feel* with Christ's heart at what is grieving Him.

> *Now as He drew near, He saw the city and wept over it, saying, 'If you had known, even you, especially in this your day, the things that make for your peace! But now they are hidden from your eyes. For days will come upon you when your enemies will build an embankment around you, surround you and close you in on every side, and level you, and your children within you, to the ground; and they will not leave in you one stone upon another, because you did not know the time of your visitation.'* (Luke 19:41-44) (my emphasis)

Intercession behoves us to dial in to God and receive from Him His call. His call on us to stand and fight. This is no picnic. This is no respectable, polite prayer meeting for those who have nothing else to do. No, this is bloody battle with the enemy who always seeks to steal, kill and destroy having first deceived us and sent us to sleep.

I believe that, *While We Were Sleeping* is God's call for his family to awake, arm up, and get into battle formation. It's never too late.

As a student in the early 1970s I knew something of intercession, but I confess, I have not always been on the battlefield since then. Brian's story at the start of this chapter and Gordon's at the start of the next, are brilliant testimonies we can all learn from. For me, I know, I am in intercession when my *heart breaks* and I don't know *why*. All I can do is pour out my heart for an individual or for the cause the Lord has given me at the time.

Welsh missionary in Africa and founder of The Bible College of Wales, Rees Howells (1879-1950) has been arguably the most inspirational intercessor in modern times. I highly commend the biography by Norman Grubb as a foundational reflection for all those keen to explore intercession. Howell taught great principles; one example will suffice:[5]

> *The New Testament makes it clear that there is a constant warfare going on in the heavenlies, and the apostle Paul, who knew this warfare well, was constantly urging his Christian converts to be aware of this, to be clothed with the heavenly armour and to fight the good fight of faith. See Ephesians 6:10-18; 2 Timothy 2:1-5; 1 Timothy 6:12.[6]*

Listen to the lyrics of most of our worship songs, the focus of most of our preaching, the prayer points of our infrequent prayer meetings and the subject matter of most of our Christian books. It's all about *me!* Seeking our needs, the rescue and recovery from our trials, and deliverance from our temptations and addictions.

Intercession takes our eyes off *me* and causes us to see with Jesus' eyes, the situation of *others* and *the world* outside our walls.

Spiritual Warfare

> *Christians in the West, of course, affirm – or should affirm – the reality of the spiritual realm, including dark spiritual powers such as Satan and demons. However, when push comes to shove, do we really believe these things? Yes, we mentally agree with biblical teaching on these matters, but one wonders if we really live as if we do, in fact, believe them.* (Muehlenberg)[7]

Spiritual warfare can and should be waged at the personal level,[7,8] but this chapter's focus is on the wider *theatre of war* that surrounds us, the world that is impacting our lives from our environment.

The argument of this book is that many of us are immature in our prayer life through want of teaching and many of our churches lack vibrant prayer ministry.[9] Or to put it another way, many of us have been lulled to *sleep* by the impossibility of the situation and by the distractions that fill our lives.[10]

The flood of evil simply keeps coming. Barely a week goes by without yet another onslaught on our senses. We become desensitised, believing we are immune, that we have a supernatural cloak that will protect us and our loved ones, but if we take a closer look at our lives, we have been, in many respects, targeted and tainted to the extent that we are *of* this world (John 17:16-18).

Rees Howell's practice of intercession and spiritual warfare are telling:[5]

> *In the pre-war years occurred a development which was to occupy a large share of the college prayers, and to lead to another great intercession. In 1938, Hitler began to persecute the Jews on an unprecedented scale and there were many Jewish orphans whose parents had been taken away to a then unknown fate. <u>The love of the Holy Spirit in him for the orphans of the Welsh village, was now manifested through Rees Howells for these children.</u> Efforts were made to rescue some from the Continent. Some were adopted into the college family; others came into the home and school for the children of missionaries. <u>Early in January 1939 Rees Howells called a special day of prayer for the Jewish people and this was to prove the beginning of the intercession which was to continue right through the war and beyond, until the day when Israel became a nation in 1948</u>. (my emphasis)[11]*

Rees *saw* what was happening through the Holy Spirit, which *drove* him and his community into prayer (spiritual warfare) and *action* towards the Jewish orphans both in Wales and in mounting projects to rescue more from out of Europe. (Chapter 15 for more detail on the role of the Jews and the land of Israel in God's eternal plan).

So much has been written about spiritual warfare. Here are some sound bites to whet our appetites.

> *A new breed of intercessors is on the move for God across the world, 'invading' countries, cloaking them in prayer and engaging in spiritual warfare.* (Cindy Jacobs)[12]

I want to talk about *taking cities and nations for God.* I think there are two opposing forces at play. The *me-first* culture, and the *globalist* agenda, have both taken our eyes off our cities and our nations. God's whole focus has always been *cities and nations*.

> *Because of the principles of authority, responsibility, free will, sowing and reaping, etc., which operate not only on an individual level, but also on the corporate level at which individuals join...The same principle of shared authority can be incrementally expanded all the way up to a national level.* (Dutch Sheets)[13]

Further, Gordon's testimony in the next chapter, highlights the imperative for *breakthrough* in prayer.[14] What is that? Picture a military campaign. The advancing army is *pinned down* in their defensive trenches by the enemy until the advancing forces *break through!* At which point there is a thunderous shout of victory as the prevailing army advances and begins to take back ground, previously lost. Breakthrough is not pretty, quiet, and orderly; it's loud and often chaotic!

> *I believe that at this time the Holy Spirit is urging the church to wake up and realise that, whether we like it or not, we are at war. We have been passive for far too long about the things that are happening around us – in our communities, across our nation. We have tended to sit back and say, 'It's none of my business.' We have become too tolerant and politically correct and not wanted to rock the boat and say no to sin. The wake-up call is: it is your business!* (Rachel Hickson)[15]

We can all recognise *breakthrough* in a physical war, but what does it look like in a spiritual war? Consider Nehemiah's spiritual warfare when he heard that Jerusalem's walls were *broken down* and its gates *burnt with fire*, the *protections for* and the *authority of* the community were shattered. He *wept, fasted* and *prayed*:[16]

> *I said: 'I pray, Lord God of heaven, O great and awesome God, You who keep Your covenant and mercy with those who love You and observe Your commandments, please let Your ear be attentive and Your eyes open, that You may hear the prayer of Your servant which I pray before You now, day and night, for the children of Israel Your servants, and confess the sins of the children of Israel*

which we have sinned against You. Both my father's house and I have sinned.' (Nehemiah 1:5-6) (my emphasis)

This was one man wrestling with God in prayer confessing the sins of a whole nation before God, he was *personally* identifying with other's sin, just as Jesus did on the cross for all of us. It is the confession of sin, literally our own if needs be, and/or the sins of others, or a nation, that God puts on us to confess before him; this is the key to *breakthrough*.

Daniel also describes spiritual warfare as the Israelite 70-year captivity was coming to an end:

> *Then I set my face toward the Lord God to make request by prayer and supplications, with fasting, sackcloth, and ashes. And I prayed to the Lord my God, and made confession, and said, "O Lord, great and awesome God, who keeps His covenant and mercy with those who love Him, and with those who keep His commandments, we have sinned and committed iniquity, we have done wickedly and rebelled, even by departing from Your precepts and Your judgments.* (Daniel 9:3-5) (my emphasis)

Spiritual warfare can be summed up as *tears*, *confession*, and *war*.

What does God say?

I am indebted to Peter Wagner for his narrative from the Book of Revelation.[16] Satan, our enemy, has a *lust for power*. He has a specific strategy for every nation and every ministry, that strategy is *deception*.

> *...and he* (the angel) *cast him* (Satan) *into the bottomless pit, and shut him up, and set a seal on him, so that he should deceive the nations no more till the thousand years were finished.* (Revelation 20:3)

No need to get side-tracked into the *when* of this prophecy, rather focus on the weapon of *deception*. How hard it is to see *deception* when we are *deceived*! It's been the weapon of choice for Satan ever since the beginning (Genesis 3:1).

Earlier in Revelation Satan's strategy, depicted as a harlot, is described:

After these things I saw another angel coming down from heaven, having great authority, and the earth was illuminated with his glory. And he cried mightily with a loud voice, saying, 'Babylon the great is fallen, is fallen, and has become a <u>dwelling place of demons, a prison for every foul spirit,</u> and <u>a cage for every unclean and hated bird! For all <u>the nations have drunk of the wine of the wrath of her fornication, the kings of the earth have committed fornication with her,</u> and the <u>merchants of the earth have become rich through the abundance of her luxury.</u>' (Revelation 18:1-3) (my emphasis)

Here we have Babylon depicted as a penal colony for the Devil and his demons. But look what they have been doing to warrant this sentence. This is why Wagner describes Satan's power as *lust*. The Bible does not mince words. The nations, and their rulers, have *gone to bed* with the Devil, and the merchants have become rich out of *partnership with him*.

Doesn't this describe the state of the nations now? This is not just our enemy, the Devil, prowling around seeking whom he may devour (1Peter 5:8), but we are up against an unholy alliance between Satan, the *rulers* of nations and their *merchants*. Do not be deceived, this is our imperative for spiritual warfare.

The warning from Jesus is so apt today:

for false christs and false prophets will rise and show great signs and wonders to deceive, if possible, even the elect. (Matthew 24:24)

We would be naive to believe that no Christians have been deceived. I would go further, those who are still asleep and cannot see the territory that has been taken by Satan, are the deceived ones of Matthew 24:24.

Jesus does not leave us hanging but goes on to give us the *Great Commission*: 'Go therefore and make disciples of all nations' (Matthew 28:19). He is saying, don't settle down, there is territory to be taken back and souls to be rescued from slavery, and what is more, they are to be discipled into the Kingdom.

If Satan is so hungry for power and control, is it any wonder he targets Christians, the church, and church leaders in particular? While we are out saving the planet and applauding global initiatives, the Devil is busy enhancing his partnerships with our national leaders. No wonder there is a war on and as Christians, by default, we have all been called up to serve in spiritual warfare.

Brian Pickering is not special. Yes, his circumstances and his leadership capacity aligned with the specific ministry God called him into, but we should not disqualify ourselves, saying *spiritual warfare* is only for the few; Ephesians 6:10-18 was written for us all.

Footnotes

[1] Corr, Brendan (2020, June 2). Inspiration Project with Brendan Corr, Episode 12. *Australian Christian College*
https://www.acc.edu.au/podcast/brian-pickering/

[2] Bush, Luis (1996, May 27-30). A Brief Historical Overview of the AD2000 & Beyond Movement and Joshua Project 2000. *Luis Bush Papers*. https://luisbushpapers.com/joshua-project/1995/11/01/a-brief-historical-overview-of-the-ad2000-movement-and-joshua-project-2000/

[3] Australian Prayer Network (n.d.). Retrieved October 23, 2025, from https://ausprayernet.org.au/home-2/about-us/

[4] Rust, Brittany (2025, July 13). What is Intercessory Prayer and Standing in the Gap? *Brittany Rust.* https://www.brittanyrust.com/blog/standing-in-the-gap

[5] Grubb, Norman (1952). *Rees Howells Intercessor*. Christian Literature Crusade
https://www.thechoicedrivenlife.com/uploads/Rees%20Howells%20Intercessor.pdf

[6] Ruscoe, Doris (2003). Rees Howells and Intercession from The Intercession of Rees Howells. *The Intercessor, 19*(2).
https://zerubbabel.org/intercessor-article/vol-19-no-2-rees-howells-and-intercession-from-the-intercession-of-rees-howells/

[7] Muehlenberg, Bill (2025, April 15). Not Just Flesh and Blood: We Are in a Spiritual War. *Daily Declaration.*
https://dailydeclaration.org.au/2025/04/15/spiritual-war/#comment-40101

[8] Savchuk, Vlad (2024, October 29). *7 Clear Signs You're Facing Spiritual Warfare*. [Video]. YouTube. https://www.youtube.com/watch?v=UmU1YnvLWHw&t=247s

[9] The 700 Club (2014, May 2). *Dr. Jack Hayford: Defeating Evil with Prayer*. [Video]. YouTube. https://www.youtube.com/watch?v=wvthOym67Sc

[10] Cahn, Jonathan (2023, August 13). *A Guide to Spiritual Warfare and Defeating the Enemy*. [Video]. YouTube. https://www.youtube.com/watch?v=FHiA59yJW2U

[11] Ruscoe, Doris (2003). Reminiscences of Rees Howells The War Years, 1939 – 1945. *The Intercessor, 19*(4). https://zerubbabel.org/intercessor-article/vol-19-no-4-reminiscences-of-rees-howells-the-war-years-1939-1945/

[12] Jacobs, Cindy (2018). *Possessing the Gates of the Enemy: A Training Manual for Militant Intercession*. Chosen Books. https://www.amazon.com.au/Possessing-Gates-Enemy-Training-Intercession/dp/080079883X/ref=tmm_pap_swatch_0

[13] Sheets, Dutch (1996). *Intercessory Prayer: How God can use your prayers to move heaven and earth*. Regal Books. https://www.goodreads.com/book/show/180733.Intercessory_Prayer

[14] Hickson, Rachel (2007). *Supernatural Breakthrough: The Heartcry for Change*. New Wine Press. https://www.amazon.com.au/Supernatural-Breakthrough-Heartcry-Rachel-Hickson/dp/1903725518

[15] Hickson, Rachel (2006). *Supernatural Communication: The Privilege of Prayer*. New Wine Press. https://www.amazon.com.au/Supernatural-Communication-Privilege-Rachael-Hickson-ebook/dp/B09DQZBCRW

[16] Wagner, C. Peter (1992). *Warfare Prayer: How to seek God's power and protection in the battle to build the Kingdom*. Regal Books. https://www.amazon.com.au/Warfare-Prayer-Protection-Battle-Kingdom/dp/0830715134

CHAPTER 14 - ISLAM

Gordon Hickson's Story

Gordon Hickson comes from a British military and business background working across the Middle East. He then worked for five years in Africa and Asia as the International Campaign Director for Reinhard Bonnke, working into a number of Islamic cities. On his return to England, he became an Assemblies of God Minister, and their Missions Director for the Muslim World. After many years of pastoring, he travelled extensively ministering with Heartcry, the Ministry developed by his wife Rachel, while she set up the London Prayernet as a 24/7 prayer shield over London. For several years he also travelled with Brother Yun, the *Heavenly Man*,[1] before finally being hi-jacked by God into the Anglican Church! In 2005 he was ordained in the Anglican Church and served for almost six years as Parish Vicar of St Aldates Church in Oxford, where he co-founded the ministry of Mahabba Network.[2] From 2012 -2019 he was the National and International Coordinator for Mahabba, motivating and mobilising ordinary Christians to unveil Jesus to Muslims. He has now released these positions to the wider Mahabba team.

Gordon picks up the narrative here:

I think that part of the reason I became passionate about working with Muslim people was due to my upbringing. My dad was a Colonel in the British Army, and for a few years, I experienced life amongst Muslims in Aden (now South Yemen). I also spent about ten years as an officer in the army, but on leaving the army I became a Business Director, working in international recruitment, mainly in the Middle East with a focus on Iraq,

Saudi Arabia, and Kuwait. I did regular trips over there and became very familiar with the Islamic world. In 1985, now married with a young child, we sold the business and responded to the call of God to work as missionaries in Africa and Asia with Christ for all Nations.[3]

One of the reasons why I became passionate about reaching Muslims, was because of my experience as the International Campaign Director with German born evangelist Reinhard Bonnke (1940–2019).[3] As a team, we had a Word from Isaiah 45:2, that God was going to go before us and that He was going to 'level the mountains and break through the gates of bronze and the bars of iron, and He was going to give us the treasures in darkness which are stored in secret places.' This scripture was such a profound Scripture to us because God showed us that many of the treasures in darkness are the millions of Muslim people, who are trapped in a system of darkness. God showed us that we had to change our perspective and no longer see them as the enemy but see them as precious people – treasures hidden in darkness. As we prayed for them, we were not to try to reach them with apologetics and polemics: rather we needed to recognise that it would take spiritual warfare to reach them. We had to recognise there was a spirit blinding these precious people. They are precious people who have been blinded by an Islamic veil: they cannot see the light of the Glory of God in Jesus. As we pray for them, something happens.

Years later, in 2006, having sold the business and in mission and ministry for many years, I was called to Oxford and became the Associate Minister of the big student church, St Aldates. When I was praying for clarity around why I had been called to Oxford, I felt God say to me, 'I didn't call you here just for the students, but for Muslims.' As a result, I was soon the co-founder of a movement called the 'Mahabba Network,' which means 'love' in Arabic. In that same year, a young man called Tim Green arrived back in Oxford: he was the son of Michael Green who had been a previous rector of St Aldates. Tim and I became very close friends and together we started Mahabba as a prayer and training movement. I was probably the main driver of the prayer, whilst the training material was largely produced by Tim. Our objective was to train Christians to reach Muslims for Christ.

We began regular prayer meetings, every Tuesday morning at 7.00 am in St Aldates. There was an extraordinary momentum in these prayer meetings. We had many students and people from so many Oxford churches. We developed what we called the Mahabba Community and began to pray and train people - but absolutely nothing happened for two years!

Then suddenly we got the breakthrough and Muslims, one by one, were getting saved. We had a wonderful young African man, who had been a senior Imam, and he was the son of a Mufti. He had an encounter with God in his mosque and became a true believer: following some intense persecution, he came and joined us in our church in Oxford: he was wonderfully gifted and often sat and debated on the streets with Saudi Arabians and other Muslim people.

Tim Green had lived in Pakistan for over 15 years, working with Interserve. He was a real expert at reaching out across the divide and bringing Muslims to Christ. The first course he developed, with Steve Bell's material, was filmed and sent out to many churches under the name 'Friendship First.' It was widely used, including in Australia. The course slowly opens people's eyes, teaching them how to reach out to Muslims. Mahabba has just re-recorded this course: it's well worth following up.[4]

Our second course was called 'Come Follow Me,' a discipleship course for Muslim believers. It teaches people how to follow us as we follow Christ (They call Jesus the Messiah - Isa Al-Masih). The third course was called 'Joining the Family': this focuses on how to integrate Muslim believers into our churches. Most of this work was aimed at the church: how to bring it out of its fear and unbelief concerning Muslims and bring them to a place of real unity and prayer.

For us it was important that we were able to inspire people to dig deep into prayer. So many people go down the route of apologetics and polemics, but if we don't get into the prayer battle, we end up winning people's minds, but we don't win their spirits. Polemics and apologetics are excellent tools, but we can't do it without prayer.

However, Hatun Tash, a Muslim background believer, became a real master of polemics and apologetics.[5] We filmed her answering all the major questions of Muslims. She led about 100 people to the Lord in her first year. She was stabbed at Speakers Corner in London, seeking to preach to Muslims, but is still reaching out to them. She is able to go into mosques and debates with imams, who seem to respect her. They love the fact that she is so passionate in seeking to unveil Jesus to them. They despise the wishy-washy form of Christianity they see in the West.

Often the battle has been created by us. In their eyes, we are the aggressors, who went out into the Middle East pursuing terrorists; over those years it became so polarised, and we became their enemy. They are not the enemy; they are precious people who are desperately searching for God. If you want to talk to anyone about God on the high streets of Oxford, look for a Muslim. To them God is a million miles away, they have no experience of Him. So, our starting point needs to reflect our love for them: if we begin with 'let me tell you my experiences of God,' something will shift in you and in them.

While working with Reinhard Bonnke, I saw that unity and prayer were the essential foundation for reaching Muslims. For example, when I went into the Islamic city of Mombasa, Kenya, I started praying against the strong Muslim presence there and I battled against the spirit of Islam. Then one-day God just stopped me and said, 'Stop doing that, that's not the problem, Islam is not the main blockage here: the main problem here is the pastors of the two big churches in Mombasa who were offended with each other. Get unity between these two and breakthrough will come.'

I invited them and their wives to a restaurant; but I didn't tell them I was bringing the other one! The men were furious that I had tricked them and sat there for twenty minutes not saying a word; the wives were fine, they were chatting away. Then, all of a sudden, the men jumped out of their seats and fell into each other's arms and sobbed. I felt God say, 'Checkmate, it's done, job's done!' Their reconciliation led to breakthrough: the next week I got a letter from the president of Kenya, to go ahead with the crusade in Mombasa, giving us his own meeting ground. There were complaints from the Muslims, but then there was a headline in the newspaper, from President Moi himself, that said, 'Leave Reinhard Bonnke alone.' When we had unity, it took off. We saw thousands of Muslims coming to Christ. I learnt there that unity and prayer were the major components for breakthrough. One of those men went on to grow a church of well over 30,000.

In my time in Oxford as a Church leader, I was responsible for organising the annual 'Love Oxford' meetings which drew together thousands of Christians. When we first formed Mahabba, we had so many churches getting behind the vision, hammering in prayer against the blindness, and then suddenly we got breakthrough. We found the coffee time after the prayer was strategic: that's when people began to share with each other what God had said. Different strategies were brought up – prayer walking the different areas; moving Christians to live in specific Islamic neighbourhoods, our people moved there and started to befriend them; knocking on doors and taking the Jesus DVD and coming back and saying can we tell you more about Jesus: we were developing a band of Christians who loved Muslims.

A major blockage in the church is fear, the fear of Islam, and sometimes almost an unbelief that Muslims can be saved. The second barrier is the thought that it takes 'experts' to reach Muslims: it doesn't take experts at all! Some people who know the least have been just as fruitful because the power of love is unstoppable. When Muslim people feel loved and valued and that we care for them as real people, they change. I say to people 'if you want to reach a Muslim, forget they are Muslim. They are a human being, they have got real needs, they have passions, they have a longing for God. Meet them as a person.' You can say to them, 'I understand you have a different culture, but whatever your needs, please let me pray for you. I'm a believer in Isa-Al-Masih.' I don't know why, but God seems to heal Muslim people much quicker than others! They get answers to prayers, so quickly. Perhaps, Father God is longing for them to really know His love.

We recognised that we have to break out of our prison of fear, unbelief and deception. It says in Isaiah 59:1 that God's hand is not too short to save. It's basically the church's problem that hinders God from reaching Muslims. We have to get into faith, into prayer, and into unity. Unity and prayer will bring the barriers tumbling down.

I have friends near Munich, Germany, in an old Dominican Monastery, that they were inspired to buy from the Catholics and set up a Prayer centre to train people in evangelism. They brought many Arabic speakers together and started to train them, and within a couple of years they had introduced 7,000 of the migrants to Christ. They went into the camps all over Germany and just loved them. A momentum grew at first, but the numbers have lessened now because as they get their roots down, they become more secure in their own faith. We have to reach them when there is a genuine hunger for God, so many are insecure. We need to wise up as a church and realise that God's arm is not too short to save - God's got this!

Before my Oxford days, I had met an Indian Imam from Kuwait who had become a believer during a direct encounter with Jesus. We became friends and in 1997 I helped him start what he called 'the Bible channel' that we beamed into North Africa through the Eutel satellite, and later on into the Middle East as well. This initiative enabled us to begin discipling people watching in their bedrooms and living rooms. We realised that there was a lot of mileage in reaching out to the Muslim world through satellite media.

For example, Iran Alive Ministries, one of many satellite programmes beamed into Iran.[6] They are constantly beaming the gospel into Iran through satellite media. They have reached tens of thousands. The underground Church in Iran, as well as Afghanistan, are two of the fastest growing churches in the world. The local people are so sick and tired of what they hear and see of Islam, and thousands are becoming believers!

During my time back in England after my time with Bonnke; I remember I was looking everywhere for real Kingdom spiritual life. I was leading a group of churches just north of London, but I did not see spiritual life I had seen elsewhere in the world, in Africa, and in Asia. So, I started going 'walkabout,' going to other churches, wherever I heard of something moving.

I ended up going to a Christian Outreach Centre (COC) church in Guildford where I met Ashley and Ruth Schmierer. When Ashley stood up, I saw the power of the Kingdom on him. I ran down the front to get him to pray for me. It felt like I was electrocuted by a million volts and thrown onto the floor and for 45 minutes the fire of God burnt through me. I couldn't walk, so my friends threw me in the car, and as I got into the car, I began to have an open vision of waves of the fire of God sweeping through Islamic nations. I began to roar and shout in tongues because I could see in my spirit, an incredible harvest of millions of souls.

Then in 2014 I was in Cwmbran, Wales, I had another extraordinary experience. I had gone there to see if it really was a revival, I felt so humbled and shamed that I had doubted. Again, I ran down the front and asked for prayer. Just like my previous encounter, it seemed as if I was being electrocuted, maybe for an hour this time. I had the fire of God burning through me and shaking me. All through that time, I just heard God say to me, 'Why won't you believe me for 30 million Muslims.' I kept on shaking my head because I thought this was stupid, I was trying to shake it off. Eventually, I shouted out, 'OK, 30 million Muslims!' As I shouted this out, the presence of God lifted off me, and I stood up knowing that God had deposited faith inside of me. This was to be the beginning of a momentum of God sweeping through the Islamic world.

I have to say that I don't believe that the Western church will have much to do with this. We have to protect Muslim believers from the sterility and compromise of Western Christianity. They need a genuine encounter, a Paul type encounter with God. As they get this, it will become like wildfire – I call it 'the heavenly virus'! If they get infected with Western Christianity, it will be a slow trudge, exactly like what happened in China. They had all those years of missionaries exporting Western Christianity to China, but it was so slow that they only had 800,000 by 1949. Then God allowed the entire religious church to be wiped out and then God began again with just the Holy Spirit moving imperceptibly in the grass roots. Brother Yun got saved during those underground years. Then in 1980 it began like a wildfire sweeping through China. I believe that in the succeeding fifty years over a 100 million people were swept into the Kingdom and it's still growing.

I think we have to realise that God is not sentimental. God may well have to close down the religious churches in the West. Either we change, or God has to start over. I think we are at a very critical moment in history. Take the Anglican Church in England, God help us, something has got to happen! Muslims will not get saved if we stay stuck in our religious traditions. This is why I wrote the book *Make God's Love go Viral*.[7] We have to get to the point where this gospel we carry is viral, it is contagious. I think Muslim people coming to Christ will be a challenge to the Western church, to bring it back to life. We will see Muslim believers so on fire for God that it will challenge our prayer life, challenge our passion, challenge our sacrifice. We currently lack any concept of sacrifice in the Western church.

This is a crucial moment; it may be uncomfortable for the Western church. God longs to see the harvest that He paid for with His own blood. We have to wake up! God has been very strong with me recently about the whole area of prayer. I believe that this begins and ends with prayer. We have to get back to radical prayer – prayer of faith that can move mountains.

Way back in the late 1970s when I was in the British Army, I remember God first challenging me. I was praying in the little chapel every single night for months for something to happen. I eventually had to go on a course in Southern Germany, and on the street one day, a young boy from Ghana walked up to me, I had never met him before. God had told him to talk to me. He said, 'God is desperate to reach through to you.' I was so angry with Him, as I was so desperate to get through to God myself! However, I swallowed my pride, and this young man took me back to his room: he said, 'Listen: God does not answer prayer, God answers the prayer of faith.' He told me, 'Your prayer is digging yourself into a hole of unbelief and disappointment. You have to go back to basics. Take a simple passage, such as Psalm 23, and as you read it and re-read it, begin to thank God for all He's promised to do. Start declaring what He has said, and suddenly faith will come.'

It took me three days of praying Psalm 23 and thanking God. The more I thanked God, the more the unbelief left, and three days later, faith came pouring into my spirit. When I felt faith come, I began to jump and run around the chapel by myself, I was totally alone at the time. Faith had come because I got into a place where the Word was alive in me. We have to get back to Romans 4:18, where it says, 'contrary to hope, (Abraham) in hope believed, so that he became the father of many nations, according to what was spoken.' We have to believe that God is able to do what He has promised. He has paid the price for these Muslim people: they are His precious people, and He has paid for them.

Prayer became the foundational building block of my life, which is why we felt called to join the team in Africa working with Reinhard Bonnke. Many years later after returning from the mission field, I became the Senior pastor of four churches just north of London. Again, prayer was our foundation: we had morning prayer in our church in those days at 6.00 am every morning. If we don't get into faith filled prayer, we develop more and more religion and more and more programmes. We have to understand the whole nature of prayer. Every revival is fuelled by a group of people who *breakthrough* in prayer.

God said to me very clearly, 'Face the facts, don't fuel the fear, find a friend.' If we do those three things, we will find Muslims coming through to Christ. It's love that never fails. Love has to work with faith and faith comes through hearing God in prayer.

I feel we are in a desperate state in the Western church; there is such a religious camp we are locked in. We have to get out and realise that God longs to reach precious Muslim people. In 1997 we created a video series called 'Treasures in darkness: God's passion for Muslim People.' At that time, I was the British Assemblies of God Missions Director for the Muslim

World. We sent that video series to hundreds of churches, to try to wake people up to God's passion to reach Muslim people. It wasn't until 2006 that we started the Mahabba Network here in Oxford, which then spread to about 75 cities in the UK and then in five years we saw the breakthrough. I started working internationally, in Norway, Denmark, France, Belgium and Germany. Then we started in Singapore and with a few small groups in Australia, and South Korea.

My encounter with God in Cwmbran, had been pivotal: I could see it was not going to happen through the Western church, and I was to start looking to the horizon for a sovereign move of God. It will be triggered sovereignly, breaking into Muslim nations supernaturally.

God is on the move: thousands of Iranians across Europe have come to faith, there are some amazing testimonies. For example, a friend called Annahita Parsan was in prison in Iran.[8] She prayed that if the God of the Bible is real, He must get her out of prison, and He did, the very next day! She escaped over the mountains with her baby into Turkey. Her baby tragically died in the freezing cold conditions in the mountains. She kept her baby's body safe in her shoulder bag, but when she got over the mountains, she had a miracle - her baby came back to life! She ended up in Sweden and is now a Lutheran pastor. She has baptised well over 1000 Muslims; she is a friend of the Queen of Sweden who is also a believer. We are in a very strategic moment.

There are many trophies like Annahita. God is on the move without us understanding it. I was recently in Cairo and met a mission leader from an Islamic nation: he had a supernatural meeting with one of the top Imam's who confessed that he is now a 'born again believer' following an encounter with 'the man in white' in his dreams. Multiple thousands have had an encounter with 'the man in white' in their dreams! It's time for the Church in Western nations to understand that God has a plan! He's not worried! He's about to draw back the veil and enable millions of Muslims to encounter the living, Lord Jesus! Come on! This could be our finest hour!

❀   ❀   ❀

Islam Examined

Gordon's testimony shook my foundations. He shattered my perception that Islam must be feared, and that Muslims are so passionate about their faith that they can't be reached with the Gospel. He has shown me how ignorant I was.

Former Deputy Prime minister John Anderson's conversation with Mark Durie and Robert Shumack, from the Melbourne School of Theology, is the raw material for this section. This section aims to provide a context for our thinking and actions towards the 1.6 billion Muslims, the second largest religion in the world.[9]

Muhammad was a man, from Mecca, Arabia, born about 600 AD. He claimed to be a messenger sent from God, firstly to the Arabs and then to the rest of the world. He used Arab armies to spread his message called Islam, which means *submission* to Allah. His campaign was extraordinarily successful, conquering all the way to the Iberian Peninsula. He was a military leader, a judge, a president, the Arabs' supreme leader.

About 25 per cent of Muslims are conservative Muslims who pursue their faith very passionately. Another 50 per cent are traditional Muslims, who may pray five times a day or once a month. They may be Ramadan Muslims who do a few things a year, but they profoundly identify as Muslims, saying, 'these are my people, this is who I am.' Finally, there is another 25 per cent who are either atheist, or non-believing. They are still thought of as Muslims but bad Muslims.

A Caliphate is the idea, or aim, that the world becomes Muslim, under Islamic law. This is the goal of traditional Suni Muslims. They don't accept a democracy but rather a theocracy, and follow Muslim law, only needing judges to interpret it. The DNA of their faith is an autocracy, and an imposition of their faith on others, by force if necessary.

It can be argued that Islam has recently had their *reformation*, the idea of going back to the roots of their faith. Waleed Aly,[10] described this as the creation of al Qaida, and Ayaan Hirsi Ali described it as the creation as ISIS.[11]

Islam is a very practical religion, you have to *do* certain things, you *follow* the law, and Muhammad is the model practitioner. So, reformation is going back to Muhammad's roots, arguably the *radicalisation* of Islam. The question is, how deep is this radicalisation? 75 per cent of Muslims are very sensitive to this move, trying to resist that radical re-shaping of their faith. But the problem is, they don't have the support of their scriptures, so they can't win.

Muslims who want more Sharia law, because they have been taught that this is good, are shocked when they see what Sharia looks like. A good example of this is what has happened in Iran. The majority Shia Muslims overthrew their Shar Mohammad Reza Pahlavi, who ruled from 1941 until 1979. He was succeeded by Ayatollah Khomeini, who became the Supreme Leader of Iran, a position he holds to this day with authoritarian, political and religious authority.

Shia Muslims, believe direct descendants of Muhammad are to be their leaders, as opposed to the Sunni, who believe the best equipped should lead. These two factions have fought since the birth of Islam. The Iranians are predominantly Shia and think they are to be the world leaders of Islam, but oddly Hamas who they support, are Sunni.[12,13]

Studying the Hadiths, namely the traditions of Muhammad, one of the books on warfare is called the *Book of Jihad.* This refers to any war against unbelievers, infidels, in order to advance the cause of Islam. However, to hold this view in the modern world casts the proponents as the enemy. So, they counter this by arguing that Jihad is not bad, rather it's a personal internal struggle for holiness; but this is a misrepresentation of reality, a contradiction of their own writings.

Michael Youssef describes three Jihads.[14] The first, 622-751 AD the initial spread of Islam through modern day, Israel, Lebanon, Jordan, and Syria, then progressing through Egypt, modern day Iraq and Iran and as far east as India. Finally, this initial Jihad conquered most of North Africa and what is now Spain and Portugal.

The second Jihad began 1302 AD with the dawn of the Ottman Empire, initially focused on the destruction of the Byzantian Kingdom, marked by the fall of Constantinople in 1453. This defeat sparked the Crusader Wars under the initiative of Pope Eugenius IV, as a just war against the invaders. The Ottoman Empire was crumbling by 1899 and was finally defeated 1924, when its territories were partitioned after WWI by the Treaty of Sèvres.

The third Jihad has already begun.[15] This time, it is primarily a *stealth war*, waged by radical ideologues against the values of Western civilization from within our own borders. To see this Jihad as isolated deadly terror attacks by crazed fanatics who do not represent the core of Islam, is to buy into one of this Jihad's most powerful weapons, the concept of Islamophobia.

Islamophobia has gripped most Western ruling elites to the extent that they don't want to be seen to offend their Muslim brothers or they will provoke all out attacks the likes of which the West has not seen yet. But this unwillingness to stand against Islam has opened the flood gates, not only to mass Muslim immigration into the West but also into the heart of Western culture.

Islam is intensely attuned to victimhood, which explains their synergy with woke ideology. Muhammad justified Jihad in terms of victimhood, it's better to kill than be persecuted. However, if we look at all world cultures and ethnicities, the Jews have been the biggest victims. We need not look further than WWII's Holocaust and the recent 7th October 2023 Hamas invasion of Israel. Yet only hours after this latest atrocity the Jews were being accused of committing genocide, apartheid, and occupation of lands not their own.

Islamic education focuses on obedience, conformity and not asking questions. So, their culture is not used to the Western idea of questioning everything. If you always feel you are a victim, it disempowers you and you don't take responsibility for yourself. Ayaan Hirsi Ali[11] talks a lot about this and sees the Muslim world held back from innovation and the potential for cultural development due to their lack of an enquiring mind, and entrepreneurial spirit.

What does God say?

We might see God's hand of blessing on Issac and his judgment against Ishmael and choose to follow the blessed and ignore the victim. But look at God's response to Ishmael and his mother, He did not dismiss the Arabs:

And God heard the voice of the lad. Then the angel of God called to Hagar out of heaven, and said to her, 'What ails you, Hagar? Fear not, for God has heard the voice of the lad where he is. Arise, lift up the lad and hold him with your hand, for I will make him a great nation.' (Genesis 21:17-18)

Islam is a relatively modern faith, founded about 610 AD in Mecca by Muhammad, much later than the beginnings of the Arabic people, approximately 2050 BC. So how does God want us to respond to Muslims?

For God so loved the world that He gave His only begotten Son, that whoever believes in Him should not perish but have everlasting life. (John 3:16)

At the start of this chapter, Gordon's emphasis was on the *love of God,* with his description of the Mahabba movement that means *love* in Arabic.[2] This is such a contrast for the Muslim to grasp, when all they have ever known is a striving to be good enough by keeping laws, a religion of *rules and works* compared to a faith of *trust and acceptance.*

One of the reasons Muslims do come to Christ, is that they *encounter* Jesus and find Him to be so radically different from Muhammad. So, the first step in leading a Muslim to the Saviour, is not to *argue* them into faith by comparing Jesus with Muhammad but rather *demonstrating* the love of Jesus. It's when they *see love in action,* Jesus, who is full of grace, forgiveness, and peace; in contrast Muhammad, who was full of hatred, revenge, and the sword. It is then that they can make the radical leap into Christ.

What holds Christian's back from sharing their faith with Muslims? The fear of the unknown, the fear of the unpredictable, so easily paralyse and blinds our eyes to the bigger picture. For example, a 2024 report (Don Shenk)[16] indicated that a million Iranians had come to Christ resulting in authorities having to shut down 50,000 out of 75,000 mosques. What is God doing and what is He saying?

We read about the various Islamic Jihads and try to get our head around the idea of the Third Jihad being a *stealth war* well underway in the West.[14,15] We see the left capitulating to Israelophobia offering an open door to radical Islam out of fear of reprisals and we inadvertently buy into the fear of the unknown.

I am sure God does not want us to be ignorant of the present dangers and wilfully blind to the devil's strategy. But rather to 'be sober, be vigilant; because our adversary the devil walks about like a roaring lion, seeking whom he may devour' (1 Peter 5:8), because 'He who is in you is greater than he who is in the world' (1 John 4:4). Islamists are to be *loved* into the Kingdom; they are not *the enemy*!

Picking up Gordon's road map, we must recognise that we are in *spiritual warfare* (Chapter 13). 'Face the facts, don't fuel the fear, find a friend.' Explore the Mahabba Network in your community, and pair up with the ones and twos who share your awakening heart for Muslims. Commit to prayer, which will be a long-term strategy requiring spiritual stamina until *suddenly* we find *breakthrough*. I have a sneaking suspicion our prayer partners will not necessarily be from our own denomination and tradition; expect to be surprised by unity! Then seek God for your local and personal strategy.

Let me finish with my own journey. In writing up this chapter, I have made connection with my local Mahabba Network, and I am praying into a local Muslim family who live near me. For many years now, they have brought us an offering of a meal each Ramadan. In the past, I have politely thanked them and felt bad that I have not returned their hospitality. But now, I am prayerfully working on ways to engage with this couple, and God is beginning to answer. Finally:

Pray for the peace of Jerusalem: 'May they prosper who love you. Peace be within your walls, Prosperity within your palaces.' For the sake of my brethren and companions, I will now say, 'Peace be within you.' (Psalm 122:6-8)[17]

Footnotes

[1] Hattaway, Paul (2002). *The Heavenly Man: The Remarkable True Story of Chinese Christian Brother Yun*. Lion Hudson Publishing. https://koorong.com/product/the-heavenly-man-the-remarkable-true-story-of_9781854245977?srsltid=AfmBOopJwkZkwu2DK59BkO2iLAR4JVb-rDUVIuFn_UCBmEwL2kXV9gID
[2] Mahabba Network (n.d.). *Welcome To The Mahabba Network*. Retrieved October 24, 2025, from https://www.mahabbanetwork.com/
[3] Christ For All Nations (n.d.). *Reinhard Bonnke 1940 – 2019*. Retrieved October 24, 2025, from https://reinhard.cfan.org/

[4] Interserve Australia (n.d.). *Would you walk with us?* Retrieved October 24, 2025, from https://interserve.org.au/learn/resources/video/

[5] Hatun Tash DCCI Ministries (2021, July 26). *Hatun Tash Stabbed at Speakers' Corner.* [Video]. YouTube. https://www.youtube.com/watch?v=QeCaTccewcM

[6] Iran Alive Ministries (n.d.). *Help Exiled Leaders Find Safety – And Keep The Gospel Alive.* Retrieved October 25, 2025, from https://iranalive.org/

[7] Hickson, Gordon (2024). *Make God's Love Go Viral: Activating 'the heavenly virus' of The Kingdom through understanding Christ's Cross.* Independently Published. https://www.amazon.com.au/Make-Gods-Love-Viral-understanding/dp/B0D7HYXXQC

[8] Parsan, Annahita (2017). *Stranger No More: A Muslim Refugee's Story of Harrowing Escape, Miraculous Rescue, and the Quiet Call of Jesus,* Thomas Nelson. *https://www.amazon.com.au/Stranger-No-More-Harrowing-Miraculous/dp/0718095715*

[9] John Anderson Media (2025, March 28). *Islam Examined - Dr. Mark Durie and Dr. Richard Shumack.* [Video]. YouTube. https://www.youtube.com/watch?v=E1GDH3GLY8o&t=1345s

[10] Aly, Waleed (2008). *People Like Us.* Picador Australia. https://www.amazon.com.au/People-Like-Us-Waleed-Aly-ebook/dp/B003R509TW

[11] Ali, Ayaan Hirsi (2021). *Prey: Immigration, Islam, and the Erosion of Women's Rights.* Harper. https://www.amazon.com.au/Prey-Immigration-Erosion-Womens-Rights/dp/0062857878

[12] Council of Foreign Relations (2023, April 27). *The Sunni-Shia Divide.* https://www.cfr.org/article/sunni-shia-divide

[13] The Telegraph (2023, November 18). *Dennis Prager: Supporting Hamas is like supporting Nazis in WW2.* [Video]. YouTube. https://www.youtube.com/watch?v=OudTXT_9CzY

[14] Youssef, Michael (2019). *The Third Jihad, Overcoming Radical Islam's Plan for the West.* Tyndale House Publishers. https://www.amazon.com.au/Third-Jihad-Overcoming-Radical-Islams/dp/1496431502

[15] Clarion Project (2015, October 28). *The Third Jihad: Radical Islam's Vision for America - HD Version.* [Video]. YouTube. https://www.youtube.com/watch?v=dytL0a5YePw&rco=1

[16] CBN News (2024, July 26). *Jesus Revolution in Iran - The Global Lane July 25, 2024*. [Video]. YouTube. https://www.youtube.com/watch?v=NDVgOdPXqDc

[17] Saul Wilks, Bonnie (n.d.). *Pray for the Peace of Jerusalem Gateway Centre for Israel*. Retrieved October 25, 2025, from https://centerforisrael.com/article/pray-for-the-peace-of-jerusalem/

CHAPTER 15 - ISRAEL

Teri Kempe's Story

Teri Kempe had a job she loved in Sydney, Australia when her life took an unexpected turn. Having just reached retirement age, she heard the unmistakable call of God to move to Fiji as a missionary volunteer. With only her aged pension for financial support, she left her family, friends, and church for five life-changing years. *Grace Upon Grace* (2020) is the story of Teri's five amazing years as a missionary.[1]

This is her story:

I was born in London, England, a Cockney. My parents bought a boat, and my first three years was spent afloat, sailing around the coast in our converted fishing trawler from Bristol, down the Bristol Channel, the English Channel and then up the Thames. Then my parents bought a house on an island in the Thames called Pharaoh's Island.

When I finished school at 16, my parents decided to emigrate to Australia; we settled in Melbourne. It was there I met and married my husband, who a few years later got a job in Fiji. I worked for the Bible Society and Scripture Union as a volunteer. We adopted two little girls, Fijian Indians, from an orphanage, and then I had my first natural born son. We returned to Australia and settled in Emerald, Central Queensland for six years, where two more sons were born. Then in 1987 we came to Sydney and sadly our family broke up and I was divorced.

Soon after that I began meeting with people I had known while in Fiji. In 2013, one of them, a pastor friend, encouraged me to come back to Fiji for a holiday. I went, and while I was there, the Lord said to me 'This is where I want you to be.' I came back to Sydney, packed up my life and went as a missionary volunteer with just my suitcase for five years, returning to Sydney just before COVID. My time in Fiji was a wonderful time of healing, of learning, of growing in the Lord and learning to trust Him for everything.

I left Fiji in 2019 thinking it would have been my forever home, but to my surprise, the Lord provided me some wonderful accommodation in Sydney through a charity. All my children and my growing grandchildren were here. Then, in 2023 my youngest son decided to emigrate to New Zealand, so I have been flying back and forth to New Zealand. I have four grandchildren in New Zealand, and eleven in Sydney.

When I went back to Fiji in December 2013, for my second stint; I was only there two weeks, when I was invited to a meeting of the International Christian Embassy Jerusalem (ICEJ) – Fiji Branch. I had never heard of them, I had no idea what they were about, but the pastor with whom I was working, was the National Director of the ICEJ, Fiji.

After the meeting, he said to me, 'You're coming to Israel'! I said, 'OK, on my pension, as if'! He said, 'someone will pay for you to go.' They had a tour going every year, since the early 1990s, for the Feast of Tabernacles each October. I was involved in planning the 2014 pilgrimage, as I had become the secretary of ICEJ, not thinking for a moment that I would be going.

Then in May of that year a missionary from Singapore came to our little mission school in Fiji. He blessed the school amazingly. As he was leaving, I was literally putting his bag into the back of the taxi to take him to the airport, he turned to me and said, 'I am putting $10,000 into your bank account for you to go to Israel.' You could have knocked me over with a feather!

He paid for everything. He paid for me, the pastor, and the school chaplain. This was the 2014 pilgrimage. I then went again, 2015, 16, 17, 18 and 19! Then there was COVID. Then in 2023 I went with ICEJ, Australia. We were there when the October 7th war started.

So here we are in 2025, and I have just resigned from ICEJ because I am now here in New Zealand, and my priorities have changed. I volunteered with ICEJ for ten years. Their mandate is, 'comfort, yes, comfort My people' (Isaiah 40:1), to comfort the Jews. They are extremely careful not to proselytise, being very conscious of the historical persecution of the Jews by Christians going right back to the Crusades, and the Holocaust.

ICEJ has poured millions of dollars into Israel. That's wonderful. I know the heart of the people who are giving, because they are so grateful to Jews for preserving the Bible and giving us Jesus. In the end the only thing to save any of us is Jesus. Jesus is the only way.

I could not have prepared myself for the impact of going to Israel in 2014. It was absolutely life changing. I have an arts degree in Biblical Studies, I have studied the archaeology of Israel, and I was very familiar with the Bible. I had read the Bible many, many times, even though I only became a Christian at 16. The Lord had regularly spoken to me through the Word. When I went to Israel, suddenly the Bible came even more alive!

I went to places where the events I had read about took place. For example, we were going along in a tour bus, the tour guide told the driver, 'Stop the bus'! We were told to leave everything on the bus to get out as we are only going to be a few minutes. The guide said, 'There is a little stream there, I want you to each to pick a round stone.' The stream was very shallow, and the stones were beautifully smooth. We each picked a stone and stood there!

The guide then pointed up the hill and said, 'There's Goliath'! This was the actual spot where David had fought Goliath. Being at the actual place was really impacting. Then going to the Garden Tomb and going inside the empty tomb. Then looking up at Golgotha. Visiting the Western Wall and praying.

I had a vision when I was at the Wall. I was praying in the lady's section. I was sitting on one of the white plastic chairs, it was the very last day of our tour. My sight started to blur. I thought I was going to faint, so I put my head between my knees. I then lifted my head. I no longer felt faint, but when I looked at the people in front of me the backs of their heads were just a blur. I thought there was something wrong with my eyes, so I put my head down again. When I brought my head up the second time I saw the people in front of me clearly, they each had around their heads a ring of diamonds.

I realised I was seeing a vision, but I didn't know what it meant. My friend who had been praying right at the Wall came back and said we must go. So we went back to our hotel, but that meant passing by the Garden Tomb. We decided to go in. I had my Bible with me at the time, and it opened at John Chapter 4 where Jesus was speaking to the women at the well, and He told her that 'Salvation is of the Jews' (v. 22). Then I understood what my vision meant. I had seen Jews with diamonds around their heads; they had been the carriers of the Word for us. It was so impacting, life changing, to experience it and to realise God was speaking to me.

To me the Word is very precious and the fact that the Jewish people have preserved it for us, means we owe them a great debt of gratitude. I was beginning to realise they were the vehicle God has used, and the Jewish people have had that responsibility. That vision was in 2018.

The Bible had really come alive for me. From then on, when I was reading the Bible, I was picturing the places where things had happened. For example, we spent a lot of time at Capernaum which is where Jesus lived, at Peter's mother-in-law house, we went to where Jesus walked on the water. We worshiped on the Sea of Galilee. All those places became so real; it was no longer just a nice story in a book. These events really happened at a place and at a time in history. Jesus was a real person like you and me.

I think the lens through which I viewed the gospel was centred on moral issues, goodness, kindness and compassion. But then I realised that Jesus was a real person who had lived, eaten, drank, walked, and taught on those streets.

When I climbed up the Mount of Olives, I realised how steep it was, and that Jesus had done this so many times. We walked to the Pool of Siloam and the Via Dolorosa where He carried his cross.

Another time in Jerusalem I had an amazing vision that was deeply impacting. There is a little chapel in the middle of the old city, on the Via Dolorosa which is where it is said Jesus stopped and put his hand on the wall. They have made it so it's like a handprint. There were thousands of pilgrims going back and forth, but I put my hand into that place, and it was as if I was the only person there and I was saying 'Crucify Him.' What would I have done if I was in that crowd? How would I have reacted knowing that everyone around me was calling for Jesus' death? That was really confronting, and I had to repent. It was so impacting to realise the sacrifice Jesus made and that no one spoke for Him.

Given the opportunity, I would say to the Christian church, that Jesus is most certainly alive. I have just been back to Fiji; we had a camp for 450 students. The theme of the camp was 'The Coming King.' Jesus is coming back next time as judge; He is not coming back as saviour. There will be no second chances when He comes back. At the camp the talks were very strongly worded, and Scripture based. On the final day of the camp there was a testimony from a young leader that I knew. I was sitting in the front row and saw everything.

Part way into his testimony, he clutched his chest and collapsed on the stage. Paramedics rushed in and took him out to perform CPR. A deathly hush gripped the crowd.

Then six men came in carrying a huge table and on top of it was a huge flaming cauldron, followed by the young man who miraculously looked just fine. He said, 'You don't want to come here, this is hell!'

It was so realistic. 450 young people were repenting, weeping, confessing all kinds of things. The speaker spoke as if he had not given his life to Christ, and he had gone to hell. Then we realised it was a drama. It certainly was very dramatic! Things like that triggered a whole lot in me, for example, that time is short. I need to be bold and courageous. I need to speak the truth about Jesus.

❀   ❀   ❀

The Arab - Jew Conflict

Teri Kempe's connection with Israel is profound. She would emphatically claim that this connection has been orchestrated by God. In order for us to understand the context, let's review some of the facts, some of the history of the Arab - Jew conflict.

The land mass of current Israel is tiny, one of the smallest sovereign nations in the world. At its narrowest point it is only 14 km E - W, and 424 km N – S.

Most of us will be familiar with Biblical history but let me highlight a few salient features. About 1000 BC King David's Kingdom was established, with Jerusalem the capital, where King Solomon built the First Temple about 957 BC.[2]

In 515 BC there was the Great Return from Babylonian exile, funded by the Babylonians, and the Second Temple established. The Romans invade in 63 BC, and the land of Judea becomes a vasal state to the Roman

Empire. The Second Temple was destroyed by the Romans in 70 AD. So, for most of Biblical times, the land of Israel was the land of the Jews.

There was a massive revolt by the Jews against the Romans in 132-136 AD known as the Bar Kochba Revolt, which was nearly successful, but in the aftermath, the Romans renamed Israel, 'Palestine' as an insult to the Jews, after their arch enemy the Philistines.

The religion of Islam was not founded until around the 7th Century AD, when the Arabs took over the land in 636 AD. The Crusades followed, a series of religious wars initiated by the medieval papacy, as a response to the expansion of Islam and the desire to reclaim the Holy Land for Christians. By 1291 the Crusaders were finally defeated, and the Muslim Ottoman Empire was established from 1517 – 1918.

Now we have arrived at the dawn of the modern era. Whose land was it Jews, or Arabs? The law of first occupation would give it to the Jews, since 1000 BC and the law of longest tenure would also go to the Jews, 11 centuries verses four centuries for the Arabs.

The Ottomans prevented any Jewish land purchases during their rule, but some Jews did manage to do back door deals with the Arabs and made some settlements there, places of refuge to flee to from parts of the world where they were being persecuted.

The First Aliyah (going up, returning to the Holy Land) was in 1882, mostly by Russian Jews escaping the pogroms in their homeland.[3] The Zionist Movement, led by Theadore Herzl, began in 1897 with the aim to establish an independent Jewish State.[4]

Britain published the Balfour Declaration in 1917, stating their intention that there would be a Jewish Homeland in Israel. After WWI, the British were given the mandate of what was then called Palestine. However, they walked back on their promise of the Balfour Declaration and divided off over half the land to the east, and gave it to the Arabs, known as Trans Jordan.

In the lead up to WWII, trying to appease the Arabs, the British restricted Jewish immigration to 75,000 per year, but despite this the Jews still sided with Britain while the Arabs went with Hitler. Post WWII the British still limited immigration despite the Holocaust.[5]

On 14th May 1948 the British Mandate ended, and Israel declared its independence. In their founding documents they asked the Arabs to stay. But all the surrounding Arab countries declared war on Israel. Their aim, to destroy the Jewish homeland at its birth. They told the Arabs living in Israel to get out so they could destroy Israel. The Jews fought back and miraculously, retained most of the land they were given when the British left.

By 1964 the Arab states decided that they needed a propaganda initiative against the Jews, so they established the Palestinian Liberation Organisation (PLO), but it soon became a terrorist group calling for the destruction of the State of Israel.[6]

Throughout my lifetime, the Middle East has been the amphitheatre for perhaps the most intractable conflicts on earth. The Jews wanting a homeland to escape persecution while the Arabs want the whole of the Middle East for themselves. This is a gross simplification even though it might be the core of the argument.

Concluding this historical overview, let's look at perhaps the most often touted peace initiative, *the two-state solution*.[7,8] This has been a dream for decades, Jews and Palestinians living side by side in neighbouring territories. Jews have always been willing to consider this, but the Arabs simply want the Jews gone from the land as they say, from the Jordan River to the Mediterranean Sea. Despite many opportunities they have never agreed to any peace settlement.

However, in line with this strategy, Israel unilaterally disengaged from the Gaza Strip and evacuating all their inhabitants, effectively creating the first Palestinian State in 2005. Almost immediately, Hamas gained power and has ruled for 18 years and created a population of sociopaths, through their control of the education system, with their single objective, the destruction of the State of Israel. What civilised nation would live alongside a neighbour that continually shoots rockets into its cities and periodically mounts the horrors of October 7[th,] 2023?

It must be said most Islamic *people* would be happy to exist alongside, or within, a Jewish state, respecting their borders, but the Iranian regime with its proxies, the Houthis, Hezbollah and Hamas are hell-bent on the annihilation of all Jews and the State of Israel.

At the time of writing, it seems that the horrors of October 7[th,] 2023, put the final nail in the two-state solution with the realisation that Israel's enemies will not rest until all the Jews are eliminated.

Replacement Theology

There is a lot of ignorance amongst Christians and non-Christians about Israel and the Jewish people, arguably on account of this wrong theology. Teri, certainly does not hold this theology, she is a most passionate Israel supporter, and I aim to show that this position is God's will for all Christians.

Replacement Theology, also known as Supersessionism, argues that the Jews are no longer the people of God and that the promises made to Israel physically in the Old Testament, are now only to be interpreted spiritually and metaphorically as applying to the Christian church.[9,10] Passages like Galatians 3:28 'There is neither Jew nor Greek,' and Romans 9:6, 'For they are not all Israel who are of Israel,' have been taken out of context and interpreted to indicate God has finished with the Jews because they crucified Christ.[10]

Pastor Gary Hamrick, has been most strident in his repudiation of Replacement Theology:[11]

> *The Catholic Church in the twelfth century believed this, and thus the Crusader Wars, marching through Europe slaughtering thousands of Jews and then headed into the Holy Land slaughtering thousands more and thousands of Muslims too in the process.*
>
> *In addition, Martin Luther did some great things, nailing his thesis on the door of the Wittenberg Church and starting the Protestant Reformation. But he also wrote a lot of anti-Semitic things, because he also believed in Supersessionism, that the church has replaced Israel, and that God no longer has any purpose for the Jewish people.*
>
> *Luther's views were so anti-Semitic that Adolf Hitler hailed him in Mine Kampf,[12] quoting him as reasons, in part, for the slaughtering of the Jews in WWII. We have to know our Bibles, as a wrong interpretation of one verse* (Romans 9:6), *has led to the slaughter of millions of Jews. God is not done with the Jewish people.*

I put it to you, while on one level the West was repulsed, and violated by the Holocaust perpetrated by the Nazi Regime against the Jews in WWII, there has always been an underlying, anti-Semitism that can be traced back to an error in an understanding of Scriptures first made by the Early Church leaders such as Irenaeus, Augustine, and Athanasius.[10]

If this is true, it might partly explain the inordinate rise in anti-Semitism the West has seen since October 7th, 2023. That being said let's examine our local church, are their undercurrents of Replacement Theology in plain sight? One way of conducting such an examination is to analyse the rhetoric from church leadership. If they are equivocal, not being able to side with either Israel or the Palestinians, that probably indicates they are accepting of Replacement Theology.

What does God say?

Teri's testimony is one of *listening* to God and being *obedient* to His call. Her going to Israel and walking in the footsteps of historic Biblical characters had a life changing impact.

I have been to Israel twice and would return like a shot if I had the chance. Have you been? If not, have you a desire to go? Israel is the birthplace of the Christian faith, 'salvation is of the Jews' (John 4:22).

Murray Dixon's (1988) *The rebirth and restoration of Israel,* is a great place to start:[13]

> *1988 marks the 40th anniversary of Israel's rebirth as a nation. Was the establishment of a Jewish homeland in 1948 merely an act of political good will by the United Nations, or a sovereign act of God, fulfilling Scripture? Has God forsaken Israel and turned his attention to the church? These and many other questions are addressed. The author illustrates the church's Jewish roots, the place of Israel in God's purposes, and most importantly of all, the responsibility of the church towards Israel.*

Further great Scriptural insight can be found in Billye Brim's, *Judgement of the nations for how they treat Israel.*[14] I also found Derek

Prince's (1915 – 2003) teaching about Israel, to be very profound and Scripture based. His teachings are still available on YouTube.[15]

Isaiah 62:6-7 calls us to be 'watchmen on your walls, O Jerusalem.' The verses go on to say they will 'give Him no rest till He establishes, and till He makes Jerusalem a praise in the earth.' That's not happened yet!

In response to Replacement Theology, I am reminded of Jeremiah 31:35-37, where God says, only if the sun and moon vanish, will Israel ever cease from being a nation before Him. Jeremiah 33:23-26:

Moreover the Word of the Lord came to Jeremiah, saying, "Have you not considered what these people have spoken, saying, 'The two families which the Lord has chosen, He has also cast them off'? Thus they have despised My people, as if they should no more be a nation before them. "Thus says the Lord: 'If My covenant is not with day and night, and if I have not appointed the ordinances of heaven and earth, then I will cast away the descendants of Jacob and David My servant, so that I will not take any of his descendants to be rulers over the descendants of Abraham, Isaac, and Jacob. For I will cause their captives to return, and will have mercy on them.' "

In other words, as long as the sun shines by day and the moon by night, God's not done with Israel and its people, and his last word is that He will have mercy on them. These Scriptures also herald the means by which this blessing will come, namely through Jesus, a descendant of Jacob and David.

I believe God most certainly has a plan for the Jewish people; He loves them dearly. Consider Romans 11:16-33. God is warning Gentile believers not to be proud, but to fear and to continue in his goodness and to stand by faith, as we were grafted into the true olive tree from a wild olive tree (v 19 & 23), and became a partaker of the root and fatness of the olive tree, blindness has happened in part to Israel until the fullness of the gentiles has come in (v 25).

Gentile believers enjoy all the promises and certainly have become partakers as believers in Jesus Christ and are coming into the commonwealth of Israel.

There are so many Scriptures that describe the relationship of Gentile Christians with the Jewish people. For example, Ephesians 2:11-13:

Therefore remember that you, once Gentiles in the flesh—who are called Uncircumcision by what is called the Circumcision made in the flesh by hands— that at that time you were without Christ, being aliens from the commonwealth of Israel and strangers from the covenants of promise, having no hope and without God in the world. But now in Christ Jesus you who once were far off have been brought near by the blood of Christ.

From 1948 the fledgling nation of the State of Israel, was surrounded by nations stronger and with armies much more powerful, but against all odds, God has been their keeper. Fulfilment of many promises to bring them back to the land and the fact that the language of Hebrew would be spoken again in that land. Zephaniah 3:8-9 reads:

'Therefore, wait for Me,' says the Lord, 'Until the day I rise up for plunder; My determination is to gather the nations to My assembly of kingdoms, to pour on them My indignation, all My fierce anger; all the earth shall be devoured with the fire of My jealousy. For then I will restore to the peoples a pure language, that they all may call on the name of the Lord, to serve Him with one accord.'[16]

I am amazed at the fulfilment of Scripture, that's unfolding right in our own time. To those that say God has done away with Israel, He hasn't! We, the church, owe so much to the Jewish people. To the Jews came the prophets, to the Jews came the patriarchs, to the Jews came Jesus our Messiah, of the lineage of the Jews. What about Revelation 21:10-14?

And he carried me (John) away in the Spirit to a great and high mountain, and showed me the great city, the holy Jerusalem, descending out of heaven from God, having the glory of God. Her light was like a most precious stone, like a jasper stone, clear as crystal. Also she had a great and high wall with twelve gates, and twelve angels at the gates, and names written on them, which are the names of the twelve tribes of the children of Israel: three gates

221

on the east, three gates on the north, three gates on the south, and three gates on the west. Now the wall of the city had twelve foundations, and on them were the names of the twelve apostles of the Lamb.

Clearly the New Jerusalem will have the twelve Jewish tribes of Israel and the twelve Jewish apostles built into the very fabric of this glorious city.

Christian tradition has it that all Jesus' disciples were martyred with the exception of Judas Iscariot who committed suicide, and John who was exiled to the Isle of Patmos and gave us the book of Revelation. So, God used Jewish people to bring the gospel to the Gentiles and they did it at great cost, persecution, and regularly martyrdom. We owe them an immeasurable debt of gratitude.

This brings a cry from my heart, why are we so silent? Why are we not standing with the Jewish people? Jesus himself came in that lineage, and when He comes again, we see in the book of Revelation, that He is to be known as the 'Lamb slain from the foundation of the world.' (Revelation 13:8), and He is also known as the 'Lion of the tribe of Judah, the Root of David' (Revelation 5:5). He clearly identifies with his Jewish roots.

Many churches today fail to focus on Biblical prophecy and the book of Revelation in particular, as they shy away from potential controversy. So, I encourage all believers to read these Scriptures for themselves with fresh eyes and ask the Lord to show us, our responsibility towards Israel and the Jews.[17,18] Right from the beginning, God said:

I will bless those who bless you, and I will curse him who curses you; and in you all the families of the earth shall be blessed. (Genesis 12:3)

Footnotes

[1] Kempe, Teri (2020). *Grace Upon Grace: My Five Amazing Years in Fiji.* Initiate Media Pty Ltd https://www.amazon.com.au/Grace-Upon-Five-Amazing-Years/dp/0648825914

[2] Shapiro, Ben (2021, June 6). *Here's the Truth About the Israeli-Palestinian Conflict (A Comprehensive History).* [Video]. YouTube. https://www.youtube.com/watch?v=dEoVzKyD_IM

[3] Jewish Virtual Library (n.d.). *The First Aliyah (1882-1903).* Retrieved October 25, 2025, from https://www.jewishvirtuallibrary.org/the-first-aliyah-1882-1903

[4] Boston University (n.d.). *The Zionist Movement: Documents.* Retrieved October 25, 2025, from https://www.bu.edu/mzank/Jerusalem/tx/zionism.htm

[5] Uris, Leon M. (1958). *Exodus.* Doubleday & Company. https://www.amazon.com.au/Exodus-Leon-Uris/dp/0553258478

[6] Charif, Maher (n.d.). *Palestine Liberation Organization (II) From the Limelight to the Backstage.* Interactive Encyclopaedia of the Palestine Question. Retrieved October 25, 2025, from https://www.palquest.org/en/highlight/6592/palestine-liberation-organization-ii

[7] Culture Wolf (2025, March 18). *Douglas Murray Addresses The Possibility of an Israel/Palestine Two-State Solution.* [Video]. YouTube. https://www.youtube.com/watch?v=ZFcz8VskdCU

[8] Heyalma (n.d.). *What are the proposed solutions to the Israeli-Palestinian conflict?* Retrieved October 25, 2025, from https://www.heyalma.com/israel-guide/what-are-the-proposed-solutions-to-the-israeli-palestinian-conflict/

[9] Jewish Voice (n.d.). *What is the source of Replacement theology or Supersession?* Retrieved October 25, 2025, from https://www.jewishvoice.org/learn/replacement-theology

[10] Harvey, Richard (2021, August 27). *Is Replacement Theology Biblical?* Jews for Jesus. https://jewsforjesus.org/answers/is-replacement-theology-biblical

[11] Hamrick, Gary (2024, May 21). *Israel: Past, Present, and Future - Romans 9-11.* Cornerstone Chapel – Leesburg, VA. [Video]. YouTube. https://www.youtube.com/watch?v=AT0mytzjtyM&t=1456s

[12] Paras, Emily (2008). The Darker Side of Martin Luther. *Constructing the Past*, 9(1). https://digitalcommons.iwu.edu/constructing/vol9/iss1/4

[13] Dixon, Murray (1988). *The rebirth and restoration of Israel*. Sovereign World Ltd. https://www.worldofbooks.com/en-au/products/rebirth-and-restoration-of-israel-book-murray-dixon-9781852400125

[14] Brim, Billye (n.d.). *Judgment of the Nations for How They Treat Israel*. Retrieved October 26, 2025, from https://billyebrim.org/product-tag/judgement/

[15] Derek Prince with Subtitles (1993, January 18). *The Uniqueness of Israel: God's Prophetic Calendar Pt 3 Of Israel, Past, Present and Future*. [Video]. YouTube. https://www.youtube.com/watch?v=y9nzMCH5bvU

[16] Twelves, Jim (2024, August 21). Western Multiculturalism – Fail! Israeli Multiculturalism – Success! *Daily Declaration*. https://dailydeclaration.org.au/2024/08/21/western-vs-israeli-multiculturalism/

[17] Behold Israel with Amir Tsarfati (2019, August 18). *Amir Tsarfati: The Deception of the Nations*. [Video]. YouTube. https://www.youtube.com/watch?v=f85M-k6inDA

[18] The Telegraph (2023, November 18). *Dennis Prager: Supporting Hamas is like supporting Nazis in WW2*. [Video]. YouTube. https://www.youtube.com/watch?v=OudTXT_9CzY&t=2232s

AFTERWORD

How has *While We Were Sleeping* made you feel? While writing this book I have been challenged, by some who have said to me; 'doesn't dwelling on all this stuff, make you depressed?' I reply, 'not at all; I have never felt so energised, and excited about the future!' Waking up for me has been liberating. My dream is that it will also be for you.

Our Christian faith continually calls us to be *strong and courageous* (Joshua 1:7), and not to be *afraid* (Isaiah 41:10) or *downcast* (Psalm 42:11), because God is with us. The issues we have considered are extremely challenging and obviously fill us with much grief; so out of self-preservation, we are naturally tempted to draw the curtains, think happy thoughts, and go back to sleep.

Wednesday 10th September 2025, Charlie Kirk, fearless advocate for conservative values, was assassinated in Utah Valley University, United States of America, while debating transgender shooters with a crowd of 3,000 young people.[1] This tragedy brought home for me that this is not a debate about political preferences but rather it is a battle for truth over lies, good over evil and love over hate. If our response to an issue is, 'that's political, I don't want to offend someone who doesn't hold my view'; we are rolling over and going back to sleep.

How can the murder of the innocents, the indoctrination of our young people with Marxist ideology, and the persecution of Jews, be dismissed as merely political perspectives?

It is cowardly to set aside challenging issues by saying, 'I don't do politics' or 'Christians are called to love and respect diversity.' We have now entered a theatre of war when, just as in Bible times, Christ followers are hated for their beliefs, standards, and lifestyles. Arguably, if we are not hated, that could indicate we have compromised and assimilated with the prevailing culture.

Let's take the imagery from the start of Joshua's leadership of the Israelites. Joshua was called to arise, with all the people, to cross the river Jordan, and possess the land promised to their fathers and to end their forty years of wandering (Joshua 1:2). They had been sleepwalked through the wilderness, living out their faith in survival mode.

Let's see Charlie Kirk's martyrdom as our *wake-up call* to rise-up, cease being apologetic and accommodating, and take back what the enemy has stolen.

Under Joshua's leadership, the ark of the covenant of the Lord, born by the Levites, moved first, and the people followed. However, they had to hold back nearly a kilometre, so that they 'might know the way by which they must go,' for they had 'not passed that way before' (Joshua 3:4). This was the first time any of them had taken such a step, therefore the call to prayer, the seeking of wisdom and direction, was vital for the success of the mission.

When all the people had crossed over the Jordan on dry land, God directed them to select twelve stones from the riverbed, one for each of the twelve tribes of the Children of Israel. They were to be erected as a monument in Gilgal, just east of Jericho, a memorial to remind them of the hand of God that had brought them into the land and a teaching tool for their children and their grandchildren and for all the generations yet to be born.

Then, Joshua looked up and saw 'a Man with a drawn sword.' He asked Him, 'Are you for us or for our adversaries?' The Man replied, 'No but as Commander of the army of the Lord I have now come' (Joshua 5:13-14). Joshua then fell to the ground and worshipped.

Prayer and worship must go before us into this battle. It seems to me that Charlie Kirk's murder, defending the gospel, is a *wake-up call* for us that is being answered around the world. How fitting that Charlie Kirk's name literally means *freeman* of the *church*. May his sacrifice pour white hot steel into our spine, filling us with unshakable resolve to stand for what is good, honourable, and true, as we *free* the *church* from complacency, and compromise:

...do not be conformed to this world, but be transformed by the renewing of your mind, that you may prove what is that good and acceptable and perfect will of God. (Romans 12:2)

I believe the loss of Charlie will go down in history as a line in the sand, a turning point, and the start of something big.[2] We cannot expect to be loved by the world. Jesus said:

If the world hates you, you know that it hated Me before it hated you. If you were of the world, the world would love its own. Yet because you are not of the world, but I chose you out of the world, therefore the world hates you. (John 15:18-19)[3]

My prayer for you is that you will be challenged and emboldened, as I have been, by these fifteen remarkable men and women. I don't believe I will ever be the same again. Every chapter has challenged me and is changing me; I have learnt so much. I call to mind the first, and only song, I ever introduced to my church, back in 1975:

> *God's got an army, marching through the land*
> *Deliverance is their song, with healing in their hands*
> *Everlasting joy and gladness in their heart*
> *And in this army I've got a part.*

Footnotes

[1] Charlie Kirk (2025, September 16). *Vice President JD Vance Remembers Charlie Kirk, Miller, Tucker, RFK Jr., Wiles, Leavitt.* [Video]. YouTube. https://www.youtube.com/watch?v=ngofqx9EfcM

[2] Turning Point USA (n.d.). *Charlie's Vision America's Future The Fight Continues.* Retrieved October 26, 2025, from https://tpusa.com/

[3] MacArthur, John (2015, October 17). *Why the World Hates Christians, Part 1 (John 15:17–25).* Grace to You. [Video]. YouTube. https://www.youtube.com/watch?v=DSeFIfCDpCI

ACKNOWLEDGEMENTS

Gilly my wife, who has sacrificed so much during the research and writing phase. Thank you for your love and understanding. Right at the end of the project, Gilly did a final proofread and made brilliant suggestions, in particular, her encouragement to start the book with the chapter on marriage.

Dr Stephen Brinton, friend and colleague for 30 years, has been invaluable as a sounding board for the more contentious issues. He had a major hand in shaping the chapters on Education and Health.

Warwick Marsh and *Kurt Mahlburg*, of *The Daily Declaration*, for their support at the start of this project. They gave invaluable suggestions from their own experience in writing and producing books.

My fifteen interviewees, *Lyle Shelton, Warwick Marsh, Dylan Oakley, Lindsey Fuchs, Akos Balogh, Ps Apenisa Ralulu, Kirralie Smith, Jodie Pickard, Leonie Robson, John Anderson, Dr My Le Trinh, Rod Lampard, Brian Pickering, Gordon Hickson,* and *Teri Kempe*. Without them *While We Were Sleeping* would still be asleep!

Sarah Chaney, my daughter for the cover design, and her out-of-the-box challenges along the way as I grappled with some of the topics.

Teri Kempe, who came on board as my interviewee for the Israel chapter, which was written quite early on. She then stayed around, becoming my editor for the whole project. She brought her wealth of experience to the table with the result being the book you now hold in your hand or read on your device.

I will not try to enumerate the army of wonderful soldiers who have supported me personally and this book project, and who will continue to uphold *While We Were Sleeping* in intercessory prayer, that it might reach the hands and hearts of those for whom it has been crafted. I am indebted to you.

Finally, I would like to acknowledge my *Heavenly Father* and the *Lord Jesus Christ*, who have been my strength, encouragement, and guide from conception to delivery of *While We Were Sleeping*.

Thank you.

ABOUT THE AUTHOR

Jim Twelves lives in Sydney, Australia, with his wife, Gillian. They have four children and six grandchildren. He has spent all his working life in education, nearly twenty years in England and twenty-six years in Australia.

Since his retirement in 2021, he has been a regular contributor to The Daily Declaration, Australia's largest Christian E-News site.

He would love to hear your thoughts about *While We Were Sleeping: A Wake-up Call for All Christians.* Please leave a review on Amazon.

Contact Jim Twelves:
Email: jim.twelves1975@gmail.com
YouTube: @jimtwelves1636
Linkedin: www.linkedin.com/in/dr-jim-twelves-990a2815
Telegram: Jim's Stand https://t.me/jimsstand
Web: https://jimtwelves.wordpress.com/

Printed in Dunstable, United Kingdom

73639419R00139